References for the Rest of Us! ®

BESTSELLING BOOK SERIES

Are you intimidated and confused by computers? Do you find that traditional manuals are overloaded with technical details you'll never use? Do your friends and family always call you to fix simple problems on their PCs? Then the For Dummies® computer book series from Wiley Publishing, Inc. is for you.

For Dummies books are written for those frustrated computer users who know they aren't really dumb but find that PC hardware, software, and indeed the unique vocabulary of computing make them feel helpless. For Dummies books use a lighthearted approach, a down-to-earth style, and even cartoons and humorous icons to dispel computer novices' fears and build their confidence. Lighthearted but not lightweight, these books are a perfect survival guide for anyone forced to use a computer.

> "I like my copy so much I told friends; now they bought copies."
> — Irene C., Orwell, Ohio

> "Quick, concise, nontechnical, and humorous."
> — Jay A., Elburn, Illinois

> "Thanks, I needed this book. Now I can sleep at night."
> — Robin F., British Columbia, Canada

Already, millions of satisfied readers agree. They have made For Dummies books the #1 introductory level computer book series and have written asking for more. So, if you're looking for the most fun and easy way to learn about computers, look to For Dummies books to give you a helping hand.

Wiley Publishing, Inc.

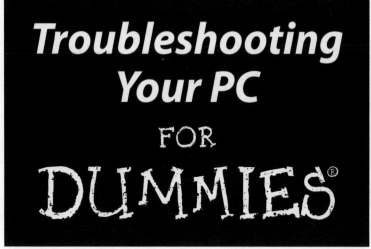

Troubleshooting Your PC
FOR
DUMMIES®

Troubleshooting Your PC
FOR
DUMMIES®

by Dan Gookin

Wiley Publishing, Inc.

Troubleshooting Your PC For Dummies®

Published by
Wiley Publishing, Inc.
909 Third Avenue
New York, NY 10022
www.wiley.com

Copyright © 2002 by Wiley Publishing, Inc., Indianapolis, Indiana

Published simultaneously in Canada

For general information on our other products and services or to obtain technical support, please contact our Customer Care Department within the U.S. at 800-762-2974, outside the U.S. at 317-572-3993, or fax 317-572-4002.

Wiley also publishes its books in a variety of electronic formats. Some content that appears in print may not be available in electronic books.

Library of Congress Cataloging-in-Publication Data:

Library of Congress Control Number: 2002108109

ISBN: 0-7645-1669-8

Manufactured in the United States of America

10 9 8 7 6 5 4 3

1O/RQ/QZ/QS/IN

About the Author

Dan Gookin got started with computers back in the post-slide-rule age of computing: 1982. His first intention was to buy a computer to replace his aged and constantly breaking typewriter. Working as slave labor in a restaurant, however, Gookin was unable to afford the full "word processor" setup and settled on a computer that had a monitor, keyboard, and little else. Soon his writing career was under way with several submissions to (and lots of rejections from) fiction magazines.

His big break came in 1984, when he began writing about computers. Applying his flair for fiction with a self-taught knowledge of computers, Gookin was able to demystify the subject and explain technology in a relaxed and understandable voice. He even dared to add humor, which eventually won him a column in a local computer magazine.

Eventually, Gookin's talents came to roost as he became a ghostwriter at a computer book publishing house. That was followed by an editing position at a San Diego computer magazine, at which time he also regularly participated in a radio talk show about computers. In addition, Gookin kept writing books about computers, some of which became minor best sellers.

In 1990, Gookin gave a publisher a book proposal. From that initial meeting unfolded an idea for an outrageous book: a long overdue and original idea for the computer book for the rest of us. What became *DOS For Dummies* blossomed into an international bestseller with hundreds and thousands of copies in print and many foreign translations.

Today, Gookin still considers himself a writer and computer "guru" whose job it is to remind everyone that computers are not to be taken too seriously. His approach to computers is light and humorous yet very informative. He knows that the complex beasts are important and can help people become productive and successful. Yet Gookin mixes his knowledge of computers with a unique, dry sense of humor that keeps everyone informed — and awake. His favorite quote is "Computers are a notoriously dull subject, but that doesn't mean I have to write about them that way."

Gookin's titles for Wiley Publishing include *DOS For Dummies,* 3rd Edition; *PCs For Dummies,* 8th Edition; and *Buying a Computer For Dummies,* 2nd Edition. Gookin holds a degree in communications from the University of California, San Diego, and lives with his wife and four boys in the rare and gentle woods of Idaho.

Publisher's Acknowledgments

We're proud of this book; please send us your comments through our online registration form located at www.dummies.com/register/.

Some of the people who helped bring this book to market include the following:

Acquisitions, Editorial, and Media Development

Project Editor: Rebecca Whitney

Acquisitions Editor: Greg Croy

Senior Copy Editor: Kim Darosett

Technical Editor: Mark L. Chambers

Media Development Supervisor: Richard Graves

Editorial Manager: Constance Carlisle

Editorial Assistant: Amanda M. Foxworth

Cartoons: Rich Tennant www.the5thwave.com

Production

Project Coordinator: Maridee Ennis

Layout and Graphics: Amanda Carter, Melanie DesJardins, Joyce Haughey, LeAndra Johnson, Jackie Nicholas, Barry Offringa, Laurie Petrone, Jeremey Unger

Proofreaders: David Faust, John Greenough, Carl Pierce, TECHBOOKS Production Services

Indexer: TECHBOOKS Production Services

Publishing and Editorial for Technology Dummies

Richard Swadley, Vice President and Executive Group Publisher

Mary C. Corder, Editorial Director

Andy Cummings, Vice President and Publisher

Publishing for Consumer Dummies

Diane Graves Steele, Vice President and Publisher

Joyce Pepple, Acquisitions Director

Composition Services

Gerry Fahey, Vice President of Production Services

Debbie Stailey, Director of Composition Services

Contents at a Glance

Table of Contents

Introduction

· ·

Welcome to *Troubleshooting Your PC For Dummies,* a book that explains how to get your PC going again when it has, for some stupid reason, decided to stop. Or maybe not stop, but just act strange. And then it decides to act normal again. Yes, even those unpredictable times of trouble can be accurately shot by using this book.

Computers aren't supposed to die or crash or hang or bomb or toss a hissy fit for no apparent reason. But as any computer owner knows, computers often don't do what they're told. In it-was-working-yesterday syndrome, for some reason your computer decides that today is a different day and so it will act up. And in the who-owns-the-problem? issue, you have to decide whether the printer isn't working because of the printer itself or because of Windows or because of the application that's trying to print. I won't even bore you with random Internet disconnect problems, dead mice, monitors thrust into stupid mode, and a myriad of other problems — because these and other issues are all adequately covered, cured, and remedied throughout this handy little book.

Oh! And that "Dummies" thing? Face it: Anyone who uses a computer feels intimidated enough. It's not that you're a dummy, but dealing with these plastic and silicon monsters certainly makes anyone *feel* like a dummy. Relax! It's the *For Dummies* approach that lets you recognize that it's *you* who is in charge of your PC's destiny. You can tame the beast! This book shows you how.

About This Book

This is a problem-solving book. After all, if *every* problem mentioned in this book were to land on a computer at one time, even I would toss the thing out the window and take up knitting or log rolling instead. The idea here is simple: You have a problem, and you look up the solution.

You can use the index to discover where solutions to specific problems lie, or you can just browse through Part II, which covers many solutions based on the particular piece of the PC that's being troubled. Each section within the chapter mentions the problem and covers potential solutions. Sample sections include

> ✔ In the presence of unwelcome silence
>
> ✔ Dealing with nasty wallpaper!
>
> ✔ The whatever-submenu on the Start menu is missing!
>
> ✔ The mouse is getting s-l-o-w
>
> ✔ Things to check when the printer isn't printing
>
> ✔ Where did the download go?
>
> ✔ Why doesn't it shut down?
>
> ✔ "Windows doesn't remember my password!"

And many, many more. You don't have to learn anything. You don't have to complete worksheets or take quizzes. Just find your problem, look up the answer, and follow a few quick and easily explained steps, and you're back on your way with a working computer in no time.

How This Book Works

This book explains how to do things in a step-by-step manner. Occasionally, solutions have a large number of steps, or sometimes you have only one or two things to do, but, fortunately, it's all numbered and explained in a cheerful and entertaining manner.

Whenever you're told to type something, that something appears in **special** type. For example:

1. Type **WINVER** in the box.

This instruction tells you to type the text **WINVER** into the box. The next step may be to click the OK button with the mouse or press the Enter key. But all you need to worry about for this step is to type **WINVER**.

2. Click the OK button.

The steps tell you exactly which button to click or which gizmo to tickle with the mouse. Sometimes these steps are shortened:

3. Click OK.

This line still means to "click the OK button with the mouse."

Keyboard shortcuts or key combination commands are given like this:

Press the Alt+F keys on the keyboard.

This line means to press and hold the Alt key on your keyboard and then tap the F key. Release the Alt key. It works the same way as pressing Shift+F is used to type a capital letter *F,* but the Alt key is used rather than Shift.

Likewise, you may use the Ctrl key in combination with other keyboard characters.

The key between the Ctrl and Alt keys in the lower-left corner of your keyboard is the Windows key, which is abbreviated as "Win" throughout this book. So when you see

>   Win+F

it means to press and hold the Win key and then tap the F key.

Choosing items from the menu works like this:

>   Choose Edit⇨Paste.

This line means to use the mouse to click the Edit menu and then click again to choose the Paste item from that menu. (You can also use the keyboard to work the menus, in which case you press the Alt key and then the underlined letter of the menu or command to choose that command.)

What You're Not to Read

I just can't help being technical at times. So when I break into a high-tech song, I let you know. Reading that material may increase your knowledge for playing computer trivia, but, otherwise, such asides and tidbits are written because — after 20 years of writing computer books — *I just can't help myself!*

The trivia and asides are always marked as optional reading. So don't bother about trying to figure out what's important and what's just the author babbling.

Foolish Assumptions

I must assume a few things about you, O dear, gentle reader: You use a computer. Specifically, you use a computer (or PC) that runs the Windows operating system. It must be either Windows 98 (First or Second Edition), Windows Me (or Millennium Edition), or Windows XP, either Home or Professional.

This book does not specifically cover Windows 95, Windows NT, or Windows 2000, though many solutions presented here work on those systems.

How This Book Is Organized

This book contains four major parts plus a few appendixes to whet your troubleshooting appetite. Each part contains chapters that help further explain the part subject. Then, each chapter is divided into individual sections that address specific issues. Everything is cross-referenced. You don't have to read the entire book, from front to back. You may start reading anywhere and receive the full enjoyment that you would if you were to start on the first page or wherever the binding falls open when you try to lay this book on its back.

Part 1: What the @#$%&*!?

The chapters in this part of the book serve as a handy introduction to the entire notion of troubleshooting your PC. I give you some explanations, some quick things to try, plus helpful tips and advice on where to go when you can't find the answers.

Part 11: Troubleshooting Minor 1rks and Quirks

The chapters in this part make up the book's core. Each chapter covers a specific aspect of the computer, either some piece of hardware or something you do, such as use the Internet. Each chapter contains general troubleshooting information and some specific (and common) questions and answers along with their possible solutions.

Part 111: Preventive Maintenance

Nothing beats being prepared. The chapters in this part tell you how to best prepare for the potential of PC peril and how to optimize your system, and you get some general good advice on what to do "just in case."

Part 1V: The Part of Tens

The traditional *For Dummies* Part of Tens contains several chapters with some good advice, all bundled into neat lists of ten.

Appendixes

This book wraps up with several interesting and handy appendixes for your reference pleasure. They include some descriptions and advice on using various Windows troubleshooting tools, how to handle Safe mode, and how to create an emergency boot disk and what do to with it.

What's Not Here

So I was sitting there in my office, merrily typing along, and all of a sudden my editor — out of nowhere (though it was probably somewhere near the navel of Indianapolis) — writes to inform me that the book *is too big!* Oh, dear! I've written another fat book. What to cut?

Fortunately, all of the book is here. I didn't have to cut anything out, nor are you being presented with a book that's lesser than the sum of its parts. On the other hand, this book can be only so big. It would be next to impossible to cover every single problem that every single PC could theoretically have. To help things out, this book has a supplemental Web page. Here's the address:

```
www.wambooli.com/help/troubleshooting/
```

On this page, you find updates, corrections, last-minute additions, plus some bonus material just for visiting my Web page. Check it out!

Icons Used in This Book

This icon flags something I would consider a tip (though just about all the information in this book falls into the "tip" category).

This icon serves as a special reminder to do something or to remember something.

This icon serves as a special reminder not to do something or to definitely not forget something.

This infamous icon alerts you to the presence of highly technical stuff discussed in the text nearby. It's optional reading only!

Where to Go from Here

Read on! If you don't know where to start, start at Chapter 1, which is why I made that text Chapter 1 and not Chapter 4.

The first part of the book does serve as a basic orientation, and Chapter 2 is an excellent introduction to some immediate troubleshooting fixes you can try. Otherwise, look up the problem and find the solution. It's in here somewhere.

As an author, I do agree to support my books. If you have any questions about this book or need something explained further, you can e-mail me at dgookin@wambooli.com. That's my real e-mail address, and I do respond to every e-mail sent to me. I cannot, however, troubleshoot your computer for you! That's what this book is for! But I can help answer questions about the book or just say "Hello, thank you for writing," if that's all you want.

I also offer a free weekly newsletter, which you can subscribe to. The newsletter offers updates, news, Q&A, how-to, opinions, and lots of supplemental information to this and all my books. It costs nothing, and it contains no ads or junk. Check it out at

www.wambooli.com/newsletter/weekly/

Enjoy the book!

Part I
What the
@#$%&*!?

The 5th Wave   **By Rich Tennant**

Arthur inadvertently replaces his mouse pad with a Ouija board. For the rest of the day, he receives messages from the spectral world.

©RICHTENNANT

YOU WILL FORGET YOUR PASSWORD. YOUR HARD DISK WILL CRASH AAAHAHAHAHA

Chapter 1

It's Not Your Fault! Well, It Might Be Your Fault (How to Tell Whether It's Your Fault)

* *

In This Chapter

▶ Discovering whether it's your fault

▶ Investigating what causes PC problems

▶ Emotionally dealing with a crash

* *

During my 20-odd years of helping folks use their computers, I've noticed one unfortunate and common belief:

> *People tend to blame themselves for just about anything that goes wrong inside a PC.*

This is not always true, of course. Computers crash for a number of reasons, and most of the time it's really not your fault. Yet, when sometimes the computer does something strange or unexpected, even I catch myself saying "What did I do now?"

Alas, the sad truth is that with a computer, you should expect the unexpected. So before you plan on doing any troubleshooting, please set the proper frame of mind. Rather than immediately jump to the what-have-I-done? conclusion, practice saying the following mantra:

Oh, my. The computer is behaving in a random and unexpected manner. I suppose that I shall have to look into this to see what can be done to remedy the situation.

Computer foul-up terms not worth memorizing

Glitch: Whenever the computer does something strange or unexpected or behaves in a manner inconsistent with normal operation, it's a *glitch.* Glitches happen to everyone. Often, you fail to notice a glitch unless it does something that directly affects what you're doing. For example, you don't notice a sound glitch until you try to make your computer squawk. The sound may have not been working for weeks, but you notice it missing only when you otherwise would expect it. Such is the agony of the glitch.

Bug: A *bug* is an error in a computer program. Despite the efforts of the best programmers, most computer software is riddled with bugs. Bugs are what cause computer glitches. Bad bugs can cause a computer to *hang* or *crash.* Note that most of the worst bugs happen when you mix two programs together and they interact in some new and unexpected way. The term

comes from the early days of computing, when an actual bug (a moth) got stuck in the circuitry.

Hang: A totally unresponsive computer is said to be *hung,* or *hanged.* You could also use the term *frozen,* though *hang* is the accepted term used by computer nerds for generations.

Crash: *Crash* is another term for a dead computer — specifically, what happens to a hard drive when it ceases operation. A crash is typically more sensational than a hang. Remember that a *hang* is a freeze. A crash is typically accompanied by spectacular warning messages or weird behavior (and it may indicate more than merely a dying hard drive). In fact, a crashed computer may still be teasingly functional. Yet only the most foolhardy continue to use a crashed computer.

There. It's totally neutral, merely an observation coupled with a determination on your behalf to fix things. With that proper attitude set, you're ready to begin your troubleshooting odyssey.

Computers shouldn't crash, of course. They're not designed to. Really! But they do, for two reasons, neither of which is really your responsibility:

- ✔ The software has bugs in it.
- ✔ There is an utter lack of cooperation.

Why It's Not Your Fault

It can be argued (and it is, by software and hardware developers) that *using* software is your fault. Yes, you can stumble across a bug. Zip-flash! The program crashes, and your data is gone, and you attempt seppuku with a letter opener. That happens. Is it really your fault? No. You were the trigger, but the fault isn't your own. Put that letter opener away!

Why do computers have bugs?

In the real world, bugs — or, more accurately, _insects_ — are a necessary part of the ecosystem. But in a computer system, bugs are an evil and entirely unnecessary thing. Yet they exist.

A _bug_ is an error in a computer program. It's an accident, caused by an oversight on the part of the programmer, by sloppy programming, or by a lack of anticipation. For example, a programmer may not anticipate that a user may have a last name that's more than 25 characters long and that when you type that 26th character, the program waltzes off into La-La Land. Or the programmer may type `variable_AM1` when he really meant to type `variable_AM2` or something similar.

No programmer creates bugs on purpose. In fact, most programming involves _removing_ bugs as opposed to writing new code. So a programmer types a set of instructions, runs them, fixes them, runs them, fixes them, and back and forth until all the bugs are (hopefully) worked out. Programmers even invite others _(beta testers)_ to check their programs for bugs. After all, the programmers can't possibly figure out every possible way their software will be used. The object is to make the final product as bug-free as possible.

When you discover a bug, which is the case with most PC trouble, you should report it to the software developers. They're the ones responsible for fixing the bug — not you!

In addition to bugs is the lack-of-cooperation issue. Software and hardware vendors can check their products in only certain PC configurations. Chances are — given the tremendous number of people who own computers and all the software and hardware combinations you can have — that somehow you will stumble across that one particular blend that wreaks havoc in the computer. Is that your fault? Technically, no, because the manufacturer should build reliable stuff.

So there you have it. The computer is a device that's not designed to crash, but through the odd chance of a software bug or some weird software-hardware mixture, it does crash, and crash often. Yes, I'd quite agree that the reason it happens is _not_ your fault.

How It Possibly Could Be Your Fault

You're not off the hook!

Rarely in my travels have I found someone who has somehow influenced the computer to go wacky. In fact, only a few things have been known to be directly related to human problems. These are covered in the following sections.

You did something new to the computer

Computers are very conservative; they don't like change. The most stable computer I have in my office is one that has only Word 2000 installed on it. Nothing else is used on that computer — not the Internet, no games, no nothing! The computer still does crash, but not as often as other systems in my office.

The key to having a more stable computer is *not* to install new software or hardware. Unfortunately, this advice is nearly impossible to follow. It's not that the mere act of installing something new causes the computer to crash. No, it's just that installing something new introduces new combinations to the system, and an incompatibility or conflict may come from that. It's what I call the it-was-working-yesterday syndrome.

For example, one of my readers writes in and says, "The sound is gone from my computer! I had sound yesterday, but today it's all gone!" The first thing I ask is whether the person installed any new hardware or software. The answer is generally "Yes," and that's what prompted the problem.

Sometimes, you can forget that you've installed new stuff, which makes the problem seem random. After all, the computer is acting goofy, and it's easy to overlook that you downloaded some corny animation from the Internet yesterday. And that one change is usually enough to alter the system.

✔ Yes, if you had one computer for every program, you'd probably live a relatively crash-free high-tech existence. But I don't recommend spending your money that way.

✔ Try to keep track of the hardware and software you add to your computer system.

✔ Perhaps create a *log file* — just a text file you can save in the My Documents folder. Add entries to the file, such as

```
March 15 -- Added soothsayer software
```

That way, you can review the changes you've made to your computer and correlate them to any new bugs the system may have. You can use the Notepad program that comes with Windows for this job. The job of this text editor is merely to create simple text files, such as a log file.

✔ If possible, do research to determine the new stuff's compatibility with your existing computer system. Do that *before* you install.

✔ These types of new hardware/software installations are why utilities such as System Restore in Windows Me and Windows XP and the Roxio GoBack are so popular. For more information, see the section in Chapter 4 about using System Restore.

You were bad and deleted files you shouldn't have deleted

Delete only those files you created yourself. It's when people go on file hunting expeditions that they can get into trouble. In fact, deleting a swath of files is typically the *only* reason I recommend reinstalling Windows. After all, if you surgically remove a great portion of your operating system, reinstalling is the only way to get it back. (For all other problems, you generally have a solution *other than* reinstalling Windows.)

Here is what's okay to delete:

✔ Files (icons) in the My Documents folder

✔ Files in any folders in the My Documents folder

✔ Any folders created in the My Documents folder or its subfolders

✔ Zip files you've downloaded and installed

That's it!

Never, ever, delete any other files anywhere else on your computer. I know that you may want to! The urge may be irresistible! You may go on a "cleaning" binge and yearn to mow down files like some crazed gardener with a high-speed weed whacker. Don't!

✔ Oh, and you can delete any shortcut icons you may find. Deleting a shortcut icon does not delete the original file.

✔ You can delete any icon on the desktop. Most of them are shortcuts anyway.

✔ You can also delete items from the Start menu, though I recommend against it.

✔ Zip files are known as *compressed folders* in Windows Me and Windows XP.

✔ Most programs you download come in zip file archives. After you extract the files, you can delete the zip file archive.

✔ I create a special folder, called Downloads, in the My Documents folder. (I suppose that I should call it My Downloads, just to fit in with everything else.) That's where I store all my downloaded files, zip files, and e-mail attachments. It's also a great folder to clean out to free up some space on the hard drive.

✔ No, I don't ever recommend reinstalling Windows. See Chapter 19 for the reasons.

Other ways to remove files you didn't create yourself

The main complaint I get with my "Delete only those files you created your-self" maxim is that people find on the computer other files that they're just itching to delete themselves. These files include

✔ Internet cookies

✔ Temporary files (especially temporary Internet files)

✔ Wallpapers and extra media files

✔ Programs that are unwanted or no longer used

✔ Pieces of Windows they want to get rid of

✔ Stuff I can't think of right now

Avoid the temptation to manually delete these files! It gets you into trouble!

"But, Dan!" you whine. "A friend said it was okay to manually delete my Internet cookies!"

Well . . . there are proper ways to delete the cookies, rid yourself of tempo-rary files, clean and scour unwanted programs, and remove things you don't need. Use those proper ways! Do not attempt to manually delete things your-self. You will get into trouble if you do.

✔ See Chapter 17 for information on dealing with cookies.

✔ Also see Chapter 21 for information on properly removing unwanted files from your computer.

✔ It's not your fault that the computer crashes — especially if you follow my advice in this section!

How old is your PC?

The older your computer is, the more likely it is to crash. I have no idea why. Systems that run stable for years may suddenly experience a growing number of glitches. It happens so often that I refer to it as "tired RAM." And, alas, no electronic equivalent of Geritol is available for your PC's tired RAM.

When your PC gets old, you have to prepare for inevitable quirkiness from it. You can try replacing the parts piece by piece, but eventually you wind up spending more on those parts than you would for an entirely new system. So, no matter how much you love your computer, when it comes time for it to go, let it go.

✔ Most PCs should last between four and six years.

✔ If you're in business, plan on replacing your PCs every four years. The boost in productivity from the new models is alone worth the expense.

✔ For the home, keep your PC as long as you can. If it still works, great! Even if you do buy a new system, you can still use the system for the kids to do homework or play games.

✔ I have a "bone yard" full of old computer pieces and parts. It's not all junk either; recently, I used parts from several old computers to create a file server for my network.

✔ The main problem with older computers: parts! I have an older PC that can only "see" 8GB of hard drive storage, yet the smallest hard drive I can find for sale is 20GB. Oops.

✔ The first things to fail on any old PC are the things that move the most, such as any disk drive, the mouse, or the keyboard.

✔ A failing hard drive is typically the sign of a PC entering its twilight years. You'll notice that the disk drive takes longer to access files and that ScanDisk (or similar disk utilities) begin to report more disk errors and bad sectors. See Part III of this book for information on what to do next.

✔ Mice can fail long before the rest of the computer. This problem may not be a portent of the PC's ultimate demise; see Chapter 13 for more mouse information.

✔ When the PC does die, bid it adieu. Salvage what you can; no point in tossing out the monitor, mouse, keyboard, modem, or other "pieces parts" that could work on another computer. Then properly dispose of the rest of the computer according to the PC disposal laws of your locality.

Things to say when the computer crashes

Frack! Wonderful, forceful, yet completely G-rated term. Sounds like you-know-what, but utterly non-offensive. Has that quasi-German feel to it.

Oh, come on. . . . As if the computer could hear you, but at least shifts the blame from yourself to the device. (My personal variation of this is "Come on, you pig!" for when the computer is behaving stubbornly slow.)

What the —? A natural and common response to an unexpected situation. Can be followed by "Frack" or a frack-like equivalent.

Please! Please! Please! Pleading with the computer is very emotional, but it really doesn't help. Most users typically follow the pleading with "Oh, you sorry son-of-a-[female dog]."

You stupid @#$%&!? piece of @#$%!! Very definitely getting it out of your system, this satisfying phrase just feels good to say. Note how blame is made entirely on the computer. That's keeping the proper perspective.

What You Can Do about It

Whether it's your fault or not, it's your job to do something about a computer glitch. This book is your best tool in helping you find a solution, so the next step is to continue reading.

Before you do, be aware that you go through certain emotional phases as you experience and deal with your computer's often irrational behavior. I've categorized them in chronological order:

- **Guilt:** Despite my insistence, just about everyone feels guilty when the computer fouls up. "Is it my fault?" "What did I do?" Even after years of troubleshooting other people's computers, I still blame myself. It must be a human gene or some instinct we have — probably proof that mankind was created by robots from another planet eons ago.

- **Anger:** Yeah, hit the monitor! Get it out of your system. "Stupid PC! Stupid PC! Why do you *always* crash when I'm doing something important! Arghghgh!" Yes, you have a right to expect obedience from your personal electronics. Too bad the guinea pigs in the manufacturer's Human Usability Labs don't express their anger so readily.

- **Fear or depression:** "This dumb thing will never work." Wrong! This book helps you eliminate your fear and get over the depression phase.

- **Acceptance:** Hey, it's a computer. It crashes. It could be your fault, but chances are that it's something else. You must deal with the problem. Be stronger and wiser than the computer.

- **Confidence:** "I have *Troubleshooting Your PC For Dummies!* I can solve any problem!" This book lists many solutions to many common glitches, but also helps you to troubleshoot just about any problem. And I've rarely met a PC problem that cannot be solved, some simply by restarting your computer.

- **Success:** Your computer is back to normal, and everything is right with the universe. World peace is just around the corner! It's raining money! And bluebirds will help you get dressed in the morning. Let's all sing. . . .

Chapter 2

Stuff to Try First

· ·

In This Chapter

▶ Testing the keyboard

▶ Using Ctrl+Z to fix file foibles

▶ Working in Windows without the mouse

▶ Restarting Windows to fix things

▶ Shutting down and starting up again

▶ Avoiding "restart guilt"

· ·

I've yet to meet a computer problem that doesn't present me with a bou-
quet of panic as I open the door. That's fine. Get over it. Then, rather than
dwell on the who's, whys, or hows of the problem, try a few of the quick-and-
dirty techniques presented in this chapter to see whether you can remedy
the situation. Then get on with your work!

Some Quick Keyboard Things You Can Do

The keyboard is the computer's ears. So after you've tried shouting at the
thing, do some typing instead. The computer will most definitely "hear" that.
Well, unless the keyboard is dead. But there are ways around that as well!

Test the keyboard

To see whether the keyboard is responding, press the Caps Lock key. If the
keyboard is alive and well, the Caps Lock light blinks on and off as you tap
the Caps Lock key. That shows you that the keyboard is alive and paying
attention.

Figure 2-1 illustrates where you find the Caps Lock key and Caps Lock light on
most computer keyboards. (Some may be exceptions.)

Caps Lock light

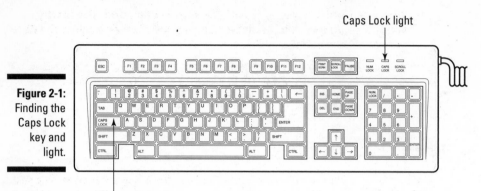

Figure 2-1:
Finding the
Caps Lock
key and
light.

Caps Lock key

✔ If the keyboard is dead, use the mouse to restart the computer, a subject covered later in this chapter. Restarting the computer awakens most snoozing keyboards.

✔ Alas, in some cases the keyboard can be alive, yet the computer is ignoring what it's saying. I've seen this situation more often with USB keyboards than with the keyboards that plug directly into a keyboard port on the PC. In these cases, the Caps Lock light does indeed blink on and off, but the computer is still deader than a doornail. Time to restart the computer.

✔ More keyboard troubleshooting information is offered in Chapter 13.

Using Ctrl+Z for immediate file relief

If you ever botch a file operation — moving, deleting, copying, renaming — *immediately* press the Undo key combination, Ctrl+Z. That undoes just about any file operation you can imagine.

✔ You must be prompt with the Ctrl+Z key press. The Undo command undoes only the most recent file operation. If you delete a file and then rename a file, the Undo command undoes only the renaming. You have to find another solution for any earlier problems that need fixing.

✔ Most people forget that editing items and submenus on the Start menu is really a *file* operation. When you screw up something on the Start menu, such as dragging an icon off the Start menu and onto the desktop, pressing Ctrl+Z fixes it right away. Remember that!

✔ Whoops! You cannot undo a Shift+Delete file operation. That's why Windows warns you that deleting a file in that manner renders the file permanently deleted.

✔ If Ctrl+Z, or the Undo command, doesn't work, give up. It means that either it's too late to undo the operation or the operation wasn't undoable in the first place. You have to try something else.

Escape! Escape!

The Esc key on your keyboard is called Escape for a reason: It often lets you out of tight situations! Most scary things that happen on a PC can instantly be cancelled or backed away from by pressing the handy Esc key.

Archaic DOS key commands

Whether you're using an old DOS program or messing around at the command prompt window, you can use two key commands to attempt to halt a DOS command run amok:

Ctrl+C. The Control-C command typically halts any DOS command or long text display.

Ctrl+Break. This command is essentially the same as Ctrl+C; however, the Control-Break combination is specifically monitored by DOS whereas the Ctrl+C combination could be overlooked. Note that the Break key shares the Pause key on many keyboards.

Older DOS programs use a variety of keyboard commands to quit or halt operations. If you find yourself stuck in a DOS program, try any of the following keys or key combinations to quit: Esc, Q, X, F10, Alt+Q, Ctrl+Q, Alt+X, or Ctrl+X.

✔ When the computer is run in DOS mode (not a DOS window), the Ctrl+Alt+Delete key combination is used to restart the computer. No warning or dialog box is displayed; the system just restarts.

✔ The DOS command to close a DOS prompt window is EXIT. Type **EXIT** and press the Enter key.

✔ To ensure that the Ctrl+Break key combination works at the DOS prompt, use the BREAK=ON command. Type **BREAK=ON** and press the Enter key to activate this "extended" Break key checking.

Using the keyboard in Windows when the mouse doesn't work

Windows needs a mouse, so if you can't get your mouse to work, you need to rely on the keyboard to finish up whatever tasks you can and then restart the computer. Here are some handy key combinations you can use in place of some mouse techniques:

Ctrl+S: Saves a document to disk. Always save! If you can't work the commands in the Save As dialog box, just save the file wherever you can; you can move it to a better location the next time you start Windows or recover the mouse.

Esc: Cancels a dialog box; closes some windows.

Enter: Does the same thing as pressing the OK or "default" button in a dialog box.

Tab: Moves between various gizmos in a dialog box. Try using the arrow keys or spacebar to activate the gizmos.

Alt+F4: Closes a window.

Win (the Windows key): Can be used to pop up the Start menu. You can then use the arrow keys and Enter to select items from the menu.

Ctrl+Esc: Pops up the Start menu if you have an older computer keyboard without a Windows key.

You can use other keys all throughout Windows to do just about anything the mouse can do, but that's missing the point here: When something is amiss, you should try to save your stuff and then restart Windows. Don't use a dead mouse as an excuse to show off your keyboard skills.

See the section nearby on restarting Windows when the mouse doesn't work. That typically fixes most mouse problems.

The Drastic Measure of Restarting Windows (Yet It Works)

Drastic is perhaps too severe of a word. To me, it conjures up images of amputation or — worse — having to drink a barium shake. Ick. Yet, for some cosmic reason, the "drastic" step of restarting Windows tends to work out many of the more frustrating and seemingly devious computer foibles.

- ✔ *Restart* is the term used by Microsoft. Old-timers may use the term *reset* or even *reboot* to describe the same thing.

- ✔ Real old-timers may even call it a *warm boot*. You have to buy the *Illustrated Computer Dictionary For Dummies* (written by me and published by John Wiley & Sons, Inc.) to find out what that word means!

Restarting Windows

Believe it or not, a simple restart of Windows can fix most problems. Try it! If it doesn't work, you can move on to other solutions offered later in this book.

To restart Windows 98 or Windows Me, follow these steps:

1. **Click the Start button.**
2. **Choose Shut Down.**

   The Shut Down Windows dialog box appears.
3. **Choose Restart for Windows Me (as shown in Figure 2-2; in Windows 98, click the appropriate radio button).**
4. **Click OK.**

Figure 2-2:
Restarting
Windows in
Windows
Me.

> **Shut Down Windows**
>
> What do you want the computer to do?
>
> | Restart |
>
> Ends your session, shuts down Windows, and starts
> Windows again.
>
> OK   Cancel   Help

To restart Windows XP, follow these steps:

1. **Click the Start button.**
2. **Choose Turn Off Computer.**
3. **In the Turn off computer dialog box, choose Restart.**

After successfully completing these steps, Windows shuts everything down and immediately restarts. Hopefully, that clears up whatever dilemma existed.

- ✔ If you have any unsaved documents open, you're asked to save them before Windows restarts.

- ✔ Be sure to remember to remove any floppy disk from Drive A; otherwise, your computer may restart from that disk.

- ✔ Close any DOS windows before you restart. Any running DOS programs halt the shutdown process in its tracks. You must properly quit the DOS program and then try to restart Windows.

✔ If you're connected to the Internet, the act of restarting Windows disconnects you. That means if you're doing anything on the Internet, such as downloading a file, the task is interrupted and you have to start over when the computer comes back on.

✔ You must restart Windows! Don't just log off. In Windows XP, don't "lock" the system. You must choose the restart option as described in this section.

✔ Sometimes you may even have to turn the computer off to fix the problem. See the section "Restarting when everything is dead," later in this chapter.

Restarting Windows when the mouse is dead but the keyboard is alive

If the mouse pointer is stuck to the screen like some dead bug on a car's windshield, you have to rely on the keyboard to restart Windows. This task isn't as hard as it seems (and I suppose I'm saying that because of my years of experience doing this):

1. **Press the Win key to pop up the Start menu.**

   If your keyboard lacks a Win key, press the Ctrl+Esc key combination.

2. **Press U to choose the Shutdown command.**

3. **Use the arrow keys to select the Restart option.**

4. **Press the Enter key.**

Maybe you want to wait for that download

If you're connected to the Internet and downloading a program, you may want to wait a bit before restarting Windows. Even if the keyboard is dead and the mouse doesn't work, sit back and watch the download. If the data is still moving, you're okay. Wait for the download to complete. Then, after the information is fully received (or sent), you can attempt to restart Windows.

The reason this strategy works is that Windows can do several things at once. Although the mouse or keyboard may be dead, the Internet connection may not be affected. Information may still fly in or out despite other parts of the computer playing possum. If you're lucky, you may get that file downloaded and not have to start over.

To tell whether the download is working, keep an eye on the progress meter. If it's moving, the data is flying. Good. Otherwise, if the meter is still for a few minutes, go ahead and restart Windows.

If you're prompted to save any documents, do so. Don't fret if you can't work the Save As dialog box; just save the document to disk and worry about relocating the file after the computer starts (and the mouse is, hopefully, back in action).

> ✔ You can also use these steps when the mouse is behaving in a stubborn or slow manner.

> ✔ Be patient! The computer may be unbearably slow. Even so, as long as you're getting a response, it's better to shut down properly than to just unplug the sucker.

Restarting when everything is dead

Ah! Life at the end of Dismal Street. The keyboard is clacking, but the computer is slacking. And you could roll the mouse to the North Pole and back, but the mouse pointer on the screen is oblivious. Time to be severely drastic:

1. **Press the computer's power button to turn it off.**

   If briefly pressing the power button doesn't work, press and hold it for several seconds. On some computers, this press-and-hold action turns off the power.

   Yes, if things appear hopeless, just unplug the PC. Or — better still — flip the switch on the surge protector (or power strip or UPS).

2. **After the computer is off, wait a few seconds.**

   Honestly, I don't know why you wait, but you should. One tech guy told me that you wait to ensure that the hard drives properly "spin down" — which is analogous to my washing machine, where I definitely don't want to stick my hand in there until the thing has done its spin-down.

   Another techy type told me that you have to wait for the RAM to drain. I do not recall whether he was intoxicated at the time, but it sounds good to me.

   Finally, I think that the wait period prevents some people from doing a quick on-off double flip of the power switch, which has the potential of damaging some of the computer's components. No, it's just best to wait a spell before turning the thing on again.

3. **Turn the computer back on.**

   Either flip the button on the computer or turn the power strip or UPS back on. If you do the latter, you may still have to punch the computer's power button to wake it up.

Hopefully, the restart resurrects your keyboard or mouse and gets you back on your way. If not, you can try ever more things, as covered throughout this book.

- ✔ Older PCs had big red switches or on-off rocker buttons that really, really, did turn off the power. Amazing.

- ✔ Some older PCs even had reset buttons, which you can use rather than the power switch to wake up a dead or even catatonic PC.

- ✔ I miss reset buttons.

What to do about "restart guilt"

Many people feel this pang of guilt when they're forced to restart their computer — even when they have no other course of action. I call it *restart guilt*. It most likely occurs because some versions of Windows come back to life with an ominous message:

```
Windows was not shutdown properly.
```

Oh, no! Which computer gods have ye offended? Peril! Doom! The wrath of Microsoft!

Relax. The message is followed by Windows running the ScanDisk program, which checks for the types of common errors that occur when the computer is improperly shut down.

Don't feel guilty about this! If you're forced to unplug the computer to get its attention, so be it. I'm sure that computer scientists in the 1950s eventually had to resort to unplugging their mammoth systems to wrest control when something went haywire. You're no different. (Well, you may not be wearing a white lab coat while you compute.)

- ✔ Windows XP dispenses with the Improper Shutdown warning message, but still runs the ScanDisk program (secretly) just as the computer starts.

- ✔ It's the duty of ScanDisk to search for "lost" file fragments on a hard drive. These bits and pieces of files (known as lost *clusters*) tend to crop up when a computer has been improperly shut down.

- ✔ Lost file fragments found by ScanDisk need not be saved. If you find any, you can select whichever option deletes them. Or, if you find files named FILE*xxx*.CHK on the hard drive, where *xxx* is some number, you may delete them as well. Those are recovered clusters, or file fragments, found by ScanDisk, and they typically contain random and useless data.

✔ Also see Chapter 20 for soothing words of advice when you just can't get the computer to quit all by itself.

✔ If the computer starts in Safe mode, you may have a hardware glitch or some other anomaly that needs fixing. Flip on over to Appendix B for more information.

✔ No, it's not required or necessary to restart in Safe mode after any crash or system reset.

What kind of idiot would just turn off a computer?

Obviously, if the computer is dead, the mouse is dead, and the keyboard is dead, what else can you do? You have to just turn off the computer. But you're not being an idiot that way. No, all the warnings and the reason for calling such a drastic step "improper" have their roots in the old days of DOS.

It was common years ago for people to use the reset button to quit a DOS program. Because DOS could run only one program at a time, pressing the reset button or Ctrl+Alt+Delete was often the fastest way to start another program. So, when some DOS user was done with WordPerfect, for example, he would whack the reset button (or rapidly flip the power switch off and on), DOS would restart and he would be off to run another program. This was bad.

It was bad because when programs are not allowed to properly shut down, file fragments and lost clusters begin to litter the hard drive. One such system I serviced had 20 percent of the hard drive wasted with lost clusters. So common was this practice that the warning message was added to Windows to ensure that people wouldn't get lazy again and just turn off their computers, as opposed to properly shutting them down. And it has worked — almost too well.

Chapter 3

Telling a Hardware Problem from a Software Problem

*I*t happens countless times a day, every day of the week: You phone technical support for your printer. After wading through the marsh of voice-mail menus, you finally get to a tech person who says "Oh, that's a Windows problem." So you phone Microsoft and they say "You really need to call your computer dealer because you didn't buy Windows directly from us." And then you phone your dealer, who says "That's a printer problem." And so it goes.

The reason for the tech support confusion (which may or may not be genuine) is that no one quite knows whether you have a hardware or software problem. If it's a hardware problem, the printer (or hardware) manufacturer can help you. If it's a software problem, the software developer should help you. When troubleshooting things yourself, knowing the hardware-software difference can save you oodles of time in tracking down the solution to the problem. This chapter shows you how.

Whose Problem Is It?

Step 1 in any troubleshooting investigation should be eliminating the possibility that you have a hardware problem. After all, if the device is working properly, you can fairly assume that it's the software controlling the device that's fouling things up.

- *Hardware* is anything physical in your computer. If you can touch it, it's hardware.

- Even the disk drives are hardware. The programs *(software)* are encoded on the disks, but that doesn't transform the disks into software.

- Software controls the hardware. Specifically, a program called a *driver* is used to control every bit of hardware in the PC. If the hardware itself functions fine, the real problem lies in the driver. Either the driver needs updating or other software in the computer is conflicting with the driver.

- Drivers are also known as *device drivers*.

Is it a hardware problem?

Specific examples of hardware and software problems (plus their solutions!) are located throughout Part II of this book. Generally speaking, however, hardware problems crop up suddenly and are not random.

For example, when the printer breaks, it stops working. That's a hardware problem. But if you cannot print when you use Outlook Express, though you can print in every other program, that's a software problem. The printer is being affected by one particular program, Outlook Express. Otherwise, the hardware apparently works just fine.

If the computer shuts itself off half an hour after you start using it — no matter which programs you run — that's a hardware problem. It isn't random. It's generally one half-hour, and it's most likely caused by something getting too hot inside the case — again, hardware.

If the tray on the CD-ROM drive no longer slides open — yup: hardware.

The Enter key doesn't work. Hardware.

Another unfortunate software problem: viruses

A sad fact of computing is that some software programs are specifically designed to do nasty things to your computer. Called *viruses* or *worms,* they can arrive piggyback on a simple e-mail message and open like a mushroom cloud, distributing havoc and chaos everywhere in your computer system.

The best way to fight viruses is with antivirus software. Windows isn't supplied with any anti-virus software, so you have to pick up a third-party product. I recommend Norton AntiVirus because it's simple to use and easy to install. It's available at most software stores or over the Internet.

Only when the problem seems more random or unpredictable is the software to blame, though that's not a hard-and-fast rule (which is one reason that troubleshooting is so tough).

How hardware fails

Hardware can fail electronically or physically. Both ways are fairly easy to spot.

Electronic failure of hardware usually happens within one month of purchase. If the electronics don't work, were cheap, were improperly assembled, or are just bad, they fail right away. That's good because the warranty on just about any computer covers such failures, and whatever goes kaput is replaced free of charge.

The physical failure of hardware happens only when the hardware moves. Fortunately, a PC has few moving parts on it: the disk drives and the keyboard.

When a disk drive stops spinning, it's dead! It needs replacement. Fortunately, the disk drive usually has a period of intermittent errors, stops and starts, and hits and misses before this happens, giving you plenty of warning.

Removable disk drives may have problems with their doors or eject mechanisms, which are obvious to spot.

Finally, the keyboard can fail. Cheap ones can go quickly, usually all at once. The better-made keyboards may lose a key here and there, but they can be fixed. Well, actually, any keyboard can be replaced, and it's inexpensive to do so.

- ✔ A cheap keyboard is one that utterly lacks a "clack" or "click" when you type; they feel mushy. That's because the keyboard is most likely a touch-membrane with spring-activated keys. If the membrane — which is like a flimsy rubber sheet — breaks, the keyboard is finished.

- ✔ Nearly all hardware is replaceable, which is often cheaper than fixing things. For example, a CD-ROM with a failed eject mechanism can be fixed, but often it's just cheaper to get a newer, better CD-ROM drive as a replacement.

- ✔ Avoid repair outfits that attempt to fix electronic components. Yes, even electronic components (the motherboard, plug-in cards, and so on) can easily and cheaply be replaced if they're damaged. I speak from experience here: I paid a guy close to $1,000 to solder new chips to an old laser printer's motherboard. The cost of a new laser? $1,200 — an expensive lesson.

Is it a software problem?

Of the two types of problems, hardware and software, software is more common because it's the software that does everything in a computer.

Alas, software trouble is more devious than hardware trouble. Consider that most software has unknown bugs in it and no software developer fully tests the programs in all possible configurations. Tracking down the problem can be *tough*.

The good news is that software problems can be predictable. If you find that choosing some option in a program causes the computer to lock up — and it behaves that way time and time again — it's a software bug. If the mouse stops working in only one program, it's a software problem.

The insidious thing, of course, is that it may not be that particular program causing the problem. For example, Internet Explorer may lock up tight whenever you visit a certain Web page, but it may be a Web plug-in that's causing the thing to crash — very nasty, but at least you've properly identified the problem as software and not as hardware.

Some good questions to ask yourself

To help determine whether you have a software problem or a hardware problem, consider asking yourself some basic questions:

- ✔ Have you installed any new hardware recently?
- ✔ Have you installed any new software recently?

Remember that computers do not like change. Change introduces new elements into the mix. Sometimes something works without a hitch. But if you have a busy computer — one with lots of software installed and many peripherals — adding something new may be that final pebble in the gears, grinding your PC to a halt.

- ✔ Adding something new introduces the it-was-working-yesterday syndrome.
- ✔ The reason for the popularity of such utilities as System Restore in Windows Me and Windows XP and Roxio GoBack is that they effectively uninstall new hardware and software, restoring your computer to the state when it last worked best.
- ✔ See Chapter 4 for more information on using the System Restore utility.

✔ Remember that adding new hardware also adds new software. Most hardware requires *device drivers* in order to work. This explains why it's tough sometimes to determine whether it's the hardware that doesn't work or whether it's just the software not cooperating.

Hardware Things to Check When You Smell Trouble

The first things to check when you suspect hardware trouble are the connections, the cables, and whatnot that link all the various pieces and parts of your PC together:

✔ Is everything properly plugged in and receiving power? (Are the power strip on-off switches in the On position, for example?)

✔ Are cables snuggly plugged into their sockets?

✔ Are cables snuggly plugged into the *proper* sockets? (The mouse and keyboard ports look identical on every PC, but *there is a difference!*)

✔ Are *both ends* of the cable connected?

I could relate a story from my old computer consulting days: Once upon a time, I made $60 in two minutes by plugging a modem's phone cord into a phone jack in the wall. The business was not happy paying my fee, but the people there learned an expensive lesson.

Listen!

Is the computer making noise? All computers have internal fans designed to regulate the temperature inside the box. If the fan goes, the computer gets too hot and fails.

Do you hear the fan? Poke your head around the back to see whether the fan is spinning, just to be sure. If not, you've got hardware trouble.

✔ Not all PCs have fans. The Apple iMac computers come without fans. I know that some older microcomputers and laptops come without internal fans. I suppose that a PC here or there could be without a fan, so if you know of one, please don't write in to tell me that I'm wrong.

✔ Some PCs can get hot even with the fan spinning. For these systems, you can get fan "upgrades" by adding a second fan to the PC's case.

- ✔ Sometimes, the fan is integrated into the power supply. In that case, you need to buy a new power supply to replace the fan.

- ✔ If you have to wait for the power supply to arrive in the mail, but still need to use the computer, you can operate it without the case's lid, as shown in Figure 3-1. See how I've used a little fan to help keep the PC's innards cool? I do not recommend this type of solution for the long term.

Touch!

Is the computer hot? Electronics do get hot, but they're designed to dissipate the heat. Heat is a Bad Thing for electronics. It causes errors. In fact, your computer manual probably had a "recommended operating temperature" guide somewhere — maybe even on the console's back panel.

- ✔ If the computer is hot, turn it off. Get it fixed.

- ✔ Also check the peripheral's power bricks to see whether they get too hot. Power bricks — more properly, *transformers* — do get warm, but should never be hot. If they're hot, then they're broken and need to be replaced.

- ✔ Heat also refers to the room temperature. Generally speaking, the hotter the room, the more likely the computer is to malfunction. If it's hotter than 80 degrees where your computer sits, turn the thing off.

Checking the monitor

To do a quick check of the monitor, first ensure that it's properly connected and turned on: A monitor plugs into both a power source and the computer. A CRT, or "glass," monitor plugs directly into a socket. LCD monitors typically plug into a power brick (transformer) and then into the wall socket.

The monitor may look dead, but the brightness may just be turned down all the way. Fiddle with the knobs to try to get a reaction.

Modern monitors are quite smart. If they don't receive a signal from the computer, they display a message telling you so. It says "No input" or "No signal" or something cryptic and obtuse, but conveys the general meaning of "I'm not connected to anything sending me a signal."

Some monitors have more than one input. My Mitsubishi monitor has an A-B switch for viewing output from more than one source. Some high-end monitors have both VGA and BNC connectors for the signal, plus corresponding buttons on the panel to choose either one.

Figure 3-1:
Don't try this
at home.

✔ It's quite common for the power light on a monitor to turn green when the monitor is up and running. When the monitor is not receiving a signal, the light turns yellow or flashes.

✔ The light also turns yellow when the computer is in Sleep, Suspended, or Hibernate mode.

Speaking of which, tap the Ctrl or Enter key on the keyboard to see whether the computer is just sleeping and has shut down the monitor.

✔ On some computers, you have to punch the Power/Sleep button to wake it up.

✔ If you still have your hearing, most CRT (glass) monitors make a high-pitched whistle, indicating that they're on. The top of the CRT monitor is also warm to the touch.

Other hardware tricks to try

This book is full of hardware tricks and tests you can use to determine whether your problem is hardware or software. See the proper chapter in Part II for more information on specific pieces of hardware.

Using Software to Check for Hardware Problems

Don't you hate it when you install some game or new piece of software in the computer and you invariably get this question: "Which type of graphics system does this computer have?" I feel like shouting at the program, "Hey! You're *in there!* Why don't you just look around and find out!?"

It's quite possible to use software to test the computer's hardware. Smart software knows where to poke around and what kind of responses are expected. If something is amiss, software can generally report it. After all, why not make the computer do the work. Isn't that what it's for?

The Device Manager

Windows comes with a handy tool called the *Device Manager,* which can be used to detect any hardware errors that are bugging Windows. You see, despite its lousy reputation, Windows is quite tolerant of sloppy hardware. Many claim that that's a fault of Windows — and it may be, but that's not my point: Checking with the Device Manager (see Appendix A) generally confirms that you have a hardware problem.

In Figure 3-2, you see the telltale sign that something is wrong with the computer: The display adapter (graphics card) in this computer isn't working properly. The circle (which is yellow) flags any misbehaving hardware right there in the Device Manager window. Further examination shows that the display adapter needs a new driver.

So is it a hardware or software problem? Officially, it's software because the Device Manager recommends getting a new driver. It seems like a hardware problem because the hardware isn't being recognized, so the device is being ignored by Windows. But it's really a software issue.

- ✔ See Appendix A for more information on how to get at and use the Device Manager.

- ✔ You can find information on how to reinstall a device driver (software) in the various chapters of Part II that deal with specific devices (video and sound, for example).

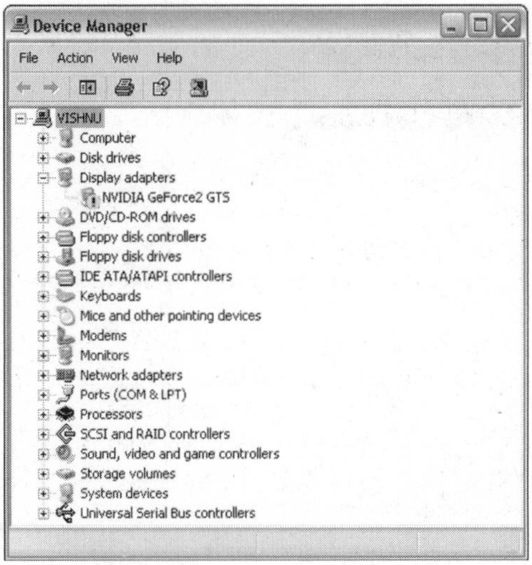

Figure 3-2:
The Device
Manager
flags a
misbehaving
doodad.

Using diagnostic tools

In addition to using the Device Manager, you can use software diagnostic tools to determine the status of just about any hardware component in your system. So when you suspect trouble, you can run the diagnostic program to determine whether your hardware is operating properly.

Because these tools are a hardware thing, they generally come with the hardware itself and are not a part of Windows. To find the tools, look for the bonus disks that came with your computer when it was new. Otherwise, you can find the disks with the hardware device inside the box it came in.

For example, my network card's diagnostic program came on the floppy disk that accompanied the network card. Figure 3-3 shows the Diagnostic tool in use. Certain video cards also come with diagnostic and troubleshooting tools. You must look for them!

The PC itself may have a diagnostic tool in its *Setup* program, the program that's run when the computer first starts. A message appears, such as "Press the <F2> key to enter Setup." (The key to press could be any key. Commonly, the Delete key or F1 are also used.) Inside the Setup program, you may find a diagnostic tool you can use to test all the PC's components.

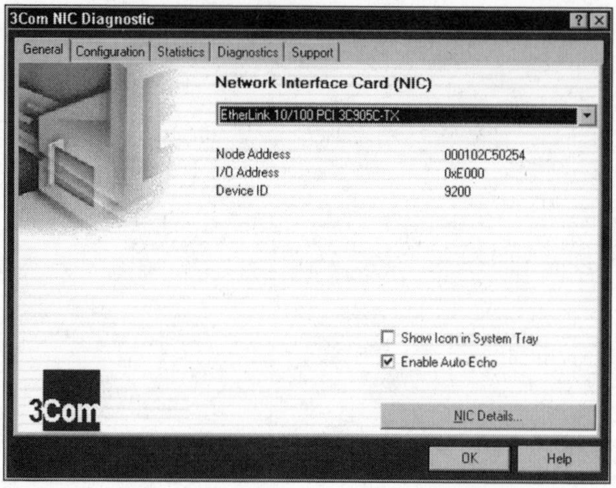

Figure 3-3:
A network card diagnostic tool.

WARNING!

✓ One thing you cannot test for in most PCs is the RAM. Programs must run in RAM, so a diagnostic program that tests RAM is a questionable thing in the first place. How can the program test memory if the program must reside in memory to begin with?

✓ Computers with failing RAM are generally a total mess anyway. It's best to have your dealer or the manufacturer test your PC's RAM; they have the proper equipment to give your computer's memory a good once-over.

✓ Diagnostic programs were all the rage in the early 1990s — not that anyone needed them suddenly; it was just one of those computer crazes. (And it's probably why the TV show *Star Trek: The Next Generation* used the word *diagnostic* more than any other computer term of the day.)

✓ You can get two types of diagnostic programs. One is only a report program. It simply reports what hardware resources you have in your computer. The program does not test anything. The other type of diagnostic program actually tests your hardware and reports the results.

✓ It's funny how the word *diagnostic* tends to lose its meaning the more you say it.

Chapter 4

The "R" Chapter (Reinstall, Restore, Recycle, Recovery)

*T*his chapter is brought to you by the letter *R*. Many happy words begin with *R*, like *recovery*. And *rescue*. Good words like *repair* and *restore*. How about *refund, rejoice,* and *recreation*? *Really!*

I don't know why most of the handy tools and helpful troubleshooting tricks are associated with R words. In fact, it didn't dawn on me until I finished writing this chapter. (Its original title was "Escape from Doom and Peril with These Fine Utilities," which is a good title, but not as catchy.) After writing about Restore, Reinstall, Recycle, and Recover, I just couldn't help myself.

Enough recess! Remember your resolve! Read on!

Restoring from the Recycle Bin

To ease the panic that sets in when you can't find a file, you need to do two things: First, use the Find or Search command to try to locate the file (this topic is covered in Chapter 9); second, check the Recycle Bin to see whether the file was accidentally deleted:

1. **Open the Recycle Bin icon on the desktop.**

2. **Choose View⇨Details.**

This step displays the Recycle Bin window, similar to what's shown in Figure 4-1. Information about the deleted files appears in four columns: name, location, date, and size. Those labels help you quickly locate files you've deleted, as covered in the sections that follow.

- ✔ The Find command does not look in the Recycle Bin for files. Keep that in mind!

- ✔ To recover a deleted file, click it and choose File⇨Restore from the menu.

- ✔ To recover more than one file, press the Ctrl key and hold it down as you click the files you want to restore.

- ✔ You must restore a file to its original location, the folder from which it was deleted. If you need to move the file to a better location, do so *after* restoring it. (But do make a note of the location to where the file is restored.)

- ✔ You cannot restore files that were deleted using the Shift+Delete keystroke. Those files cannot be recovered by using any of the tools in Windows. (Various third-party tools, such as the Norton Utilities, may be able to recover these files.)

- ✔ *Rubbish* is yet another R word, underused by Americans but right at home in the commonwealth.

Restoring a file you deleted recently

To find a file that you suspect was just deleted, click the Date Deleted heading in the Recycle Bin window. When the triangle next to Date Deleted points *down,* the most recently deleted files appear at the *top* of the list: scroll to the top of the list and pluck out the files you want recovered.

Note that in Windows 98 or Windows Me a triangle does not appear next to the Date Deleted column header; you just have to check the dates after clicking to ensure that the files are sorted the proper way.

Restoring a file when you know its name

To locate a file by name, click the Name heading in the Recycle Bin window. That action sorts the files alphabetically by name, either from A to Z or from Z to A, depending on how many times you click the Name heading.

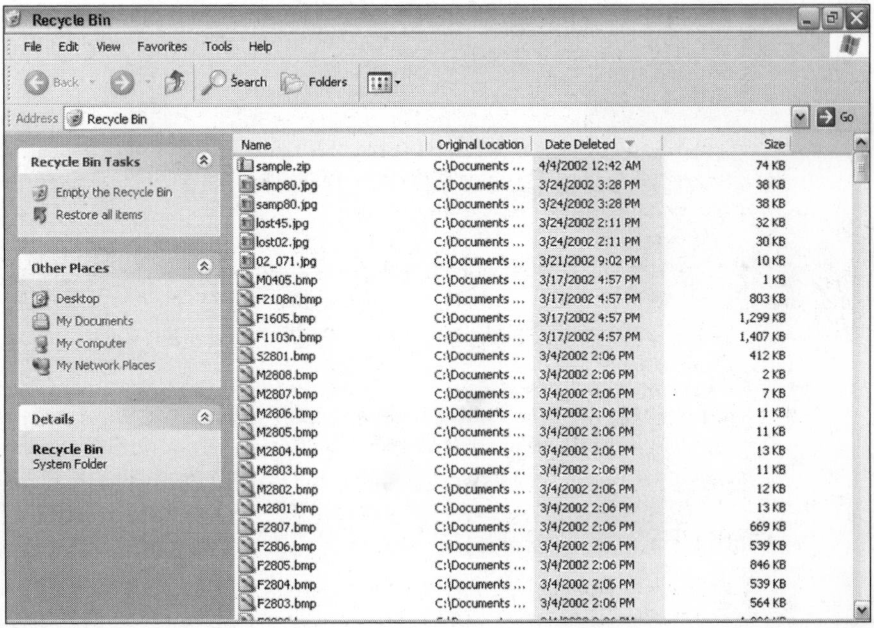

Figure 4-1:
Setting up
the Recycle
Bin for file
recovery.

Restoring a file when you know which application created it (by file type)

Searching for files by type allows you to locate a file when you don't know its name but you do remember which program created it. To do so, click the Type heading in the Recycle Bin window to sort the files by their file type (or by which program created them).

✔ To see more columns in Windows XP, such as the Type column, choose View➪Choose Details from the menu. Then, in the Choose Details dialog box, put a check mark next to the columns you want to see in the Recycle Bin window. Click OK to close the Choose Details dialog box.

✔ In Windows Me, choose View➪Choose Columns to select which columns you want visible in the Recycle Bin's window.

Using System Restore

The System Restore program in Windows Me and Windows XP is an excellent way to recover from just about any mishap, but specifically it works best for those it-was-working-yesterday situations. With System Restore, you can turn back the clock on your entire computer system — yes, back to the good old days.

When to set restore points

The System Restore utility lets you take your computer back in time only by setting various *restore points*. Windows sets them automatically as you use your computer. More importantly, you should set them yourself *before* you make any extensive changes to the system.

For example, set a restore point before you add or upgrade any hardware or software. Set a restore point before you mess with any Windows settings — graphics, sounds, or wallpaper. Set one before you modify your Internet or network settings or when editing the Start menu, rearranging files, uninstalling programs — before doing just about anything other than getting your work done, set a restore point. You'll thank yourself later.

Setting a restore point

Never rely on Windows automatically setting a restore point for you. To do the job manually, heed these steps:

1. **Start System Restore.**

   From the Start menu, choose Programs➪Accessories➪System Tools➪ System Restore.

2. **Choose the option labeled Create a restore point.**

3. **Click the Next button.**

4. **Enter a restore point description.**

   The restore point description appears when you later use System Restore. Therefore, you should be descriptive here.

   Good restore point descriptions are "Installing new Zip drive," "Changing resolution for new monitor," "System acting funny," and anything that may remind you in the future of what the problem could be.

   Bad restore point descriptions are "Installing" and "Stuff" and "Chad is singing again and if I pretend I'm busy doing something on the computer, perhaps he'll go away."

5. **Click the Create button in Windows XP; in Windows Me, it's the Next button.**

The new restore point is created, and the current day, date, and time appear on the screen. Nifty.

6. **Click the Close button in Windows XP; click OK in Windows Me.**

And you're done.

Now you can proceed to mess with your system or add a new gizmo or application. Those are the times when the system may not behave as you've expected. Not to worry! You have the safety net of a recent restore point, which you can bring the system back to if things don't work as expected.

REMEMBER

✔ Don't neglect using the restore point description! It's valuable information that may come in handy later if something goofs up.

✔ Windows attempts to create automatic restore points as long as you leave the system on for a length of time. I leave my computers on 24 hours a day, so I notice restore points created just about every day, typically around midnight.

Restoring the system

When things don't go as planned or your PC suffers from it-was-working-yesterday syndrome, you can attempt a system restore. (My first advice is to restart Windows, which is covered in Chapter 2, and then do a system restore.)

Follow these steps to restore your system:

1. **Close any open windows or programs, safely saving any unsaved information.**

   Restoring the system restarts the computer, so it's best to close and save now before you begin the restore process.

2. **Start System Restore.**

   Refer to Step 1 from the preceding section for starting System Restore in Windows Me or Windows XP.

3. **Choose Restore my computer to an earlier time.**

4. **Click the Next button.**

5. **Pick the date you want to take the computer back to.**

   If you've set a specific restore point, choose the date where you set that restore point.

   If more than one restore point is set on a date, as shown in Figure 4-2, choose it from the list.

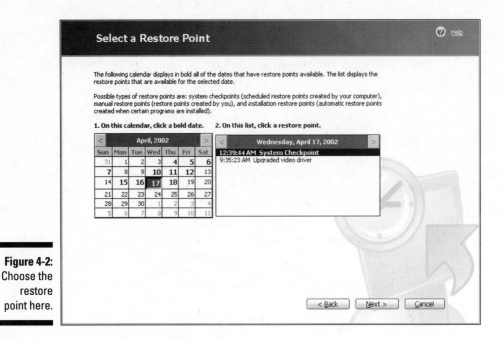

Select a Restore Point

The following calendar displays in bold all of the dates that have restore points available. The list displays the restore points that are available for the selected date.

Possible types of restore points are: system checkpoints (scheduled restore points created by your computer), manual restore points (restore points created by you), and installation restore points (automatic restore points created when certain programs are installed).

1. On this calendar, click a bold date.   **2. On this list, click a restore point.**

Figure 4-2:
Choose the
restore
point here.

Sometimes, System Restore may fail if you choose a restore point too far in the past. In that case, consider selecting more recent restore points and working your way back to restore the system to an earlier date.

6. Click the Next button.

Read the scary warning. The bottom line is that the System Restore process is fully reversible, so if System Restore makes things worse, you can undo its changes.

In Windows Me, click OK to make the scary warning go away.

7. Click the Next button.

Windows restores, restarts, and. . . .

Hopefully, things wind up just fine and the kinks are worked out of the system. After the system restarts, a screen eventually appears, telling you "Restoration Complete," with a summary of what happened.

8. Click the OK button.

I've suggested this operation to many of my readers with computer problems, and most of the time it meets with tremendous success. If not, further troubleshooting is needed. In fact, if System Restore doesn't fix the problem, it's most likely a hardware problem that needs further attention (replacement, for example).

TIP

"But I have Windows 98 and don't have a System Restore utility! Waaa! Waaa!"

Fret not, gentle Windows 98 reader — as well as Windows Me and Windows XP users who may not find that System Restore cuts the mustard: Better tools are out there for everyone. One program is GoBack, available from Roxio, Inc. (www.roxio.com/). I recommend it.

Undoing a System Restore

If the System Restore operation fails to address the issue or you just would rather have not performed the operation in the first place, you can undo the changes: Start System Restore and on the first screen select the option Undo my last restoration. Click the Next button and continue through the steps to undo whatever it was that System Restore had done.

Restoring Files from a Backup

Backing up a hard drive used to be a required (though bothersome) necessity for anyone using a computer. In the early days, hard drives were not only expensive, but they were also often unreliable. Backing up your data ensured that a safety copy existed.

Backing up is more of a lost art today. I bemoan this topic even more in Chapter 22. See that chapter if you want to hear my caterwauling about why people don't back up.

Of course, if you do back up, you have the benefit of owning that second, safety copy of your stuff. It means that you can *restore* files or even your entire system from the backup copy.

Information in the following sections describes how to restore files from a backup. This information is based on the Windows 98 backup program, though it's loosely similar to all backup programs. (I apologize that I cannot be more specific, but not having a standard backup program for Windows is a problem.)

✔ *Backing up* is the process of creating a duplicate of the information on your computer's hard drive. The backup itself is the copy. See Chapter 22 for more detailed information.

✔ Tools such as System Restore would be completely unnecessary today if more people made backups of their hard drive.

✔ Windows 98 comes with a backup utility, as does Windows XP Professional.

✔ Windows XP Home and Windows Me do not come with backup programs. Ack! You've been robbed! Sorry, but you must purchase your backup software separately (which is usually better than the stuff that comes with Windows anyway).

✔ For the restore operation to work, you must have a recent backup handy.

Restoring a single file, folder, or folders

If you can't find a particular file or have lost it or permanently deleted it, you can always recover it from a recent backup. Follow these (general) steps:

1. **Start the Backup program.**

   To start Microsoft Backup, click the Start button and choose Programs⇨ Accessories⇨System Tools⇨Backup. If you don't see it there, your version of Windows doesn't have it. Don't be surprised.

2. **Enter Restore mode.**

   In Microsoft Backup, you choose Restore backed up files when the program first starts. In other programs, you may have to click the Restore tab or switch to whichever part of the program deals with restoring files from the backup archive.

   Some backup utilities may even have a restore program run separately from the main backup program.

3. **Select the backup media or location.**

   Backing up can be done to a special tape drive, second hard drive, disk drive on the network, Zip disk, CD-R or CD-RW disk, or any removable disk. This step involves not only inserting that media into the drive (or device) but also telling the backup program where to look for it.

4. **Choose the backup set.**

   Often, multiple backups are stored on a single disk. This step involves choosing the most recent backup from which you will restore files.

5. **Wait as the program catalogs the backup.**

   The backup program takes a few seconds to read the backup information and, eventually, presents you with a list of the files stored inside the backup archive.

   Figure 4-3 illustrates the Microsoft Backup program in Windows 98. The files and folders that are backed up appear on the left side of the window. The folder DrivewayCam is selected, and its contents appear in the right window. That's where single files are restored.

6. **Browse to find the files or folders you want to restore.**

   Navigate through the folders that were backed up. Note that not all backups may contain all the folders on your system. If you can't find the folder you're looking for, you need to choose another backup.

7. **Click to select the files or folders you want to restore.**

8. **Choose a location to restore the files.**

   This step may not appear in all backup programs: Sometimes, you're given the option to restore the file to its original location or to another location. You would choose another location, for example, if you want to review an older version of a file without overwriting the current version.

   If you do elect to overwrite any existing file, a warning dialog box is usually displayed. My advice: Overwrite the file only if the one you're restoring is more recent.

9. **Click the Start or Go or Restore button.**

   Perform whatever operation is necessary to make the restore take place.

   If the files are stored across several disks, you're asked to replace disks as the restore operation continues.

   And you're done.

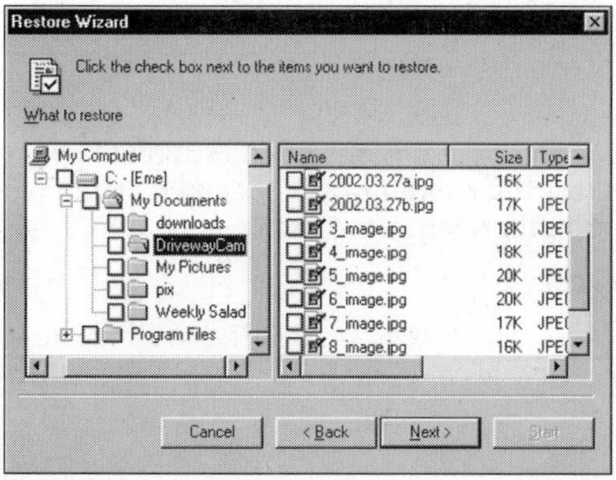

Figure 4-3:
Choosing
a file to
restore.

I would say that of all the utilities I've ever used on any computer, the restore half of Backup is the most satisfying. It's not enough knowing that you have the backup copy. It's a great feeling when you actually get to restore a file and recover something that you thought was lost forever.

Be careful about overwriting existing files when you restore a folder! Make sure that you *really* want to restore the entire folder and all its contents before you choose a Replace All option. (You cannot recover any file that has been overwritten.)

Restoring an application

Alas, it's fairly difficult to pluck out a single application from a backup disk set. Applications in Windows don't really install themselves in a specific place. Therefore, trying to locate all the bits and pieces of a program that may be scattered all over a hard drive is a questionable operation.

Rather than restore an application, just reinstall it. See the section "Reinstalling applications," later in this chapter.

Restoring the entire hard drive

When disaster strikes, you can use your backup disks to restore your entire hard drive — for example, if your computer is infected with one of those nasty, nonremovable viruses (such as Nimda or Code Red). Or suppose that your 12-year-old "computer genius" cousin decided to "optimize" your Windows folder. It's those severe times that call for a full hard drive restore operation.

Restoring a full hard drive involves these steps:

1. Create special *boot disks* to reinstall the operating system, or disks you can use to run the backup program and restore files.

2. Reformat the hard drive.

3. Boot with the special boot disks to restore files from the backup to the hard drive. Or reinstall the operating system and then the backup program to restore the hard drive.

4. Restore from any partial or incremental backups since the last full hard drive backup.

Those steps are not only scary, they're also time-consuming! That is why I don't recommend this operation for silly things. Unfortunately, most of the tech support people working today recommend the reformat-restore operation like it's routine. It's not.

✔ Most backup programs do come with a special boot disk, or they let you create your own disk, so that you can start the computer, run the program, and restore files when the hard drive may be utterly corrupted.

✔ Most new PCs come with a boot image, or restore, CD, which you can boot on the computer to reinstall the system the way it appeared when you first bought the computer. Just stick the CD into the drive and restart the computer. If you're presented with the option to start from the CD, do so. That restores the entire system. After that point, you can reinstall your backup program and then restore the rest of your computer system from the backup disks.

Reinstalling Stuff

Sometimes, the solution to a problem is as easy as reinstalling software. You just find the original copy or distribution disks or CDs, pop 'em in the computer, and reinstall. Problem fixed (most of the time).

✔ A special instance where reinstalling isn't what I recommend is for your computer's operating system, Windows. Too often, "reinstall Windows" is presented as a solution by lazy tech support people — especially when a better, less time-consuming and less-destructive option is available. (Reinstalling Windows is one of my pet peeves, which I shall bemoan throughout the rest of this book.)

✔ Another thing to reinstall is a *device driver*. That's the software used by Windows to control a piece of hardware. Because reinstalling a device driver is specific to the hardware you're troubleshooting, that information is located elsewhere in this book. Use the index to locate the hardware for which you need a new device driver.

Reinstalling applications

Consider reinstalling an application for any of the following reasons:

✔ The application is behaving in a manner inconsistent with the way it once behaved.

✔ All the files "owned" by that application are now owned by something else, something you don't want them to be owned by.

✔ Files belonging to the application were deleted so that the application either no longer runs or displays error messages as it starts.

✔ The application was accidentally uninstalled.

✔ The application was infected with a virus.

✔ The application develops a longing to tour the world's beaches and find "the perfect wave."

There may be more reasons as well. In my experience, I've had to reinstall only two programs. One was a graphics program that apparently didn't like another graphics program I later installed. Reinstalling the first program fixed the incompatibilities. The second instance was an older program that no longer worked, but somehow reinstalling it fixed things up nicely.

To reinstall your application, simply insert the Install or Setup disk into the proper drive. Just go ahead and install the program over itself; you rarely have any need to remove or uninstall the original from the hard drive. (Only if the Setup program tells you that the original needs to be removed do you need to do so.)

✔ Generally speaking, consider visiting the Web page for the application's developer. Check for a FAQ list or any tech support you can find online that maybe has a specific solution to your problem.

✔ The support Web page for all Microsoft products is
`http://support.microsoft.com`.

Bringing back bits of Windows

For problems involving Windows applets (Calculator, Paint, and FreeCell, for example), the solution is often to uninstall and then reinstall the program. This trick has worked on many occasions — especially with WordPad in Windows 98. I have no idea why WordPad tends to cause trouble for so many people, but it does.

The first step to reinstalling a Windows applet is to uninstall it. Follow these steps:

1. **Open the Control Panel's Add/Remove Programs icon.**

   An Add/Remove Programs dialog box appears.

   In the Windows XP category view, click the Add or Remove Programs link to open the Add/Remove Programs dialog box.

2. **Click the Windows Setup tab.**

   In Windows XP, click the Add/Remove Windows Components button on the left side of the window.

3. **Choose the main category from the scrolling list.**

   You find most applets in the Accessories categories, though with each release of Windows the exact locations of things do change. You may have to poke around a bit.

4. **Click the Details button.**

   This step displays whatever group of programs is held inside a category. In Windows XP, the Accessories and Utilities category contains both the Accessories and Games categories. (It's funny that no Utility category is in there.)

5. **When you finally get down to the bottom level, locate on the list the program you want to uninstall.**

6. **Remove the check mark by that program, as shown in Figure 4-4.**

   This step selects the program for removal.

7. **Click OK to close the various dialog boxes until you return to the main Add/Remove Programs dialog box, and then click OK to close that one.**

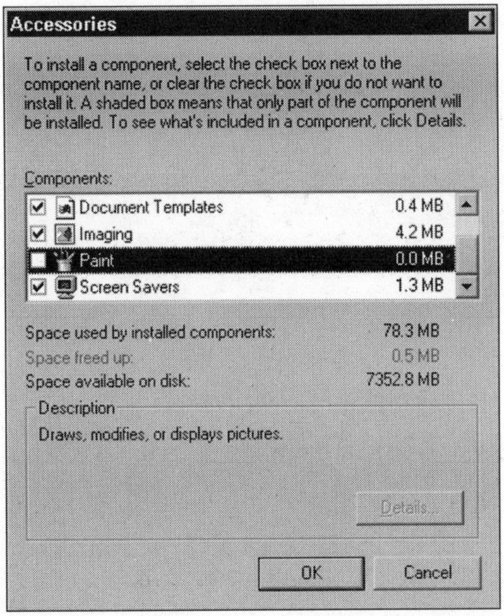

Figure 4-4:
Uninstalling
a Windows
applet.

| Accessories | ☒ |

To install a component, select the check box next to the component name, or clear the check box if you do not want to install it. A shaded box means that only part of the component will be installed. To see what's included in a component, click Details.

Components:

☑ 📄 Document Templates	0.4 MB	▲
☑ 🖼 Imaging	4.2 MB	
☐ 🖌 Paint	0.0 MB	
☑ 💻 Screen Savers	1.3 MB	▼

Space used by installed components: 78.3 MB
Space freed up: 0.5 MB
Space available on disk: 7352.8 MB

Description
Draws, modifies, or displays pictures.

Details...

OK   Cancel

8. **Restart Windows.**

   This step is optional, though it does officially remove the files previously installed. If you do not restart Windows, the files may still be on the hard drive. Better not chance it: Restart Windows. (Refer to Chapter 2 for the details.)

   After restarting your computer, you reinstall the program, giving Windows a fresh — and, hopefully, better-running — copy:

9. **Repeat Steps 1 and 2.**

   You want to be in the Windows Setup part of the Add/Remove Programs Properties dialog box.

10. **Repeat the steps you just took to remove the applet (Steps 3 through 6), but this time add the applet back in (reinstall).**

    For example, in Windows 98, you select Accessories and then click the Details button. Then put a check mark by the WordPad item. This step sets up the system to reinstall WordPad.

11. **Click OK to close the various sub-dialog boxes.**

12. **Click OK to close the Add/Remove Programs Properties dialog box.**

    Windows may ask for the CD-ROM to be inserted so that it can reinstall the programs. If your computer came with Windows preinstalled, the files are found on the hard drive.

After reinstalling, the program should work just fine. At least, that has been my experience.

- ✔ If Windows is unable to locate the files, try looking in the Windows\Options\CABS folder on Drive C for them.

- ✔ Uninstalling unused programs is yet another way to conserve hard drive space. This topic is covered in Chapter 19.

Chapter 5

Your Last Resort: Tech Support

· ·

· ·

*W*hen you buy a computer, purchase software, or sign some type of agreement for a service (such as the Internet), you should get some form of support. I recommend service and support over brand names and discounts any day of the week. Support is there to help you if things don't work as expected and to fix things when stuff invariably breaks. It's a good thing; worth the extra expense.

Alas, the quality of technical support has dwindled over the past several years. It has grown expensive and often intolerant, especially of the needs of beginners. Although you find good support departments here and there, technical support for computers is rapidly getting a reputation as bad as the computer manuals of days gone by.

This chapter shows you the ups and downs of technical support and why you should use it only as a last resort.

✔ In the computer biz, there is a difference between technical support and customer service. Customer service deals with sales, sale support, product questions before purchase, and product return. Technical support is where you go when you have questions or problems with the product. Know the difference before you make the call!

✔ Looking for proper service and support is the fourth of five steps to take when buying a computer. See *Buying a Computer For Dummies,* which I wrote (and Wiley Publishing, Inc., published) for more information.

When to Use Tech Support

This advice is simple: Use tech support as a last resort, if at all.

✔ Most problems are easily fixable without having to call support.

✔ Use this book to help you troubleshoot many of the common computer foibles that everyone experiences.

✔ Technical support is also available for any peripheral or add-on hardware you may buy. In that case, call the manufacturer, as listed in the manual or on the invoice.

✔ Above all, you *paid* for support when you bought the product. They owe it to you. If you can fix it yourself, great. But don't feel guilty about calling support when you need it.

Boring tech support history you don't have to read

In the old days, technical support was purely technical. By that, I mean that the only people who would call tech support were technicians themselves, the office computer guru, a programmer, or a hacker. They knew computers. And the folks giving the technical support were typically the software programmers or product engineers themselves. They knew the answers, but more importantly, the people calling knew the right questions to ask. The system worked rather well.

As computers became more of a consumer commodity, tech support changed to accommodate more beginners. In fact, the folks at the old DOS WordPerfect toll-free tech support line told me that the most common phone call they received was by someone who hadn't yet taken the product out of the box. Sure, those people needed help, and the WordPerfect folks were willing to help them. In the end, the bean counters took over, and WordPerfect had to cut back on its technical support.

Eventually, companies had to justify having technical support. The toll-free numbers disappeared. Then, free support almost dried up. Today, support is often free for the first 90 days, and then you pay for a flat-rate toll after that, a per-call fee, or a per-minute fee. Even then, the fee doesn't guarantee that your problem will be solved or even that you won't have to wait on hold.

Before you call tech support

Using a computer is a tough thing. These beasts are not simple. Anything can and does go wrong. The tech support people know this, and they brace themselves for anything. They have to! Callers range from the timid beginner who still has the computer in the box to the hacker whose computer has been utterly disassembled and desoldered. You can make the tech support person's job easier by doing a little research before you call.

Find out who owns the problem. Narrow things down. Is it hardware or software? That way, you can call the proper place. Refer to Chapter 3 for more on making this determination.

Try as many solutions yourself as possible. Use this book to help you troubleshoot as much as possible. Tech support people are blown away if you've already looked in the Device Manager or worked in the System Configuration Utility. They may have you look there again — if so, be patient. (They're typically following a script and must check things off before taking you to the next level.)

Determine whether the problem is repeatable. Be prepared to demonstrate to tech support that the bug isn't random and can be reproduced. I did this once, and the tech support guy was amazed when the same foul-up happened on his computer.

Be prepared to give information, and lots of it. Do your homework before you call. This book tells you many places to look for solving problems. Go through those steps and gather as much information as possible. You don't have to spill it all to the tech support person at once, but have it ready for when they ask.

One important thing to relate to tech support is which version of Windows you have. It also helps to know the version of any application or utility you figure is causing the problem.

Yes, there is a time limit

Technical support is often "farmed out" now to businesses other than the original manufacturer or developer. So although you think you're calling the software developer, hardware manufacturer, or online service, you may end up being connected to some other company, one that specializes in handling technical support.

For the most part, the people answering the phones are knowledgeable about the product and capable of solving the problems. Unfortunately, because they base their business on the number of calls answered per hour (or per shift), their financial goal is to beat the clock as opposed to solving a problem to your satisfaction.

The average amount of time the typical tech support person has to deal with your problem is 12 minutes, more or less. After that, they are under tremendous pressure to "dump" you. I've

experienced this too often myself. And my readers have related to me the disappointing results of being dumped: After 12 minutes, the tech support person simply says, "Reinstall Windows" or "Reformat the hard drive" and then hangs up. Most definitely, that is *not* the solution to your problem. But it's the solution to their problem, which is to get rid of you before the 12 minutes are up.

So when you phone tech support, keep an eye on the clock. If it's over 12 minutes and no solution is working or the tech support person suggests reinstalling Windows or reformatting the hard drive, you should protest. Ask to speak to a supervisor. Often, the supervisors are not under the same time limitations as the grunts who have to answer the phones. That should lead to an answer.

To find out the Windows version, follow these steps:

1. **Right-click the My Computer icon on the desktop.**

2. **Choose Properties from the pop-up menu.**

   The General tab in the System Properties dialog box lists all the information about Windows that you need to know, as shown in Figure 5-1. Beneath the System heading are listed the Windows version (or release) and then below that the edition and then the specific version.

   In Figure 5-1, the computer is running Windows XP, Home Edition, Version 2002.

3. **Close the System Properties dialog box.**

To find out the version of any specific application, choose the Help⇨About command. (The About command is usually followed by the program's name.) That displays a dialog box with the program's full name, release, and version information — and maybe even a quick button to click for connecting to tech support.

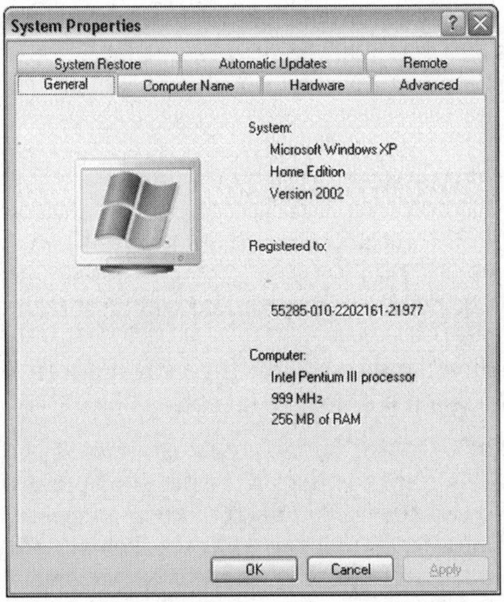

Figure 5-1:
Windows
version
information.

Finally, it pays to know which number to call. This is something I find frustrating: The tech support number is typically hidden somewhere in the manual. Sometimes, it's right up front or in a tech support index. But most often it's in a not-so-obvious place.

✔ When you find the tech support phone number, flag it! Highlight it. Better still, write it in the front of the manual. Add it to your Address Book. Spray paint it on the wall!

✔ See Appendix A for more information on the Device Manager and the System Configuration utility (MSCONFIG).

✔ Although it helps to gather information such as microprocessor speed, hard drive capacity, and total RAM, don't bother passing those figures on to tech support unless they ask for it.

✔ If Windows 98 lacks an edition line, it's Windows 98, First Edition. The Second Edition says "Second Edition" right below the line that reads "Microsoft Windows 98."

✔ Also see Chapter 23.

Make the call

Phone up tech support. Wait on hold. Listen to the silly music.

Be prepared to talk to a screener before you get true tech support. Sometimes, an initial person breaks in and gets your name, phone number, customer, and serial or registration number and a description of the problem before you speak with an actual tech.

Do some doodling in the Paint program while you wait.

When the tech answers, calmly and politely explain the problem. Then follow the instructions as best you can. Don't bother saying "But I already tried this." Just follow along and hopefully your problem will be solved.

- ✔ For some reason, when you opt to pay for the tech support, it happens sooner and faster than when it's "free" support.

- ✔ Keep an eye on the clock. Do this for two reasons. First, if you're paying for the call, you probably want to check the time you spend waiting on hold. Second, after the call starts, you need to keep an eye out for the 12-minute period to elapse and then see whether tech support is giving you the brush-off. (See the sidebar "Yes, there is a time limit," earlier in this chapter.)

Tech Support on the Web (Better than You Think)

As long as your problem isn't with the Internet in the first place, you can find some excellent tech support available freely on the Web. Most software developers and hardware manufacturers have support areas on their Web sites. There, you can review common questions and answers, troubleshoot products, e-mail questions, or download new software solutions. In fact, it's only after checking the Web that I bother calling tech support by phone.

Finding the manufacturer's Web site

After discovering whether the problem is hardware or software, your next step is to find a Web site to seek out technical support. Sometimes, this part is easy: Choose Help⇨About or Help⇨Support from the menu, and often the developer's Web page is listed right there. Neat-o.

For hardware manufacturers, the problem is a bit rougher. First, if the hardware came with the computer, contact the computer manufacturer.

It's common for the computer manufacturer to list contact information in the System Properties dialog box:

1. **Right-click the My Computer icon.**

2. **Choose Properties from the pop-up menu.**

   The System Properties dialog box dangles open.

3. **If necessary, click the General tab.**

4. **Click the Support button.**

   A dialog box is displayed, listing tech support and contact information.

If this trick doesn't work, you have to hunt down the hardware manufacturer using a search engine like Yahoo! or Google:

```
www.yahoo.com/
www.google.com/
```

Just type the manufacturer's name into the text box and click the Search button on the Yahoo! or Google main page. Somewhere within the results is the page you're looking for.

When you get to the manufacturer's page, look for a technical support link. Then you can begin the process of searching for whatever information you need.

- ✔ You should also use these steps for finding support information for any extra hardware you buy for your computer. If the tech support Web page isn't listed in the manual, use the Internet to search for the Web page.

- ✔ Be sure to use as few words as possible when you search for information on the Internet. Be direct: "S3 graphics driver upgrade" or "missing icon."

- ✔ Another tip: If you search broadly at first, check to see whether any options can refine your search or "search within results." For example, if the search results on the tech support Web page yield 400 answers, consider searching through those answers for something more specific to your situation.

- ✔ If you bought the computer locally, just phone the dealer for support. This is one case where it's easier to call and bug them than to use a Web page. But for manufacturers, going to the Web page is easier by far.

- ✔ Also check on the manufacturer's Web page for an FAQ — Frequently Asked Questions — list.

Using the Microsoft Knowledge Base

Microsoft has perhaps the most extensive and exhaustive troubleshooting database on the Internet. They call it the Microsoft Knowledge Base, and it's similar to information the Microsoft tech support people use when you phone them (and pay) for an answer.

Visit the Knowledge Base, at `http://support.microsoft.com/`. Choose an operating system or application from the drop-down list, and then type a brief, punchy question or problem description. Click the button, and soon a list of potential solutions appears, one of which will perhaps save your butt.

- Definitely, definitely, most definitely use the Microsoft Knowledge base *first,* before phoning up Microsoft.

- Much of the information in the Knowledge Base is rehash from what you find in the Windows help system.

- Note that some problems have multiple solutions. For example, the nefarious Windows 98 Shutdown Hang Problem has perhaps two dozen solutions. Each one is for a different system configuration.

- It helps to know Microsoft-ese when typing questions for the Knowledge Base. For example, you may use the word *hang,* but the Knowledge Base uses the word *freeze.* Be sure to try another, similar word if your initial search yields no results.

Downloading a new driver

Occasionally, your Internet search ends with the task of installing new software to make things work right. For example, to fix that CD-ROM glitch, you may need new software — a driver. To get rid of a printer problem or to make your printer happy with other software, you may need a new printer driver. Whatever the reason, your task is to download and install new software. Here is my advice for getting that done:

- Bookmark the Web page! Press the Ctrl+D key combination to add the Web page to your favorites list. You do this just in case things go wrong and you need to return.

- Print any instructions for installing the new software.

- When you've found the software you need, you click a link so that the software can be sent to you online *(downloaded).* A Save As dialog box appears. In that dialog box, choose a memorable location for the file. I use a folder named Downloads, which is created in the main My Documents folder.

✔ If the download fails or Windows tells you that it's "corrupted," you have to try again. If the file is still corrupted after the second download, contact the developer and tell someone there that something is wrong with the file.

✔ Drivers control hardware, so to learn more about installing specific drivers, see the index for the hardware in question. Instructions for installing or updating drivers are included throughout this book.

✔ Drivers should be free of charge. I've found only one Web site where they wanted to charge me for a new driver — and for hardware I already owned. I immediately tossed out the hardware and bought something else. I wrote a letter to the hardware manufacturer's president — not that it did any good. Don't be suckered into paying for a driver or software upgrade.

Windows XP and Remote Assistance

I've answered technical and troubleshooting questions from my readers for more than a dozen years now. The biggest hurdle in trying to help someone is not being able to see what they see on the screen.

For example, someone may write "The buttons are wrong; they're all over the screen." After two or three exchanges of e-mail, I discovered that the reader's taskbar was on the top edge of the screen, not on the bottom. Had I been standing right there looking at the screen, it would have been a click and a swipe of the mouse to fix things. But via e-mail, it took four or five messages to get things right.

Being there is a big part of getting proper tech support. To help out, Windows XP has a feature called Remote Assistance. By using Remote Assistance, you can allow anyone on the Internet who also has Windows XP to take control of your computer and see what you see on the screen. That makes it a heck of a lot easier to fix things, as the following sections demonstrate.

✔ I recommend using this feature only if you really, really trust the person who's looking at your computer. If so, you might find a ready solution for some of your PC's problems.

✔ Remote Assistance isn't worth diddly squat if your computer cannot connect to the Internet.

✔ Speaking of the Internet, the faster the connection, the more effective Remote Assistance is. I've done it with 56K modems at about 49 Kbps true speed, and it was tolerable but not ideal.

Setting up your system for Remote Assistance

Obviously, you don't want just anyone barging into your PC to give you "assistance." No, the person must be properly invited. Follow these steps:

1. **Find someone to help you!**

   Ideally, the person must be another Windows XP user signed up for the Windows Messenger program. That way, the operation works smoothly on both ends (and that's the only configuration I've tested).

   Phone that person up and tell them to get online and to connect into the Windows Messenger program. Then they need to wait while you set things up on your end.

2. **Get on the Internet.**

   Connect to the Internet as you normally do.

3. **Summon the Help and Support Center.**

   You can choose Help and Support from the Start menu or press the Win+F1 key combination.

   On the right side of the Help and Support Center window, you see a heading titled Ask for assistance.

4. **Click the link Invite a friend to connect to your computer with Remote Assistance.**

   A special, Remote Assistance screen opens.

5. **Click the link Invite someone to help you.**

   The next screen is used to choose who will help you.

6. **Pick your pal out of the Windows Messenger list.**

   The person should appear on the list, per your instructions from Step 1. This is the easiest way to get help from someone. You can try sending them an e-mail message, but things just work better when both of you are online and connected with Windows Messenger.

7. **Click the link Invite this person.**

   A message is sent to your pal, who is fortunately already connected per Step 1. They have to accept the invitation, in which case you see a Waiting for a connection dialog box.

   Eventually, you're asked whether you want the person to view your screen and chat with you.

8. **Click the Yes button.**

   The Remote Assistance dialog box appears, as shown in Figure 5-2. This is your control panel for granting the person access to your computer. It's also where you can chat with them while you're connected.

   On the other system, the person is receiving a snapshot of what your screen looks like.

   The person may chat with you via the chat window (see Figure 5-3) and have you do things, which they can see on their computer. Or, they may opt to control your computer for themselves, in which case they can move your mouse and type things. If so, you see the dialog box shown in Figure 5-3.

9. **Click the Yes button to allow the other person to control your computer.**

   You can cancel what the other person is doing at any time by pressing the Esc button on your keyboard.

   Hopefully, everything goes well and they fix your problem without discovering where you hide the filthy pictures on your computer.

10. **When you're done, click the Disconnect button in the Remote Assistance dialog box.**

11. **Close any windows you may have opened.**

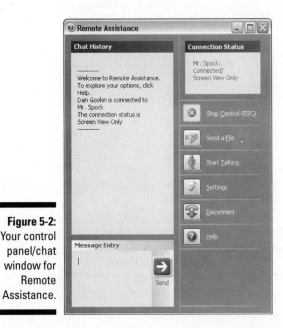

Figure 5-2:
Your control
panel/chat
window for
Remote
Assistance.

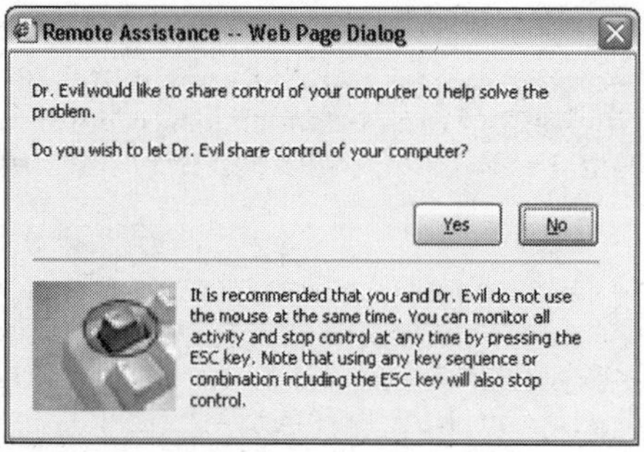

Figure 5-3:
Allowing
the other
person to
control your
computer.

Hopefully, whatever problems you've had were solved by the nice Remote Assistance person.

- ✔ If you have Windows XP, you probably have already signed up for your .NET ("dot-net"), Passport, and Windows Messenger accounts.
- ✔ No one can get into your computer unless you invite them.
- ✔ You can cancel the connection at any time by clicking the Disconnect button or pressing the Esc key.
- ✔ If you don't want the person to meddle with certain areas of your hard drive, such as your personal finance folder, let them know ahead of time.
- ✔ Yes! It's *slow* over plain modems! It's very slow, but workable.

Performing Remote Assistance on another system

To help out another Windows XP user, start by arranging the Remote Assistance session. The person should let you know when you need to be online and ready to help. Follow these steps:

1. **Connect to the Internet.**

2. **Start up the Windows Messenger.**

   The person contacts you via the Windows Messenger program. You have other ways to contact people, such as by sending them e-mail and so forth, but it's much easier if you're already on Windows Messenger.

3. **Wait for the invite to appear on the screen.**

   It appears like any other pop-up message in Windows Messenger.

4. When the invitation appears, click it.

A Conversation (chat) window appears, similar to the one in Figure 5-4. But unlike in a normal chat window, you find an invitation to help the other person via Remote Assistance.

5. Click Accept.

The connection is made to the other computer, and the Remote Assistance window appears, which details what the other person sees on their screen, as shown in Figure 5-5.

At this point, you can type in the Chat History window (on the left side of the window in Figure 5-5) and tell the other person to do things. What they see on their screen shows up in the window so that you can see what's going on.

Click the Actual Size button to see the image clearly; otherwise, the Scale to Window option squishes everything down to fit in the Remote Assistance window.

6. To take over the other computer, click the Take Control button.

This step allows you to use your mouse and keyboard to manipulate the other computer. The results are displayed in the Remote Assistance window. Note that the person has to say Yes to the Take Control question before you can take over.

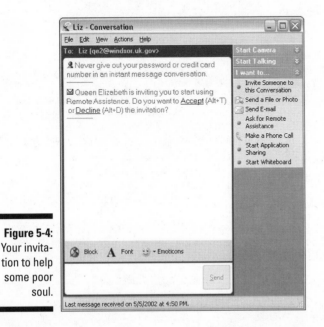

Figure 5-4:
Your invitation to help some poor soul.

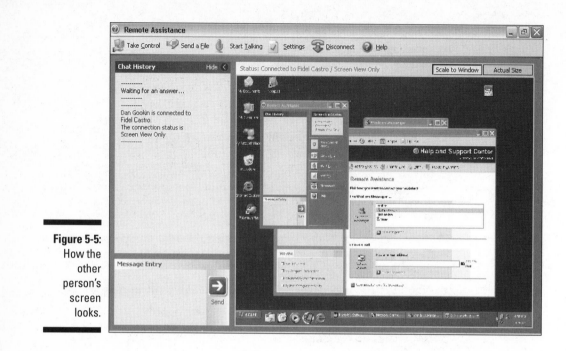

Figure 5-5:
How the
other
person's
screen
looks.

7. **Press the Esc key when you're done controlling the computer.**

8. **Click the Disconnect button to break the connection when you're done troubleshooting.**

   Be sure to close any other windows that may be left open.

Again, the idea here isn't to mess with the computer, but rather to *see* what they see. In fact, it's often better to tell the person what to do and then watch the results than try to work a mouse over a slow modem connection.

Part II

Troubleshooting Minor Irks and Quirks

The 5th Wave By Rich Tennant

Maintenance is chagrined to find out the squeak in Clark's disk drive is really a whistle in Clark's nose.

In this part . . .

Face it: Even at times of brutal desperation, human beings are essentially lazy. It's nothing to feel guilty about, and nothing worth "getting over." It's just one of those random and ugly facts about people. For example, only in the movies will the good guy go back and rescue his stumbling girlfriend when the monster is chasing them. In real life, the guy runs to the shelter and bends over all red-faced, panting and wheezing. Then, only after someone hands him a cold beer will he wonder, "Hey! Where's Linda?"

So why experience the solution when you can just look it up instead? It's human nature to prefer the ready-made solution. After all, so many computer problems are common or similar enough that someone somewhere must have had the same thing happen to them. Then all you need to do is look up that answer and get on with your life. That's the function of the chapters in this part of the book. They're organized into problem areas, scenarios, or specific hardware or software. Look up a common question. Get an answer. Get on with your life.

Chapter 6

"This Just Bugs Me!"

● ●

In This Chapter

▶ Hearing weird things

▶ Fixing the display's "dumb mode" resolution

▶ Updating your graphics device driver

▶ Removing icons from the system tray

▶ Working around Scandisk and Defrag

▶ Dying in sleep mode

▶ Removing the Logon dialog box

▶ To Open With or not to Open With

▶ Undoing a file's read-only persuasion

▶ Getting out of DOS mode

● ●

I suppose that every computer glitch falls under the category of This Just Bugs Me. Even so, I tried to compile a short list of my top ten favorite annoying PC or Windows problems plus their solutions. Obviously, I couldn't list *everything* that bugs you with your computer; there aren't enough trees in the world to produce the paper needed to print *that* particular book.

✔ Yes, even though a particular problem may be on your personal This Just Bugs Me list, it may not be here.

✔ See the index or use the table of contents to discover in which chapter the problem and solution lie.

Funny Start-Up Noises

Oh, those start-up noises just make me laugh!

Well, no, not really. I suppose I should say *peculiar* or *unexpected* noises as opposed to funny noises. No, if the computer made funny noises, the troubleshooting process would be far more enjoyable.

Officially, the computer makes only the following noises when it starts (I leave it up to you to determine whether you think they're funny):

- ✔ The fan comes on, keeping the console cool but also making a soft, warbling drone.

- ✔ The hard drive spins up to speed, which makes a high-pitched humming sound that few people over 40 can hear.

- ✔ The computer beeps once as it comes to life. The single beep means that everything is okay. It's like the computer gets all excited and — golly, gee! — if this were an MGM musical from the 1940s, the computer would burst out into song and have a big dance number with all the other office equipment. But, no: It's just a beep. That's the best Mr. PC can do.

The computer could make additional noises, funny or no:

- ✔ The monitor may honk when it comes to life. The larger the monitor, the louder the honking noise. Actually, it's more of an "UNK" noise than a car horn tootling.

- ✔ Also, the monitor makes a high-pitched whistling sound. Again, if you're over 40, there's no point in trying to hear it.

- ✔ The printer may hum a few bars of "Oink-grunt-oink" as it comes to life.

- ✔ Zip drives honk and whir when they're first initialized.

- ✔ The scanner may also power up and play "Clink, grindily grind."

That's pretty much it for the morning computer cacophony. You're most likely familiar with all these noises and note that something's wrong when a noise goes missing or a new noise gets introduced.

In the presence of unwanted noises

Noise problems are invariably hardware related, especially at start-up. New noises generally indicate a problem with whichever device seems to be making the noise. Alas, these problems must be fixed by your dealer or the computer manufacturer. Especially if the computer is still under warranty, avoid a homebrew solution.

- ✔ If the computer beeps more than once, the beeps indicate a problem with the start-up BIOS. This problem must be fixed by your dealer or the manufacturer. Tell them what the beep pattern was: several short beeps or long-short beeps, for example.

- ✔ Beeps may also sound off after you upgrade some hardware. That's simply the computer's acknowledgement that its basic configuration has changed. The extra beeps are typically accompanied by a text message on the screen explaining that new hardware has been found (or something like that).

✔ Hard drives can get louder over time. That means that their bearings are giving out. Of course, the real question is *when* will they give out. I had a hard drive in one system that was loud for an hour after turning the computer on, but then it got quiet. So the problem could be intermittent. See Part III of this book for more disk drive information.

✔ A squealing monitor needs to be fixed by a professional. Or replaced. Or told that squealing doesn't work.

✔ You can replace a pinging fan yourself, if you're good with electronics. In some cases, however, replacing the fan involves replacing the entire power supply, which can be done by anyone handy with a screwdriver or who has ever set up a backyard barbecue. Even so, if the system is still under warranty, have the dealer or manufacturer fix it.

✔ Another good way to repair a noisy fan: Clean it! Unplug your computer and open its case. Then take a vacuum and suck out all the dirt, hair, and byte-bunnies that accumulate in all PCs. Ensure that you also clean the vents that the fan blows air through.

✔ Never open or try to repair a PC's power supply or the monitor. Despite whatever noise they make, these items cannot be fixed by mere mortals.

In the presence of unwelcome silence

Whether the computer makes too much noise or no noise at all, it's still a hardware problem, one most effectively repaired by your computer dealer or manufacturer. Worse, a missing sound typically means a dead something-or-other inside your computer. Pee-yew! So the unwelcome silence is followed by more error messages and trouble. Take the thing in and get it fixed.

✔ Some computers do not beep when they first start up. Other computers may beep only if they are connected to speakers.

✔ One day, the sound stopped entirely in my old IBM PC. I heard no beep at start-up and no music when I played my favorite game. The next time I opened the case, I discovered the problem. I was living in a rather decrepit apartment in El Cajon, California, and a mouse family (the rodent type) moved into my computer and built a cozy nest atop the warm hard drive. The speaker apparently bothered them, so they *ate* the speaker's cardboard cone. I solved the problem by moving to another apartment complex.

The Display Is Stuck in "Dumb" Mode

I believe dumb mode to be the lowest possible resolution on a modern computer monitor: 640 by 480 pixels. This mode renders everything on the display *very large,* and it doesn't give you much screen real estate to get any work done. Obviously, it's a problem that needs fixing.

✔ Dumb mode may also be caused by your computer entering Safe mode when it starts up. You see the words *Safe Mode* appear in the four corners of the screen. If so, turn to Appendix B for what to do next.

✔ Yes, I am aware that even lower graphic resolutions are available (320 by 160, for example). The 640-by-480 resolution is the lowest mode supported by Windows. So there.

Checking the resolution

Before jumping to any conclusions, see whether you can fix the resolution the way Microsoft intended:

1. **Right-click the desktop.**

2. **Choose Properties from the pop-up menu.**

   This step summons the Display Properties dialog box, which you can also get to via the Control Panel.

3. **Click the Settings tab.**

   In the bottom of the dialog box, you find a slider gizmo, used to change the resolution from Less to More. Figure 6-1 gives you an idea of what's where (though in Windows XP, the slider gizmo is on the left side of the dialog box).

4. **Adjust the resolution higher.**

   Grab the slider gizmo and try moving it to the left. The resolution displayed below the gizmo tells you the potential screen resolution. The preview window gives you an idea of how the new setting affects the display.

   If nothing works, you need a new display driver. See the next section.

5. **Click the Apply button to test the new setting.**

   Unlike the OK button, the Apply button lets you preview your changes without closing the Display Properties dialog box.

   If you don't like the new settings or they don't seem to work, return the resolution to its old setting.

6. **Click the OK button.**

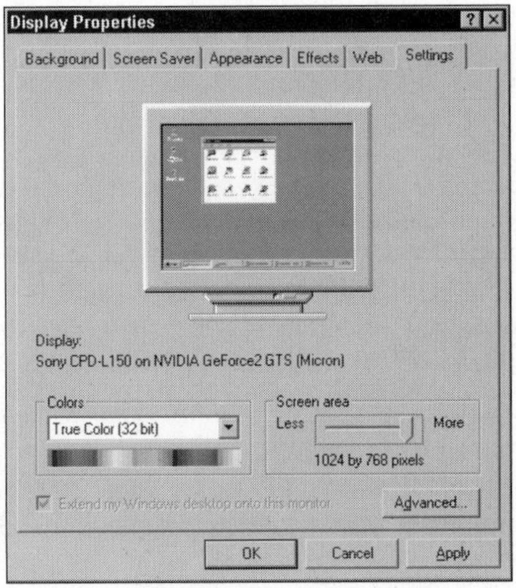

Figure 6-1:
Setting the
proper
screen
resolution.

In the long list of who-does-what in Windows, you are the one in charge of screen resolution. You can pick and choose whichever resolutions the Display Properties dialog box lets you. No program, not even Windows itself, can change that resolution to something else. After you've made a setting, it sticks that way.

The only time the resolution does change is if a problem occurs with the display driver or, occasionally, if some games change the resolution and then don't change it back after you close them. (That's becoming less of a problem, however.)

✔ More is not always better. If you set the resolution too high, you may lose the number of colors available.

✔ Higher resolutions also tend to flicker more and cause eyestrain. Only the highest-speed, high-memory graphics adapters can handle the higher resolutions. If you're in doubt, don't set the resolution over 1024 x 768.

✔ LCD monitors are optimized to handle specific resolutions, such as 800 x 600 or 1024 x 768. Trying other resolutions yields damn ugly results.

Updating your graphics device driver

Dumb mode is often caused by Windows losing track of your PC's graphics device driver. Without a specific driver, Windows uses what's known as the standard VGA driver, which gives you only 640 x 480 boring pixels to play in — not enough.

Fortunately, although Windows has lost track of the video driver, the driver most likely still exists on your computer. The solution is to go to your graphics adapter's Properties dialog box and reinstall the existing driver software. You can do that in a number of ways.

If you have Windows XP, you can do a System Restore to reinstall the video driver: Go back in time to when you remember the display working properly. It could be yesterday or last Friday or whenever you last used the computer. Refer to the Chapter 4 discussion on using System Restore.

You can also try a System Restore in Windows Me, though I know people who would rather shoot their own thumb with a bow and arrow than use System Restore in Windows Me.

For Windows 98, or for Windows Me and Windows XP when System Restore doesn't work, you can follow these steps to manually replace the graphics device driver:

1. **Display the Device Manager.**

   See Appendix A for information on using the Device Manager. It's a utility program you must be familiar with if you plan on troubleshooting your own computer.

2. **Open the Display adapters item.**

   This step lists your computer's display adapter hardware, as shown in Figure 6-2. Some computers can have more than one display adapter, in which case two of them appear on the list.

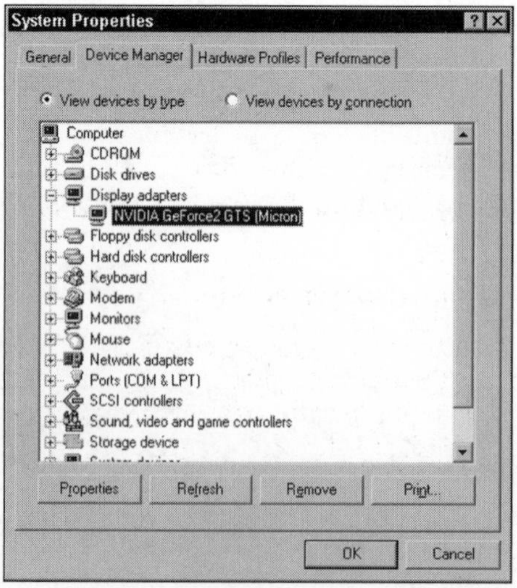

Figure 6-2:
Displaying the video adapter hardware.

3. Double-click your display adapter.

This step opens the adapter's Properties dialog box.

On the General tab is a Device Status area, which tells you right away about any known problems with the adapter. Heed those instructions! However, if the screen is stuck in dumb mode, you're most likely directed to update the driver (which is what you're in the middle of doing anyway).

4. Click the Driver tab.

Though each graphics adapter's Properties dialog box is different, all of them have a Driver tab, similar to what you see in Figure 6-3.

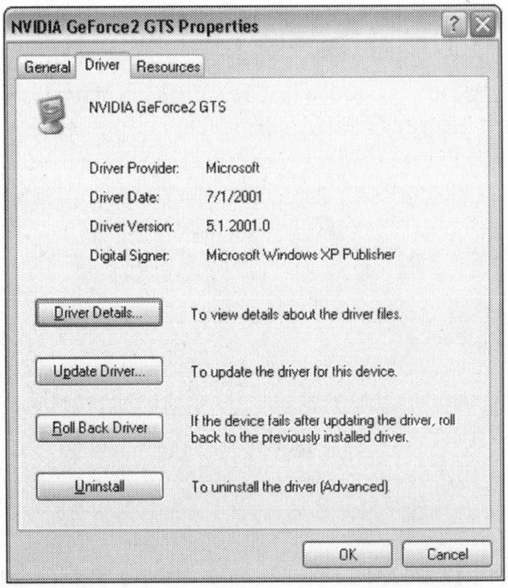

Figure 6-3:
Install or update the video driver here.

5. Click the Update Driver button.

This step starts a wizard, which looks for a better driver than the silly one you're using now.

6. Ensure that the Recommended option is chosen.

The phrasing is different with each Windows release. In Windows 98 and Windows Me, the option says something like "Search for a better driver." In Windows XP, it states "Install the software automatically."

In some versions of Windows, you must click the Next button first to see this option displayed.

7. Click the Next button.

Windows attempts to locate a better driver for your graphics adapter. Chances are, for this problem, that Windows will find the driver already on your computer. If so, use that driver, and everything will be fine.

8. Take whatever steps are necessary to finish installing the driver.

This step may include finding the original Windows CDs or the CDs that came with your computer that contain drivers. It may also involve restarting the computer.

In some cases, Windows may not be able to find a better driver. If so, it may urge you to connect with the Windows Update service to look for a new driver. If that doesn't work, you need to consider visiting the Web page for the graphics adapter or the computer manufacturer to see whether you can find and download a newer or better device driver.

✔ If your computer does have two display adapters, it's a guessing game to determine which one is the one that requires a new driver. My advice: Update them both.

✔ If the display is still in dumb mode after you restart Windows, visit the Display Properties dialog box to see whether you can then change the resolution to something higher (refer to the preceding section).

Annoying Programs in the System Tray/Notification Area

One of the most vexing issues that vexes even the most vexless PC user seems to be those ugly little booger icons in the *system tray,* or what Windows XP calls the *system notification area.* Whatever. It's littered with teensy icons like dust bunnies under the sofa.

Although many people seem to tolerate the miscellaneous miscreants, a few downright can't stand the boogers and want to stomp them out of existence. If that's you, heed the advice given in the following sections.

So what the heck are those icons, anyway?

Each icon appearing in the system tray or notification area represents some program running in Windows, usually a utility or some other "background" operation. The icon offers you a way to check that program's progress or to get quick access to its settings or more information. And that sounds really nice.

In real life, however, the system tray/notification area has become an electronic commune for any old random icon that wanders by. After about ten or so icons, I begin to think "What the heck is this?" It's from that thought that the urge to purge grows into an obsession.

WARNING!

Beware of utilities to help you manage system tray icons

When I present the system tray/notification area icon problems in my free weekly newsletter, a few people respond that tools are available to help manage the icons for Windows 98 or Windows Me. Beware of these tools! I've tried a couple, and I was not happy with the results.

One such utility interfered with the way some of my programs operated, forcing me to delete the

utility in order to save my sanity. Another program merely hid the system tray, which wasn't a very good solution.

My advice is to try my techniques described in this chapter before you resort to some other solution.

Required icons for the system tray/notification area

What do you need to have in the system tray/notification area? Nothing. There is no requirement, and if you're crafty enough, you can eliminate *all* icons from that area. (A blank box remains, but that's it.)

Killing off teensy icons in Windows 98

Icons in the system tray are controlled from one of two places: the Control Panel or the Options (or Preferences) dialog box of the application that owns the icon. So it's possible to disable the icons without shutting down the program that displays them — though quitting the program is also a valid way to remove the icon.

First thing to try: Right-click the icon and check its pop-up menu. If you're blessed and it's a good day and the sun is shining and the check is in the mailbox, an item on the pop-up menu says "Hide this icon" or something similar. Hallelujah.

Second thing to try: Right-click the icon and check for a Properties, Preferences, or Options menu item. Choose it and look for a setting that disables the icon from showing up in the system tray.

Third thing to try, though drastic: Right-click the icon and see whether you can find a Close, Exit, or Quit command. Choose it. Unfortunately, this method has the side effect of disabling whatever it was the little booger was doing. Be sure that you want that feature turned off — or, to put it another way, is the annoyance of having the little icon greater than the benefit the little icon can give you?

Fourth, close-to-desperate, thing to try: Find and open the program associated with the icon. See whether you can find any option to turn off the System Tray icon. For example, you may find on a program's Tools⇨Options menu a setting that switches the icon display off.

 Fifth thing to try for the volume control and time settings only: To switch off the volume control, open the Multimedia icon in the Control Panel. Remove the check mark by the option labeled Show volume control on the taskbar. Click OK.

To disable the time display, right-click the time and choose Properties from the pop-up menu. Then, in the Taskbar Properties dialog box, remove the check mark by the option labeled Show clock. Click OK.

Sixth, and last, thing to try: Locate the program that initializes the System Tray icon and prevent it from starting. The problem here, of course, is that you don't know which program summoned the little ugly guy in the first place. Oh, but you can guess.

The first spot to look in is the Startup menu: From the Start menu, choose Programs⇨StartUp. If the offending program is there, you can disable it. (This subject is covered in Chapter 8.)

The second spot to look is the Startup tab in the System Configuration utility's window. See Appendix A for more information.

 The idea is to disable the icon without deleting the program. Sometimes, that task involves stopping the program, but most of the time you have a way to disable the System Tray icon without stopping the program — definitely without uninstalling or deleting the program that displays the icon.

Removing the annoying boogers from Windows Me

Most of the tricks for disabling the icons in Windows 98 also apply to Windows Me. Additionally, Windows Me has the Language Bar icon, which may show up in the system tray.

The Language Bar icon is used to show you that keyboard language switching is available and that you can press certain keys on the keyboard to switch between foreign language keyboards and English keyboards. The icon appears as a black square with the letters *EN* on it.

To disable the Language Bar's icon, right-click it and choose Close Language Bar from the pop-up menu.

The more elegant Windows XP icon-hiding solution

Apparently, word got to Microsoft that the system tray was bugging people, so the company made two changes. First, they changed the name from system tray to notification area. Whether the new name makes sense, it's definitely more descriptive than system tray.

Second, Microsoft provided a feature, built into Windows, where you can manually hide all the icons, no matter what. Here's how to get there:

1. **Right-click the mouse in the notification area.**

   Do not click an icon in the notification area — click in the notification area proper. If this step confuses you, just click the time shown in the notification area.

2. **Choose Properties from the pop-up menu.**

   If you don't see the Properties command, you've clicked an icon and not in the notification area proper.

3. **Ensure that the Taskbar tab is up front in the Taskbar and Start Menu Properties dialog box.**

   The bottom part of the dialog box deals with the notification area.

4. **If you don't want the clock to be displayed, uncheck the box by the Show the clock option.**

5. **Click the Customize button.**

   The Customize Notifications dialog box appears, as shown in Figure 6-4. This box is where you can permanently hide any or all of the icons.

6. **To hide an icon, click to select it.**

   This step displays a drop-down list in the Behavior column, as shown in Figure 6-4.

7. **Choose Always hide from the drop-down list.**

8. **Repeat Steps 6 and 7 for all the icons on the list that you want hidden.**

9. **When you're done hiding the icons, click the OK button.**

10. **Click OK again to close the Taskbar and Start Menu Properties dialog box.**

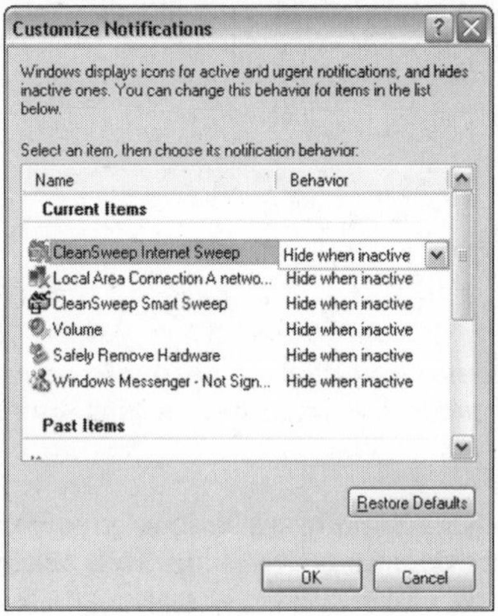

Figure 6-4:
Here is
where you
hide the
icons in
Windows
XP.

Note that even with everything hidden, the notification area does not vanish completely. The Hide/Show arrow on the left lip of the notification area still appears, which does allow you to see the icons. But at least they're not "on stage" all the time.

Scandisk Poops Out, Defrag Poops Out, We All Poop Out Now

The versions of the ScanDisk and Disk Defragmenter that came with Windows 98 and Windows Me often poop out before they're done. The message is that ScanDisk or Defrag has discovered that some other program has altered the hard drive, so everything must start all over. On and on it goes, and neither program ever seems to finish.

This problem has frustrated millions. Some say that the solution is to run ScanDisk or Defrag in Safe mode. Poppycock. The best solution is *not to run* ScanDisk or Defrag. Instead, invest in a good third-party utility package, one where the programmers are wise enough to anticipate information being written to the hard drive so that their utilities don't poop out all the time.

 ✔ I personally recommend the Norton Utilities versions of ScanDisk and Defrag as a vast improvement over what Windows 98 and Windows Me offer. The Norton programs not only complete the job, but they also seem to do things more thoroughly than their Windows versions.

 ✔ Windows XP does not seem to have these ScanDisk and Disk Defragmenter problems.

✔ If you do opt into using Norton Utilities for Windows XP, make double-dog sure that you get the version made specifically for Windows XP. Using an older version of any disk utility on Windows XP can be disastrous.

✔ I'm thrilled every time I get to write the word *poop* in a book.

The PC Can't Recover from Sleep Mode

Some computers go to sleep and never wake up. The problem was so bad with Windows 95 that I recommended *not* using sleep mode! But since then, things have gotten better.

✔ If you have any problems with your computer sleeping or going into Suspend mode, contact your computer's manufacturer. Ask for a patch or update to make your version of Windows more compatible with the sleep system hardware.

✔ Another alternative to putting the entire system to sleep is merely to "sleep" the monitor. Leave the system and its hard drives on, but after a given interval have the computer shut off the monitor for you.

✔ Sleep mode is controlled from the Power Options or Power Management icon in the Control Panel.

Oh, That Annoying Logon Dialog Box!

Must you log in to Windows? I'm afraid that the answer is "Yes" pretty much all the time. Sorry!

I once recommended removing or bypassing the Logon dialog box. Just press the Esc key and get it out of the way. But there is a problem with that method, especially if you use the Internet.

When you log in to Windows, something called the *password chain* is activated. Sounds dungeony, right? But the password chain is where Windows stores all your passwords — all of them.

When Windows recognizes your account (the name you used to log in), it opens the password chain, which contains any other password you use in Windows — including your Internet access and e-mail passwords. So if you log in properly, you can click the Save Password button in the various Internet dialog boxes, and Windows remembers your password.

If you neglect to log in, Windows does not remember your password. The password chain is never loaded! Therefore, when you go to connect to the Internet or to read your e-mail, Windows prompts you for your password *and* the Save Password check box is unavailable. Bummer.

✔ If you don't see a logon dialog box when you use Windows 98 or Windows Me, choose the Log Off command from the Start menu. That helps reactivate the Logon dialog box for you.

✔ You need to log in to the Windows network if you're using any type of broadband Internet connection, such as DSL or a cable modem. In that case, the logon is necessary because you use Windows networking to access the Internet.

✔ In Windows XP, you do not have the option to neglect the Logon prompt. There's no way around it! And I do recommend that you password-protect your account in Windows XP.

You Can't Open a File, or the Open With Fiasco

Some files were not meant to be opened. They're data files or support programs for other things you do on your computer. There's nothing wrong with poking around and trying to double-click every file you find. It's just that you had better be prepared to reset if anything new and wacky happens to your PC while you're poking around.

Open With in Windows 98 and Windows Me

Most of the time when you try to open a file that Windows doesn't recognize, you see the Open With dialog box, as shown in Figure 6-5.

Here's what you need to do:

1. Click the Cancel button!

When you see the Open With dialog box, it means that the file you're trying to open does not have a companion application. Or, to phrase it another way: You cannot open the file, so don't even try.

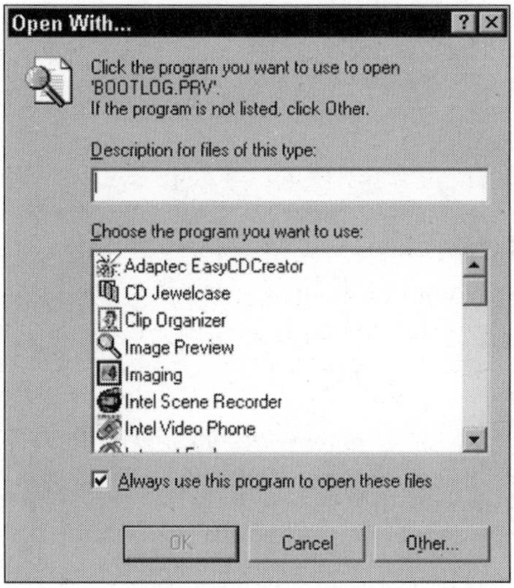

Figure 6-5:
The dreaded
Open With
dialog box
(in Windows
Me).

- ✔ It's when people accidentally try to use a program on the list to open an unknown file that they get into trouble.

- ✔ I think the problem is that the Open With dialog box seems to demand that you select a program to open the file. That's wrong. There is no need to do so.

- ✔ To open the file, you need the program that created it. So if a friend on the Internet e-mails you a Photoshop image (a PSD file), and you don't have Photoshop, you can't open the file.

- ✔ The real solution for the Open With dialog box, especially when receiving e-mail attachments, is to have whoever is sending you the file send it in another, more common format. I recommend JPG for graphics and RTF for text documents. See the nearby sidebar "Common file formats your computer can read" for more information.

- ✔ The Open With dialog box also appears when you attempt to open a data file or a file that can't really be opened by any other program (a file that shouldn't be messed with).

Open With in Windows XP

Windows XP utterly lacks an Open With dialog box. When you attempt to open an unknown file, you get the "I cannot open this file" dialog box, as shown in Figure 6-6.

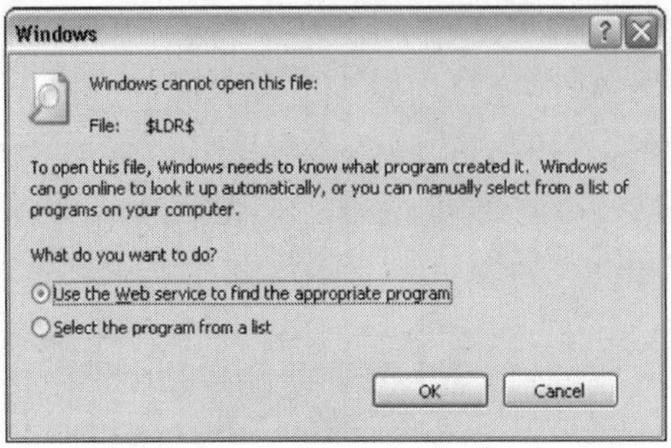

Windows   [?][X]

Windows cannot open this file:

File: LDR

To open this file, Windows needs to know what program created it. Windows can go online to look it up automatically, or you can manually select from a list of programs on your computer.

Figure 6-6:
Windows
XP is at
a loss.

What do you want to do?

◉ Use the Web service to find the appropriate program
○ Select the program from a list

[OK]   [Cancel]

The *modus operandi* here is still the same: Click the Cancel button.

Sure, you could have Windows venture out to the wilds of the Internet and search for *whatever*. Windows may find a program to open the file, so if you're curious, take a look. I've never done this myself. I either give up or, if someone e-mailed me the file, ask that person to send me the file again in a format my computer can read.

You definitely don't want to select a program from the list. If the icon can't be opened now, it won't be opened then either.

Also in Windows XP, Open With appears as a submenu on the pop-up menu for most applications. You can use the submenu to choose which program you want to use for opening any icon:

TIP

Common file formats your computer can read

Most of the time, I hear about Open With programs because of strange e-mail attachments or files downloaded from the Internet. If you can't open the file, do what I do: Request that the person resend the file in a format your computer can read. Here are some of those common formats that just about any PC can read:

GIF: This common graphics file format can be viewed by the Paint program or Internet Explorer.

HTML: These documents are actually Web pages, which can be read by Internet Explorer. Just about any major application can save its documents in HTML format.

JPG: This is another common graphics file format.

PRN: The old Lotus 1-2-3 printer file format can be used to exchange spreadsheet data and some database information between programs.

RTF: Using the rich text format for documents, any word processor can read these documents, which makes RTF even more common than HTML.

TXT: With plain-text documents, nothing gets simpler.

1. **Right-click an icon.**

2. **Choose Open With⇨to display the Open With submenu.**

   The submenu displays a list of programs qualified to open the icon.

   Or you can select the Choose program command to view a list of applications and choose one to try to open the file.

I find this aspect of Open With in Windows XP most handy. It not only lets you specify which program to use for opening known files, but it also lets you experiment with opening unknown files without utterly lousing up the system. Yes, it's the newer, *safer* Open With dialog box!

That Wicked File Is Read-Only

Read-only is one of a handful of file *attributes* that can be applied to a file. In this case, the read-only attribute tells Windows that the file can be opened, examined, printed, and copied, but cannot be changed in any way — look, but don't touch, like the snake pit at the zoo.

Read-only files happen for two reasons. First, they're created that way. For example, any file on a CD-ROM disk is read-only, which it inherits from the read-only aspect of the CD-ROM drive (where the RO in ROM means Read Only). Second, you can change a file's read-only attribute at any time by using the file's Properties dialog box. That is also how you remove the Read Only attribute from a file and restore it to normal.

Follow these steps:

1. **Right-click the file's icon.**

2. **Choose Properties from the pop-up menu.**

The Microsoft Word read-only bug

Microsoft Word has a bug in it (although Microsoft doesn't call it a bug, I do). When you open a document created by another word processor, Word automatically makes that document read-only. It does this to ensure that you do not overwrite the original, non-Word document with a Word document. To overcome this bug, simply change the name of the document when you save it back to disk; use the File⇨Save As command and enter a new name as well as a new file type for saving the document.

3. Remove the check mark by the Read Only option.

See Figure 6-7, which shows the file's Properties dialog box for Windows XP, though it's similar to the older versions of Windows as well.

4. Click OK.

The file is restored to non-Read Only status.

Do keep in mind that the read-only status may be set on a file for a reason. It is one of the few ways you can protect a file in Windows.

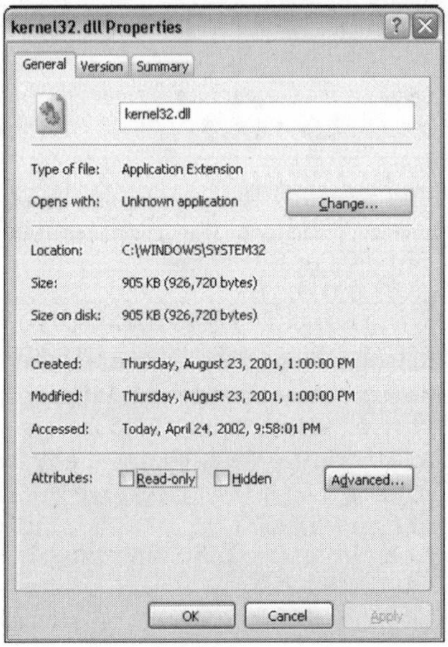

kernel32.dll Properties

General | Version | Summary

kernel32.dll

Type of file:	Application Extension
Opens with:	Unknown application Change...
Location:	C:\WINDOWS\SYSTEM32
Size:	905 KB (926,720 bytes)
Size on disk:	905 KB (926,720 bytes)
Created:	Thursday, August 23, 2001, 1:00:00 PM
Modified:	Thursday, August 23, 2001, 1:00:00 PM
Accessed:	Today, April 24, 2002, 9:58:01 PM
Attributes:	☐ Read-only ☐ Hidden Advanced...

OK   Cancel   Apply

Figure 6-7:
A file's
Properties
dialog box.

Full-Screen DOS Prompt

If you ever find yourself facing a computer that's showing an ugly text screen — not beautiful, graphical Windows — you've stumbled into the World of DOS. It's text, man — text!

DOS screens don't pop up as much as they used to. Still, it can happen. The first thing to try is pressing the Ctrl+Enter key combination. This keyboard command switches a DOS window from full screen to *windowed* mode, where DOS just looks like any other window (but uglier). After you're in windowed mode, you can close the DOS prompt window like any other window.

"But my computer always boots into DOS!"

Don't despair if your computer always boots into DOS. The problem can be fixed — well, unless you have an old DOS computer that doesn't even load Windows. But if you have Windows 98 or Windows Me, you can easily fix the boots-into-DOS problem.

First, at the DOS prompt, type **WIN** to start Windows. After you're in Windows, run the Notepad program. Choose File➪Open to display the Open dialog box.

In the bottom of the Open dialog box, choose All files from the Files of type drop-down list. Then, in the File name box, type **C:\MSDOS.SYS**. Type

that command exactly as I have written it here: C, colon, backslash, MSDOS, period, and SYS, and then click the Open button. This command opens a special boot file into Notepad.

In the file that appears on the screen, look for the line that reads `BootGUI=0`. That line is under the [Options] area. Change the 0 to a 1 so that it reads `BootGUI=1`. That's the command to start Windows rather than DOS.

Choose File➪Save to save your change. Then quit Notepad. Restart the computer, and it will boot into Windows rather than DOS.

✔ You must quit DOS programs before you can close the DOS window. If not, a horrible error message appears, telling you just that. Even so, if the window is something you need to close, click the Yes button to terminate the DOS program.

✔ You can use your keyboard to close any DOS window: Type **EXIT** and press Enter at the DOS prompt.

✔ If you try pressing Alt+Enter and typing **EXIT** and nothing happens, somehow the computer was started in DOS mode. In that case, simply restart the computer; turn it off, wait, and then turn it on again.

✔ If the computer appears stuck in DOS mode, type **WIN** and press the Enter key to run Windows.

Chapter 7

"Gosh! This Is Embarrassing!"

. . . .

In This Chapter

▶ Dealing with the recent documents list

▶ Erasing evidence from the history list

▶ Working around the AutoComplete feature

▶ Covering up nasty wallpaper

▶ Instantly hiding anything on the screen

. . . .

*N*othing makes you yearn for instant assistance like something unexpected and, well, *embarrassing!* This situation happens because the computer is programmed to indiscriminately remember just about everything you do. Remember that time you walked into the kitchen naked and your great aunt was sitting there? So does the computer.

Well, maybe it's not that bad. But remember how handy it has been in the past for the computer to recall a file you just opened or to remember a Web page or someone you just sent e-mail to? That's computer convenience! Alas, the computer isn't discriminating with the stuff it remembers. Sometimes, places you didn't really intend to visit can pop up again — just like your aunt in the kitchen!

This chapter summarizes some of the many places where, well, "evidence" can be found that you've been somewhere shameful. Remember that the computer doesn't judge intent; no, it merely keeps track of your wanderings. If that concerns you, the tips and techniques presented in this chapter will help you eliminate any potential cause for embarrassment.

  ✔ This chapter covers how to remove remnants of places you've been and files you've opened or saved, mostly from the Internet, but also from the daily operation of your computer.

  ✔ Generally speaking, Windows 98 and Windows Me have very similar commands for keeping track of things. Windows XP, however, is quite different. If you use Windows XP, be sure to note which sections in this chapter specifically apply to you.

✔ One of the best ways to prevent unwanted Internet filth and slime from invading your PC is to use a tool such as NetNanny or CyberSitter. Visit www.netnanny.com/ or www.cybersitter.com/.

Deleting Recent Documents from the Documents Menu

Windows 95 introduced the My Documents menu on the main Start menu. I don't know why. I've rarely used it. I've written about it. I can see how it could be handy. But I can also see how it can be a security risk. Why would you want to advertise to anyone else using the computer which documents you've been working on recently?

The terrible part about having the My Documents menu is that you have no way to turn the sucker off — not in Windows 95 nor Windows 98 nor Windows Me. So you must deal with it, as the following sections describe.

The My Documents menu still exists in Windows XP, though you can easily turn the menu off. See the section "Disabling the thing in Windows XP (at last!)," later in this chapter.

Scrubbing out the My Documents list

Although you can't stop it, you can erase the My Documents submenu contents. It's not the easiest thing to do, but in Windows 98 and Windows Me it can be done if you carefully follow these steps:

1. **Right-click the taskbar.**

2. **Choose Properties from the pop-up menu.**

   If you don't see the Properties command, you right-clicked the wrong spot on the taskbar. Try again.

   This step opens the Taskbar Properties dialog box.

3a. **In Windows 98, click the Start Menu Programs tab.**

3b. **In Windows Me, click the Advanced tab.**

   In both operating systems, it's the tab on the *right.* Figure 7-1 shows the Windows 98 version, which is cleaner than the ugly Windows Me variation.

4. **Click the Clear button.**

   This step not only removes all the documents from the My Documents submenu, but it also clears any personal history list in Windows — such as the drop-down list for the Run command or the Address bar and just about any other place you can type a filename in Windows.

5. Close the dialog box.

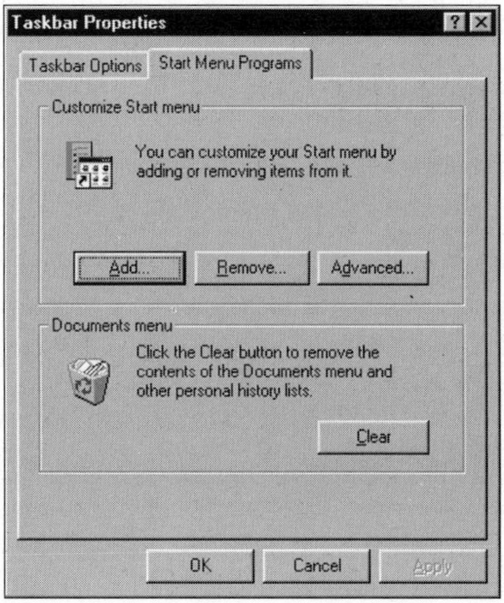

Figure 7-1:
Where the
Clear button
lurks.

Of course, the problem doesn't go away. Things are cleared, but they start to come back the second you go off and open some document.

✔ Using the Clear command as described in the preceding steps generally cleans out all lists of recently typed stuff just about everywhere in Windows.

✔ Note that older DOS and Windows programs may not have their documents appear on the My Documents menu. In fact, some newer applications are security-conscious and prevent their documents from being listed there as well. Check with your application's help file to see whether you can find an option to disable the Recent Document List feature.

Disabling the thing in Windows XP (at last!)

In Windows XP, the Documents submenu is called My Recent Documents. The submenu is an entirely optional thing to have on the Start panel. To remove it, follow these steps:

1. Right-click the Start button.

2. Choose Properties from the pop-up menu.

This step displays the Taskbar and Start Menu Properties dialog box, which you can also open through the Control Panel.

3. Ensure that the Start Menu tab is selected.

I'm also assuming that the Start menu option is chosen. If you choose the Classic Start Menu option, the options available when you click the Customize button are similar to the Windows 98 and Windows Me options shown in the preceding steps.

4. Click the Customize button.

The Customize Start Menu dialog box wanders in.

5. Click the Advanced tab.

No, *Advanced* doesn't mean scary or forbidden! It's a general term for options they couldn't figure out where else to put. In this case, as shown in Figure 7-2, the Recent Document List options are stored there.

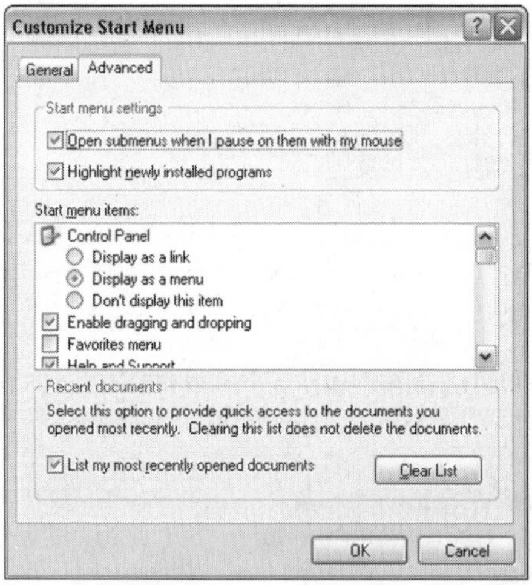

Figure 7-2:
Changing the settings for the Windows XP Recent File List.

6. Click to remove the check mark by the option labeled List my most recently opened documents.

That step disables the list. It's gone!

7. Click OK.

8. Click OK to close the Taskbar and Start Menu Properties dialog box.

Now you can check the Start menu, and the My Recent Documents menu is gone.

And we all sing and dance a merry song of thanks.

> ✔ Note that there is a difference between the My Recent Documents menu and the My Documents shortcut that may also appear on the Start menu. One is a shortcut to the My Documents folder. The other is a sub-menu that lists recently open documents.

> ✔ If you want to merely clear the list, click the Clear List button after Step 6 in the preceding steps.

Historically Speaking

Wherever you go on the Web, Internet Explorer (IE) makes a note of it, like some busybody neighbor or relative who must check up on you all the time. Internet Explorer notes which Web sites you visit and which pages you look at. At least it doesn't nag you about wearing a sweater. . . .

Supposedly, all this checking is done to make it easier to retrace your steps if you want to go back and visit someplace again. But it also serves as a trail of bread crumbs that just about anyone can follow to see what it is you look at on the Internet — obviously a potential source of embarrassment.

Clearing places from the history

To remove any Web site or specific Web page from the Internet Explorer history list, follow these steps:

1. **Click the History button in Internet Explorer.**

   The history list appears on the left side of the browser window, as shown in Figure 7-3. Web sites appear as folders. The pages you visit in the site appear as Web page icons beneath the folder, as shown in the figure.

2. **Right-click on any item you want to delete.**

3. **Choose Delete from the pop-up menu.**

4. **Click Yes in the warning dialog box if you're asked to confirm.**

   And the offending entry is gone.

Alas, the entry still may appear on the Address drop-down list. If so, try using the Clear button, as described earlier in this chapter.

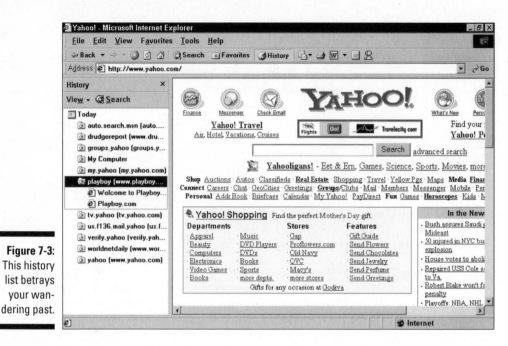

Figure 7-3:
This history list betrays your wandering past.

✔ The Ctrl+H key combination can also be used to hide or show the history list.

✔ The number of days the history list keeps track of is initially set to 20. This value can be adjusted, as covered in the section "Disabling history altogether," just ahead in this chapter.

✔ Removing a history item is not the same thing as removing an Internet cookie. For cookie information, see Chapter 17.

Clearing all the history

People who don't read history are doomed to repeat it. And why not? Let's just go and make those same mistakes over and over. It builds character, or something like that.

When the entries on the history list appear to be overwhelming, consider zapping them all:

1. Open the Control Panel's Internet Options icon.

Or, from Internet Explorer, choose Tools⇨Internet Options. This step displays the Internet Options dialog box, as shown in Figure 7-4. On the General tab, you can control the history.

Figure 7-4:
You control
history here.

2. **Click the Clear History button.**

   And that removes everything.

Of course, if your spouse or computer partner is astute, they will have recognized that you zapped the history list. If so, be honest: Just tell them that things were in there that you'd rather no one else see. Nothing wrong with that — it happens to everyone.

Disabling history altogether

If the history list is a complete and utter bother, just get rid of it: On the General tab in the Internet Options dialog box (refer to Figure 7-4), set the Days to keep pages in history option to zero. Click OK.

Although this technique does eliminate history tracking for previous days, note that Internet Explorer still keeps track of the history *today*. So if you've been somewhere today and you don't want anyone to know about it before midnight, you still have to manually delete the entries, as covered in the section "Clearing places from the history," earlier in this chapter.

Undoing the AutoComplete Nightmare

Remember that really smart-but-annoying person you once worked with? Any time you started a sentence, he finished it off for you. You'd say "Let's go back to. . . ." and he would hurriedly say "The drawing board!" That saved you excess thinking time and tongue energy molecules, but frustrated your brain because you could never complete a sentence. I suppose that the fellow believed he was being handy. Call the chap Otto — Otto Kompleet.

In Windows, the AutoComplete feature is one of those nifty utilities that makes typing long, complex things — like Web page addresses — easier. What Windows does is to keep track of the places you've been and the addresses (and filenames) you've typed. When you start typing again, Windows automatically completes the address for you, guessing what it is you want to type. Or, a drop-down list of alternative suggestions may appear.

Suppose that late one night Phil's wife wants to visit Mary's Boutique on the Internet. She starts typing `Marysbo` — and suddenly the Address bar is filled with `Mary's Bondage and Discipline Dungeon`. Oops! It's time she had a talk with Phil!

Yes, AutoComplete can also be a source of embarrassment. Fortunately, you have several ways to deal with it, as covered in the sections that follow.

Turn off AutoComplete

When anything vexes you in Windows, the direct solution is usually to turn it off. Why not? Such features should be optional. On my computers, I find AutoComplete to be annoying; I'm startled when some other Web page spelling or suggestion comes up. No problem. AutoComplete can be turned off (or at least curtailed) by following these steps:

1. **Open the Control Panel's Internet Options icon.**

2. **Click the Content tab.**

3. **Click the AutoComplete button.**

   The AutoComplete Settings dialog box appears, as shown in Figure 7-5. Did you notice the two happy buttons labeled Clear?

4. **To turn off AutoComplete, uncheck everything.**

   Click. Click. Click. Click.

5. **Also click the Clear Forms and Clear Passwords buttons.**

   That removes anything stored in AutoComplete's memory. In fact, you can just perform this step (and Steps 7 and 8) to remove things stored in AutoComplete's memory.

   Did you notice the annoying message about the Clear History button? How hard would it have been for Microsoft to add a second Clear History button right there in the AutoComplete Settings dialog box? It was apparently too hard, so you must exercise your mouse-clicking muscles yet again:

AutoComplete Settings

AutoComplete lists possible matches from entries you've typed before.

Use AutoComplete for
- ☑ Web addresses
- ☐ Forms
- ☑ User names and passwords on forms
  - ☑ Prompt me to save passwords

Clear AutoComplete history

[Clear Forms]   [Clear Passwords]

To clear Web address entries, on the General tab in Internet Options, click Clear History.

[OK]   [Cancel]

Figure 7-5: Changing the Auto Complete settings.

6. **Click OK.**

7. **Click the General tab.**

8. **Click the Clear History button.**

   Now everything is gone from AutoComplete.

Theoretically, this technique should work. No previous addresses or other information appear on the Address bar as you type. If something still does, you can see the next section for a more direct and drastic solution to the problem.

- ✔ Using AutoComplete for Web addresses means that Windows remembers any address you've typed or the address of all Web pages you've visited, which can be recalled as you type new addresses.

- ✔ Using AutoComplete for forms means that any Web forms you complete that have similar fields (Name, Address, and Telephone, for example) are also filled in automatically as you visit various Web pages.

- ✔ Of course, the Forms option also covers entering information in search engines. So if you've been searching for ladies undergarments in extra-large gentlemen's sizes, that too would appear if you have the Forms item checked.

Removing an MRU list

MRU is Microsoft-spiel for Most Recently Used. This concept is the root of the drop-down list dilemma or the AutoComplete quandary. Those files or text you type are kept in various MRU lists and stored in a very dark and dank — and technical — place in Windows called the *Registry*.

Hopefully, the commands listed earlier in this chapter help you to get rid of the things you don't want on the various MRU lists. If not, you can venture into the Registry and manually delete things on your own. It's not that hard, but it does take a certain amount of intestinal fortitude:

1. **Click the Start button.**

2. **Choose Run.**

   The Run dialog box pops up.

   You can quickly summon the Run dialog box by pressing the Win+R key combination on your keyboard. (Win is the Windows key.)

3. **Type** REGEDIT **into the Open text box.**

4. **Click OK.**

   The Registry Editor shows up on the screen, as pictured in Figure 7-6. It looks — and works — like a Windows Explorer window. You open various folders to display more folders and eventually display the entries in the Registry itself.

```
Registry Editor
Registry  Edit  View  Favorites  Help
My Computer                         Name          Data
  HKEY_CLASSES_ROOT
  HKEY_CURRENT_USER
  HKEY_LOCAL_MACHINE
  HKEY_USERS
  HKEY_CURRENT_CONFIG
  HKEY_DYN_DATA



My Computer
```

Figure 7-6:
The Registry Editor.

To remove MRU items, you need to know where they are. This process involves being able to read a path to the MRU list and understanding which folders to open to get there. For example, here is the location where the addresses you type in Internet Explorer are stored:

```
HKEY_CURRENT_USER\Software\Microsoft\Internet
                Explorer\TypedURLs
```

Here's how to get there:

1. **Open the HKEY_CURRENT_USER folder.**

2. **Open the Software folder.**

3. **Open the Microsoft folder.**

4. **Open the Internet Explorer folder.**

5. **Open the TypedURLs folder.**

Refer to the path again. Note how each item in the path represents a folder to open. The folders are all separated by backslash (\) characters. Now look at the screen. What you see is the list of recently typed URLs or Web page addresses or anything you typed into the Address box. Figure 7-7 shows what it looks like on my screen, though it's a rather brief list because I just cleared my history.

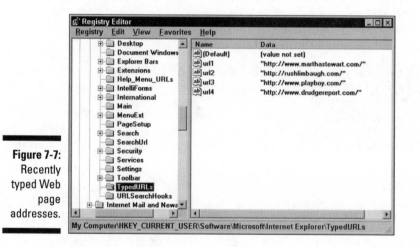

Figure 7-7: Recently typed Web page addresses.

To delete a specific entry, such as that offensive Martha Stewart Web site, select it and press the Delete key. (Click on the "ab" icon to select an entry.) Click the Yes button when you're asked whether you're sure that you want to delete the value. You're sure.

Table 7-1 lists a few other places in the Registry where you can also find MRU lists. You can use these items to go in and pluck out specific files that may be offending people — or stuff you just don't want other folks to know about.

Note that it's assumed that each location in Table 7-1 begins with
HKEY_CURRENT_USER\Software.

Table 7-1	A Few MRU Lists in the Registry
Program	*List Location*
Adobe Acrobat	...\Adobe\Acrobat Reader\4.0\AdobeViewer
Excel 2002	...\Microsoft\Office\10.0\Excel\Recent Files
FrontPage	...\Microsoft\FrontPage\Explorer\FrontPage Explorer\ Recent File List
Kodak Imaging	...\Kodak\Imaging\Recent File List
Media Player	...\Microsoft\MediaPlayer\Player\RecentFileList
Paint	..\Microsoft\Windows\CurrentVersion\Applets\Paint\ Recent File List
Run dialog box	...\Microsoft\Windows\CurrentVersion\Explorer\RunMRU
WordPad	...\Microsoft\Windows\CurrentVersion\Applets\Wordpad\ Recent File List

If you don't see your application listed in Table 7-1 (and I don't have the space to list everything), use the Ctrl+F key combination to summon the Registry Editor's Find command. Search for a bit of text you've seen in the recently used file list. For example, if you've just opened the file NAUGHTY.DOC, you can search the Registry for that name. When you find it, you probably also find the MRU list for that application. If so, you can delete the entry manually.

Be sure to close the Registry Editor when you're done.

- ✔ Avoid the temptation to monkey with the Registry beyond my simple words of advice offered in this book.

- ✔ No, I can't recommend any other good book on the Windows Registry. I get this question often via e-mail, including requests that I write that Windows Registry book myself, but there really isn't that much to the Registry, and it can be a scary place if you're not careful.

- ✔ Set a system restore point before you do any messing around in the Registry (refer to Chapter 4).

Dealing with Nasty Wallpaper!

When you right-click an image on the Internet, you see on the pop-up menu an option called Set as Wallpaper (or something similar). That command turns the image into wallpaper you can see when you use Windows. Sometimes, this is an accident. It need not be a nasty image, but whatever image it is, you probably want it off the desktop. Here's how:

1. **Right-click the desktop.**

2. **Choose Properties from the pop-up menu.**

   This step conjures up the Display Properties dialog box, which you can also get to through the Control Panel.

3. **In Windows 98 and Windows Me, ensure that the Background tab is selected; in Windows XP, click the Desktop tab.**

   The Background tab is what sets an image, pattern, or straight color to use for the background or wallpaper (see Figure 7-8).

   You see the current, nasty image selected on the scrolling list.

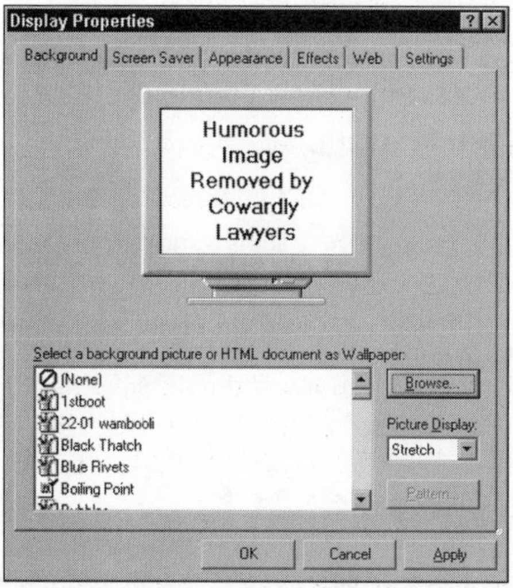

Figure 7-8:
Removing
an image
from the
desktop.

4. **Choose a new background from the scrolling list.**

   Or select None if you want a solid color.

   In Windows 98 and Windows Me, you can also click the Pattern button to create a background pattern.

5. **Click the Apply button.**

   The background on the desktop changes, removing the old image and replacing it with a new one.

   In one instance, this step doesn't work in Windows 98 and Windows Me. If you're using the Active Desktop to display a GIF or JPG image as your desktop, that image covers up the background image chosen in the Display Properties/Background dialog box. In fact, you may see the first image "flash" on for a second before the Active Desktop image takes over.

The solution for the dual-image problem is to disable Active Desktop:

a. Click the Web tab.

b. Remove the check mark by the option labeled Show Web content on my Active Desktop.

c. Click the Apply button.

That should fix the problem.

6. Click OK to close the Display Properties dialog box.

Generally speaking, that should fix whatever nasty images you have. If you want to permanently remove the nasty image, go find that file and delete it for good.

- ✔ Images set as wallpaper from Internet Explorer are given the name Internet Explorer Wallpaper and saved in this folder:

  c:\Windows\Application Data\Microsoft\Internet Explorer

- ✔ Also see Chapter 9 for more information on finding files.

- ✔ Windows XP changes the name of the Background tab to Desktop, though it still functions the same way as the dialog box shown in Figure 7-8.

- ✔ Windows XP also lacks the "second" desktop image you often see with Windows 98 and Windows Me.

Hiding Something on the Screen

I'm sure this never happens to you: You're looking at something diverse and interesting on the computer when someone else walks into the room. Do you panic? Do you freak out and yell at them? Or do you quickly and stealthily know how to hide the entire contents of the screen?

Hopefully, you know the trick to instantly hide everything on the screen: Press the Win+M key combination, where Win is the Windows key.

Win+M automatically *minimizes* every open window, leaving only the desktop displayed.

- ✔ Alas, you have no Win+M key equivalent if your computer's keyboard lacks a Windows key.

- ✔ The mouse equivalent for this command is to right-click on the taskbar and choose Minimize All Windows from the pop-up menu. Alas, sometimes that's just too slow.

- ✔ Oh, and you can always switch off the monitor, though that does tend to arouse suspicion.

Chapter 8

Start-Up Problems

*I*t must take more oomph for a computer to get up in the morning than any human being alive. Consider the computer's electronic contemporaries: The television has no problem turning on. (Indeed, if there is a TV problem, it's not turning the thing off!) The toaster? Starts right up. VCR player? Works — sometimes even turns itself on when you shove in a tape. But the computer? It must be a Herculean effort — a full-on electronic brawl — required to get the thing going.

The fact that the computer starts at all should be considered miraculous, especially considering the sheer number of things that go on in order to get the beast up and running. There's no reason for the delays, of course; because we tolerate a lengthy start-up time on our computers, there is no rush for any manufacturer to speed up the process. Yet, for some reason, the delay is always long enough to build up some anxiety. Will the thing start? Why won't it start? And what the heck does that message mean? All those issues are covered in this chapter.

How the Computer Starts

If you understand how the computer starts, you had better be able to pinpoint various problems that can occur during the start-up process. This chapter isn't required reading, but it does help if you're familiar with what happens where and how to be properly able to point the finger of blame.

Computer hardware is dumb. It needs software to tell it what to do. The problem, however, is that it's the hardware that starts up first. So the hardware in a PC is geared toward immediately finding and loading an operating system so that the computer can become a useful tool and not a kingdom of confused characters searching for more instructions.

First: The first software the computer runs is encoded on a ROM chip inside the computer's memory. That program is called the *BIOS,* and it does two things: First, it performs a diagnostics text called the Power-On Self Test, or POST. This test ensures that all the basic input/output devices (monitor, and keyboard, for example) are working.

> **If it goes right:** Various copyright text appears on the screen.
>
> **What can go wrong?** When the BIOS fails the POST, the computer either beeps several times or, if the monitor is working, an error message is displayed. Note that any error you get at this stage is a hardware error.

Second: The second thing the BIOS does is to look for an operating system on one of the disk drives.

> **If it goes right:** The operating system takes over and continues starting up the computer.
>
> **What can go wrong?** If an operating system isn't found on any disk, a "Missing Operating System" error is displayed. Or the text "Non-system disk" is displayed.

Third: The operating system begins loading.

> **If it goes right:** You see the pretty Windows start-up logo, or splash screen.
>
> **What can go wrong?** Anything at this point can go wrong because software is in charge of the system. For example, in Windows a problem can be detected and you're thrust into the dreaded Safe mode. Or Windows may detect new hardware and attempt to install it. Or . . . just about anything!

Fourth: The operating system loads other start-up programs, such as device drivers, start-up applications, antivirus utilities, and the Task Scheduler.

> **If goes right:** Eventually, you're prompted to log in to Windows and start your merry Windows day.
>
> **What can go wrong?** Lots and lots of things: missing devices or bad device drivers, an improperly uninstalled program can display various "missing file" error messages, and on and on.

Fifth, and finally: You can start using your computer.

If it goes right: There is rejoicing throughout the land.

What can go wrong? Everything.

It's important to know these steps because a different solution exists for the various problems that can occur as the steps progress. For example, a blank screen with a blinking cursor when you first turn on the computer means that even the BIOS program hasn't started. That makes the solution relatively easy to find because you eliminate every other possibility.

✔ The BIOS does not directly run the operating system from disk. Instead, it runs a program called a *boot loader*. Boot loaders can often do more than merely load another operating system from disk. On some computers, the boot loader lets you select an operating system to start.

✔ System Commander, Partition Magic, or even the Linux program LILO are all examples of boot loaders that let you select an operating system to start.

Immediate Trouble

Nothing beats a novel that gets into the action right away, or a film that begins in the middle of things with a chase scene (*Star Wars* comes to mind). With a computer, nothing beats instant trouble. No sense in waiting for a long, dreary process to find out that something is wrong or missing. No, instant trouble is right there on the screen before you even have a chance to mangle the mouse.

On the down side, instant trouble is often the unfortunate sign of impending expensive repair or replacement. Not always, but often.

"I see nothing — just a blinking prompt!"

When the computer first starts, text should be displayed on the screen. Typically, you see a copyright notice. The computer make and model number may be displayed. Traditionally, a memory count takes place. Perhaps some internal hardware options are rattled off: hard drive, mouse, and video adapter, for example.

Eventually, the parade of text ends with a prompt to press a certain key to enter the computer's Setup program. Then the operating system takes off and displays that colorful, graphic "Windows" logo. That's the way it's supposed to happen.

When all you see is a blinking prompt, it means one of the following things:

Problem: A motherboard failure has occurred. Something is wrong with the motherboard — an electronics fault, no power, or some other type of corruption. Or, the problem could be as specific as a failure of the BIOS chips.

Solution: Take the computer into the dealer and have them replace the motherboard. That can be expensive.

Problem: The computer is too hot. You can tell by feeling the case or checking to see whether the fans are spinning. A computer doesn't operate if its internal temperature is too hot.

Solution: Fix the fans. Some microprocessors have fans, and these can be replaced. Ensure that your dealer replaces only the microprocessor fan and not the entire microprocessor, which would be expensive. (However, if the dealer replaces the fan and the microprocessor is damaged, the microprocessor needs to be replaced as well.)

Problem: The hard drive has no operating system. This problem happens on those systems that show logos and not start-up text. Occasionally, you may even see a "Missing Operating System" error.

Solution: See the section "The dreaded Missing Operating System message," a couple of sections from here.

✔ Some computers, such as eMachines, start with a graphic logo. You can change this in the computer's setup program so that you can see the start-up text. That's a good option to choose if you're experiencing start-up trouble.

✔ Make a note of which key combination starts the computer's setup program. Text on the screen informs you of which key or key combination to press to enter this program. On most PCs, it's the Del or Delete key, F1, F2, Alt+S, or F10. Whatever the key, make a note of it, for example, in the manual that came with the computer.

✔ Sometimes, cables come loose, which may lead you to believe that you have a major component failure, but it's just not the case. If you're bold enough, unplug the PC and venture into its case. Check to ensure that all the cables are properly connected and that all expansion cards are properly "seated" into their slots.

The nefarious Non-System Disk error message

The exact wording of the error message varies, but the cause is the same: You've left a nonbootable floppy disk in Drive A. The solution: Remove the disk and press the Spacebar to continue booting from the hard drive.

✔ This error can also happen if you attempt to boot from a nonbootable CD. Same solution.

✔ If you get the CD error often or dislike the floppy drive error, you can fix it on most PCs. See the section "The computer stupidly starts from another drive," later in this chapter, for information on changing the boot order.

✔ If a hard drive produces this error, it means that the hard drive lacks an operating system. See the next section.

The dreaded Missing Operating System message

The most terrifying error message I've ever seen is "Missing Operating System." It's a BIOS error message, though it could also be a boot loader message. Basically, it means that no operating system is on disk to load. Uh-oh.

There are many things you can do, however:

Use the emergency boot disk. Hopefully, you made an emergency boot disk with Windows 98 or Windows Me. You can use this disk to start your computer (see Appendix C).

The emergency boot disk can confirm that your computer still works; if it loads up and runs, you may just have a problem with the hard drive. Furthermore, you can use the disk to check the hard drive to see whether it's intact. Some tools can also recover a hard drive if something ugly has happened to it.

✔ The Norton Utilities, as well as other programs — such as backup or system recovery tools — also urge you to create a type of emergency boot disk to be used in dire crisis.

✔ If you have the Norton Utilities, use its emergency boot disk instead of the one Windows creates.

✔ Some disk partition utilities come with recovery disks as well. If you're messing with disk partitions and you get the "Missing Operating System" error message, use the disk partition utility's disk to help you get the operating system back.

Boot from a bootable CD. For example, your computer may have come with a recovery disk, or you may have another bootable Windows CD. If so, try to start the computer with it. Again, this technique confirms that the computer is working fine; the problem may only be with the hard drive.

Reinstall your computer system. The final step, which is most drastic and terrible, is to merely start over and attempt a full system recovery. Most PCs come with a recovery CD, which you can use to reinstall basic system software and return your computer to the same state it was in when you took it out of the box.

I wish that I had better news on this error message. Generally speaking, the only way your operating system (Windows) can disappear and go for a powder is if you've somehow messed with it. This situation can happen if you attempt to modify or change the hard drive's partition tables, boot sector, or master boot record or, well, if you just up and delete all of Windows.

- ✔ Another culprit? Computer viruses. The Monkey virus can delete the FAT resource on a hard drive, which is the map that tells Windows where to find files. When the FAT is gone, so is the hard drive.

- ✔ Norton has a utility that may recover a hard drive if the FAT is damaged — but don't bet your data on it: Back up the hard drive and use antivirus software as a precaution.

- ✔ Hardware-wise, this problem may occur if the hard drive fails outright. However, that problem generates a BIOS error message on most systems when the hard drive fails to initialize.

- ✔ Does this scare you? Then it's a good time to consider a backup strategy (see Chapter 22).

The computer stupidly starts from another drive

Starting the computer from a disk drive other than the hard drive isn't really trouble, though it can often be annoying and may lead to some surprise. Traditionally, the PC boots first from the floppy drive A, checking for the presence of a disk there and, if so, an operating system on that disk. Then Drive C is checked.

Today's computers often check Drive A, the hard drive, and a CD-ROM drive. I've noticed that if I keep a CD-ROM in the drive, some of my test computers quiz me when they're started: "Do you want to boot from the CD?" or "Press any key to boot the CD." This option is valuable if anything happens to the hard drive.

If you'd rather not mess with such messages, you can change the boot order. Most computers let you do this through their Setup program: Read the screen when the computer first starts. Take note of which key (or keys) to press to enter the Setup program.

In the Setup program, look for boot information. You may see an option there to change the boot order, specifying which disk drives you want the PC to check for an operating system and in which order.

Be sure to save your selection to the Setup program's memory if you make any changes.

✔ Not every PC's Setup program has boot options that let you change the order of which disk is checked for an operating system.

✔ I generally disable booting from Drive A on my computers; that way, I can be lazy and leave a disk in the drive and it doesn't stop up my computer's boot process.

✔ If you have an emergency and you need to boot from a floppy or CD, you can rerun the Setup program and, once again, change the boot order. That way, you can use an emergency boot disk, if the need arises.

Dealing with the Boot Menu

It's entirely possible to have multiple operating systems on the same computer. For example, one test PC I have has Windows XP, Windows Me, Windows 3.1, DOS, and Linux all on the same system. This arrangement is accomplished through a software program I use called System Commander, but it can also be done in Windows XP (and also Windows 2000, though it's not specifically covered in this book).

When you have your system set up to boot into multiple operating systems, you see a boot menu appear as the computer starts. (On a computer with one operating system, you would see that sole operating system start.) You can then select from a list which operating system you want.

Normally, this choice is a good thing. After all, today's hard drives are roomy, and the ability to support several operating systems is entirely possible.

In Windows XP, the Boot menu feature is controlled from the Startup and Recovery dialog box, as shown in Figure 8-1.

Here's how to display that dialog box:

1. **Right-click the My Computer icon on the desktop.**

2. **Choose the Properties command from the pop-up menu.**

   The System Properties dialog box appears.

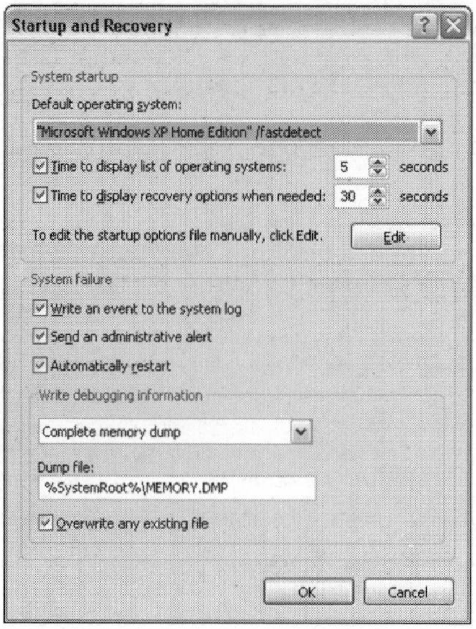

Figure 8-1:
Controlling
the boot
menu in
Windows
XP.

3. **Click the Advanced tab.**

   Advanced doesn't imply anything dangerous or scary. I view it as a word Microsoft uses to throw in all the leftovers it couldn't stick in any other category.

4. **In the Startup and Recovery area, click the Settings button.**

   It's the lowest of the three Settings buttons in the dialog box. This step displays the Startup and Recovery dialog box, as shown in Figure 8-1.

   The drop-down Default operating system list displays the available operating system on your computer. (At least, it displays the operating systems that Windows itself knows about.) This is where you choose which operating system you want to boot from automatically; for example, when you're away from your computer when it starts.

   The Time to display list of operating systems option tells Windows how many seconds to display the list before the default operating system is automatically chosen.

5. **To disable the menu, remove the check mark by the option Time to display list of operating systems.**

   This way, Windows always boots into the operating system you've selected.

6. **Click OK when you're done making changes to this dialog box.**

Again, the list of operating systems appears only if you've installed multiple versions of Windows on a PC and Windows itself is managing those operating systems.

✔ If you're using another system to control which operating system starts, such as System Commander or the Linux LILO program, you have to check its documentation for the various options and settings.

✔ Now would certainly be a good time for a hot, soft peanut butter cookie.

Getting at the Startup Menu

The Startup menu differs from the Boot menu. The Startup menu is a special menu suited for troubleshooting Windows, one that lets you turn off certain options when the computer boots, boot into a DOS session, or start the computer in Safe mode.

To see this menu, press the F8 key immediately after you hear the computer beep or you see the menu to select an operating system or you see the "Starting Windows" message on the screen.

You have to be quick! If you're too late, you don't see the Startup menu.

The Startup menu typically displays the following items, though not all versions of Windows display the same ones and some versions of Windows display more options than these:

✔ **Command Prompt:** Start the computer in DOS mode. None of the Windows drivers is loaded, in case they're causing problems. Choose this mode only if you really know how to work in DOS to fix whatever is wrong. You can also choose it to run older DOS programs that may be incompatible with Windows.

✔ **Logged/Enable Boot Logging:** A text file is created as the computer starts, listing which programs or processes start and whether they're successful. For Windows 98 and Windows Me, the file is named C:\BOOTLOG.TXT. In Windows XP, it's NTBTLOG.TXT, found in the Windows folder. The file is used to pinpoint problems the computer may have when starting, though the information there is decipherable only by highly trained tech support people or Vulcans.

✔ **Enable VGA Mode:** Select this option if you're having video troubles in Windows XP. It looks similar to Safe mode, but unlike Safe mode, the rest of the computer starts up normally (only the video driver is disabled). That way, you can fix a video problem and still have the rest of the computer in working order.

✔ **Last Known Good Configuration:** For Windows XP, this option uses a type of System Restore "on the fly" to return the computer to a state where it last started properly. This option is good to choose if you're unable to start the computer to run System Restore after some upgrade. Alas, unlike a real System Restore, this option does not fix or uninstall bad drivers or missing files. (You need to run System Restore in Safe mode for that to happen.)

✔ **Reboot:** Restart the computer.

✔ **Return to OS Choices Menu:** On computers that have multiple Windows operating systems (OSs) installed, this option returns you to the operating system selection menu (or the boot menu, as covered in the preceding section).

✔ **Safe Mode:** The computer is started, but Windows doesn't load any specific hardware drivers. Please see Appendix B for all the details and reasons why.

✔ **Safe Mode with Command Prompt:** The computer is started in DOS mode in Windows XP, using only basic configuration files.

✔ **Safe Mode with Networking:** This option is the same as Safe mode, but with networking abilities enabled, so you can use the network and, possibly, restore a network backup or download updated files from a server.

✔ **Step-By-Step Confirmation:** This option in Windows 98 displays a Yes-No confirmation prompt during each step of the start-up process. This option can be used to disable known problems, such as bad drivers or unknown commands in the CONFIG.SYS, AUTOEXEC.BAT, or other start-up configuration files.

✔ **Normal/Start Windows Normally:** Just continue loading Windows as though you didn't press F8 to see the Startup menu.

Make your choice based on your troubleshooting needs. Various sections elsewhere in this book recommend choices and options to take for this menu.

✔ On some computers, you can press and hold the Ctrl key rather than the F8 key.

✔ In Windows 98, you could press the F5 key to force the computer to start in Safe mode.

✔ If you see the "Please select an operating system to start" menu (the Boot menu), you have to press the F8 key again to get at the Startup menu.

✔ Any additional options not mentioned in the preceding list are generally advanced configuration items. Mess with such options only when directed to do so by a support technician.

✔ If you do have an older DOS program that is incompatible with Windows, starting the computer at the DOS prompt may not turn the trick. In some cases, you need to run an older version of DOS on the computer to make the program work. For that, I recommend using disk partition software, such as System Commander, to set things up for you.

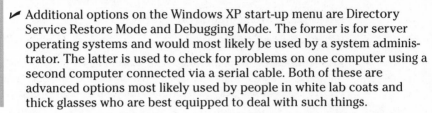

✔ If the computer starts in Safe mode no matter what, see Appendix B for more information.

✔ Additional options on the Windows XP start-up menu are Directory Service Restore Mode and Debugging Mode. The former is for server operating systems and would most likely be used by a system administrator. The latter is used to check for problems on one computer using a second computer connected via a serial cable. Both of these are advanced options most likely used by people in white lab coats and thick glasses who are best equipped to deal with such things.

Hunting Down Mystery Start-Up Messages

Suppose that the computer starts as it normally does. However, along its tired journey, some oddball messages pop up. It's stuff you've never seen! Is Windows causing the message? Is the message something to be concerned with? And, most importantly, how do you get rid of the dumb message?

For some reason, Selective Startup is on

Selective Startup is a debugging tool set by the System Configuration Utility (MSCONFIG). Simply uncheck Selective Startup in the System Configuration Utility window by choosing Normal Startup instead. That fixes the problem.

See Appendix A for information on the System Configuration utility.

Blah-blah in CONFIG.SYS

For Windows 98, where the old DOS CONFIG.SYS file still holds sway, you may see a message about a bad line or missing driver in the CONFIG.SYS file. Whatever the message, if it says CONFIG.SYS is the problem source, follow these steps to remove the message:

1. **Make a note of the message.**

   Write down exactly what the message says. Sometimes, it may list a line number — that's good! Sometimes, it may name a driver or SYS file. Write that down.

2. **Click the Start button.**

3. **Choose the Run command.**

4. **Type** MSCONFIG **into the box.**

5. **Click OK.**

   The System Configuration utility appears.

6. **Click the Config.sys tab.**

   The Config.sys tab lists the contents of the CONFIG.SYS file, as shown in Figure 8-2. It was originally used by DOS to load device drivers, but exists in Windows only for compatibility with older programs.

   The message you see is caused by a typo or a command left behind by some DOS program you uninstalled. Either way, disabling the command removes the error message.

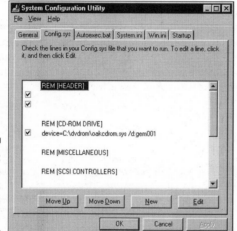

Figure 8-2:
Perusing the
CONFIG.SYS
file in
Windows 98.

7. **Remove the check mark next to the offending command.**

   Find the command using the information you wrote down in Step 1. If it's a specific command, search for that text in CONFIG.SYS. If it's a line number, count down that many lines; the first line is Line 1.

8. **Click OK to close the System Configuration Utilities window.**

9. **Restart Windows.**

   Do this step even if you're not prompted to do so when you close the System Configuration utility's window.

When the system restarts, the message is gone. If not, it wasn't a CONFIG.SYS message to begin with. See the next few sections for more troubleshooting info.

✔ Windows Me and Windows XP do not use the CONFIG.SYS file, so these types of messages don't appear in those operating systems, nor does a Config.sys tab appear in their System Configuration Utility dialog boxes.

✔ If the Config.sys tab is blank, the message is coming from somewhere else; see the next few sections.

Bogus text screen messages

Most text screen error messages I've seen deal with CONFIG.SYS or the AUTOEXEC.BAT file, two DOS start-up files that were still active in Windows 98 but are defunct in Windows Me and Windows XP.

Refer to the preceding section for undoing mystery CONFIG.SYS messages.

For AUTOEXEC.BAT messages, click the Autoexec.bat tab in the system Configuration Utility dialog box. (To summon the System Configuration Utility dialog box, work through the first five steps in the preceding section.) The Autoexec.bat file appears in the window, as shown in Figure 8-3.

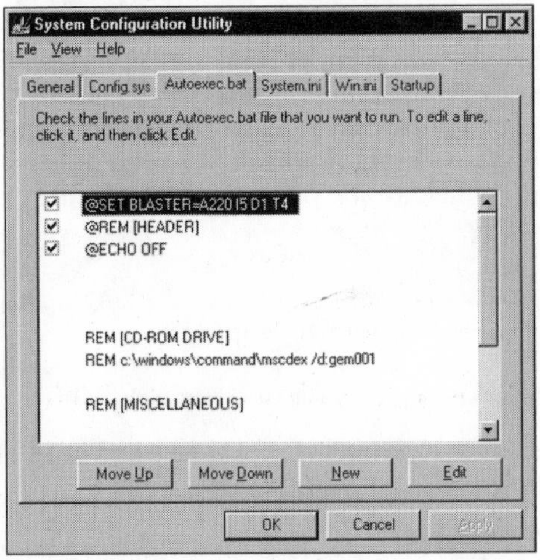

Figure 8-3: The lovely AUTOEXEC. BAT file.

As with CONFIG.SYS, look for the offending line in the AUTOEXEC.BAT file. When you find that line, disable it by removing the check mark.

Some AUTOEXEC.BAT commands display messages on the screen. If you see any line starting with ECHO, you can disable that command. Any line that starts with PAUSE can also be disabled without affecting anything.

The first line in the AUTOEXEC.BAT file is usually @ECHO OFF. This command turns off the text display for the remaining commands. If @ECHO OFF is not the first command (if it's the second command, for example), you can change things as follows:

1. **Click to select the @ECHO OFF command from the list.**

   Just click the command; do not click to remove the check mark.

2. **Click the Move Up button.**

3. **Keep clicking that button until @ECHO OFF is the first command on the list.**

Note that some programs display messages that appear and then go away. For example, the old SoundBlaster driver file displayed a text screen message and then switched back to the Starting Windows banner. Other programs do the same thing, especially in Windows 98: You see the Windows 98 splash screen, and then text, and then the splash screen again. This is normal! There is no need to disable or remove anything in that case.

The missing DLL or VxD file mystery

A typical nontext message that crawls under your skin appears in a dialog box. Windows 98 and Windows Me announce to you that a DLL or VxD or some sort of file is missing or doesn't exist. As with most text screen error messages, this one means that something wasn't installed or was uninstalled properly. The idea is to find which idiotic program is displaying the message and squelch it.

The System Configuration utility is the best tool for tracking down the causes of unknown messages. Follow these steps to employ it:

1. **Write down as much as you can about the message.**

   If the missing file has a name, write it down. If another program is mentioned, write it down.

2. **Search for the file in question.**

   See Chapter 9 for information on finding files. You know the file's name; it was displayed in the warning dialog box. Now you need to check to see whether the file exists. If you can find it, note in which folder it lives.

3. **Start the System Configuration utility.**

   Refer to Steps 2 through 5 in the section "Blah-blah in CONFIG.SYS," earlier in this chapter (or see Appendix A).

   Your job now is to try and find the program associated with the bum start-up program. It may be started directly or run when another program starts.

What is a DLL file?

The DLL file is one of the most regrettable mistakes made by the people who originally created Windows. The idea seemed worthwhile and wholesome: much of computer programming involves the redundant rewriting of the same routines. For example, most applications use the Open, Save, Print, and several other common dialog boxes. Rather than re-create that programming code over and over, the wise programmers at Microsoft decided to save everyone time and bother. So they created the Dynamically Linked Library (DLL) file concept.

A DLL file contains common routines to be used by all programs. For example, the COMMDLG.DLL file contains the programming needed to use the Open, Save, Print, and other common dialog (COMMDLG) boxes. Other DLL files were created so that programmers could link into them and everyone could share all the same code and be happy and go on to live lives of religious and spiritual fulfillment.

Alas, the DLL solution became a problem in itself because just about everyone figured out how to make better DLL files. There were conflicts! There was competition! There was hoohaw! And eventually the simple solution turned out to be a gigantic pain in the rear. I've heard a rumor that the next version of Windows will do away with DLL files altogether. If so, there will be much rejoicing.

The name of the folder in which the missing file exists can be your clue to which program "owns" the file.

4. **First, check the Startup tab.**

   Scroll through the list of programs and see whether you can find the "bad" one in there.

   If you find the bad program listed, remove the check mark. This step prevents that program from starting and the error message from being displayed.

   In Windows Me, just click the Cleanup button to remove any unknown programs from the list.

5. **Second, check the Win.ini tab.**

   WIN.INI is an older Windows initialization file, used before Windows 95 introduced the concept of the Windows Registry, yet it's still a source of trouble.

6. **Open the** `[windows]` **folder.**

7. **Look for the** `run=` **or** `load=` **entries.**

   Those two entries are used to specify start-up programs, such as

   ```
   load=ptsnoop.exe
   ```

If either one lists your program, uncheck that entry to remove the program and the error message.

8. **Close the System Configuration utility when you're done.**

These steps should help you eliminate the programs that cause most of the annoying "missing DLL" file messages. If not, you can also check the Programs⇨ Startup menu to see whether the errant program appears there. See the next section, "Stopping Programs from Automatically Starting."

✔ Missing DLL/VxD file messages appear right after installing or uninstalling a program. If you just installed a program and you get the message, try installing the program again. If that doesn't work, phone the developer and have someone there fix the error.

✔ See the Microsoft Knowledge Base on the Internet for information regarding missing DLL files for Windows. Visit http://support.microsoft.com/ and select your version of Windows. Search for the DLL or VxD file's name, and any information about the file appears in the search results, along with information on how to fix any problems. (Also see Chapter 5.)

Stopping Programs from Automatically Starting

Windows can stick programs in three places to start them automatically. The first two are covered in the preceding section; the System Configuration utility's Startup tab lists programs that Windows itself automatically starts for you. And the [windows] section of the old WIN.INI file could also be used to secretly start programs.

Where else do start-up programs lurk?

The StartUp folder is obviously not the only place Windows tucks programs that automatically start. No, Windows is pretty sneaky about knowing where to hide programs that can start — and it has quite a few of them.

The place to disable these programs is the System Configuration utility, which is covered throughout this chapter as well as in Appendix A. But what the System Configuration utility shows you is merely information that exists deep within the Windows Registry. One such place is the devious Run entry. Here's the key:

```
HKEY_LOCAL_MACHINE\Software\
    Microsoft\Windows\
    CurrentVersion\Run
```

This isn't the last word, of course; many spots in the Registry list start-up programs. Don't bother deleting them or messing with the preceding key; the System Configuration utility is the one, central place to disable the nasty start-up files.

For you, a mere mortal user, you have the StartUp folder on the Start button's Programs menu: After clicking the Start button, choose Programs⇨StartUp. The menu you see lists a bunch of programs designed to start automatically when the computer starts — a nifty thing to have.

Well, it's nifty until a program is in there that you don't want to start automatically. In that case, I recommend either deleting the program or moving it to a NotStartUp folder.

✔ In Windows 98 and Windows Me the folder is named StartUp. In Windows XP, it's named Startup (no big *U*).

✔ Also, in Windows XP, the folder is on the All Programs menu. In Windows 98 and Windows Me, the menu is called Programs.

Deleting a program from the StartUp folder

To delete the program, right-click its entry on the StartUp menu. Choose Delete from the pop-up menu, and the program is gone.

✔ Actually, only a shortcut icon is deleted. The program isn't removed from the hard drive. (To remove a program, you must uninstall it.)

✔ If you make a mistake, press Ctrl+Z right away, and your deleted menu item is yanked back.

Creating a NotStartUp folder

Better than deleting a StartUp menu item is disabling the program from starting. You do that by moving the menu item from the StartUp folder to a special folder you create called NotStartUp. Here's how to create that folder:

1. **Right-click the Start button.**

2. **Choose the Open command from the pop-up menu.**

   This step opens a window into the Start button's menu folder. That's where folders appear as submenus and shortcut icons appear as menu commands. It's very sneaky, but also a very good way to edit the Start menu.

3. **Open the Programs folder.**

   You see menu items (shortcut icons) and menus (folders), including the StartUp folder.

4. **Choose File⇨New⇨Folder from the menu.**

   The new folder appears highlighted in the window.

5. **Type** NotStartUp **as the folder's new name.**

   If this step doesn't work, reselect the New Folder icon by clicking it once with the mouse. Press the F2 key, and then you can rename the folder.

   The NotStartUp folder is now a new menu off the main All Programs (or Programs) menu. You can pop up the Start button and look at the menu to confirm this, if you like. Or, you can continue by moving those items you want disabled from the StartUp folder to the NotStartUp folder.

6. **Open the StartUp folder.**

7. **Click to select the program you don't want to run when the computer starts.**

   If it's more than one program, press the Ctrl key as you click the mouse. This step lets you select more than one icon.

8. **Choose Edit⇨Cut from the menu.**

9. **Click the Up button to return to the main Programs folder.**

10. **Open the NotStartUp folder.**

11. **Choose Edit⇨Paste.**

    The shortcut icons are moved — and disabled from starting up every time Windows starts.

12. **Close the Programs window.**

The beauty of this system is that you can easily reenable the programs by moving them from the NotStartUp folder back to the StartUp folder. Nothing is ever lost.

Finding more start-up files in Windows XP

Windows XP has many StartUp folders. Greed? Perhaps. But their purpose is more than likely to serve the multiple users XP can handle than any overt avarice on behalf of the computer.

In any event, don't be surprised if you try the trick from the preceding section and discover that the Startup folder is empty. That's because Windows XP is also copying in programs from the All Users Startup folder. Fret not! You have a way to fix that folder as well.

Repeat the steps from the preceding section, but in Step 2 choose Open All Users from the pop-up menu. The programs you see in the Start Menu window are menu items and submenus common to all the users on your computer. (Remember that Windows XP supports multiple users, even if you're the only person using the computer. I realize that's like driving a city bus when all you need is a moped, but that's how XP works.)

From this point on, you can continue, creating a NotStartUp folder and moving files from the Startup folder into that new folder. Keep in mind that these changes affect all users on your computer.

Chapter 9

Finding Lost Files and Things

· ·

· ·

*I*n the top drawer of the Windows treasure chest is a wonderfully powerful file-finding command. It's fast. It's convenient. It's always correct. Alas, with each new release of Windows, it changes in a weird, frustrating, and utterly different way.

For example, in Windows 98 the command is the Find command. Find. That makes sense. And it appeared in a handy little dialog box with all the options arrayed in a logical, sensible manner. You could find files narrow and wide with that handy Find dialog box. Mm-mmm.

Then, in Windows Me, the handy Find dialog box morphed into the Windows Explorer program. Find became Search. And the Search panel, appearing on the left side of the folder window, listed handy options and such, making searching for files similar to manipulating things. An improvement? Perhaps.

Then along comes Windows XP with its clown makeup and balloons. The Search command from Windows Me is still there, but the interface is hidden beneath an interactive system that quizzes you about the lost file, hiding many of the useful options and renaming all the familiar and handy ones? Oh, Microsoft. . . .

This chapter covers some quick tips for finding lost files, downloads, missing programs, and other things that drift off or turn invisible. Because of the twisted and changing nature of the Find command in Windows, each section contains three different sets of steps for each of the three versions of Windows covered in this chapter. Sorry about that.

Finding and Searching

Little Bo Peep has just downloaded some sheep. But, alas, she knows not where to find them! She looks up. She looks down. She turns the PC around. But that stupid sheep file is no where to be found.

Files disappear for two reasons: You forgot where you put the file, or the file was deleted. In the case of downloads, sometimes the files never appear. That's because you're supposed to *save* the download to disk as opposed to *open* the download — but that's a sorrowful woe for another chapter. Right now, you probably want to find your sheep, er, file.

The Quick Find or Search Command

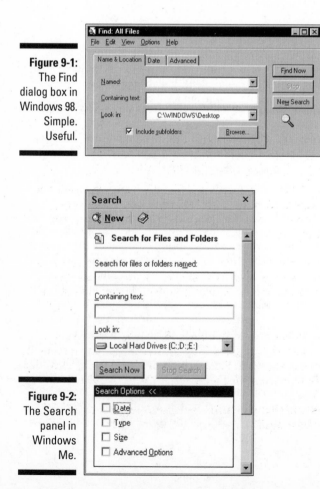

Figure 9-1:
The Find dialog box in Windows 98. Simple. Useful.

Figure 9-2:
The Search panel in Windows Me.

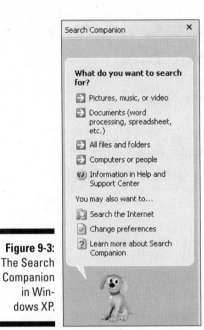

Figure 9-3:
The Search
Companion
in Win-
dows XP.

In a hurry? You can use tricks to immediately search for stuff. Two key commands come to mind:

Win+F   Pressing the Windows key plus the F key summons the Find or Search command in all versions of Windows.

F3   Pressing the F3 key brings up the Find or Search command, but only when no other windows are open or when a Windows Explorer window is open. For example, click the desktop and then press the F3 key.

Also, in Windows Me and Windows XP, you can click the Search button in any Windows Explorer (folder) window to start searching for files. Press the Ctrl+E keyboard shortcut to display the Search panel on the left side of the window.

Configure the Search Results window in Windows Me and Windows XP so that Details view is showing. That's the best way to sift through the results. If you don't see Details view (as shown in Figures 9-4 and 9-5, a little later in this chapter), choose View⇨Details from the menu.

The next few sections assume that you have the Find dialog box or Search panel ready to go and look for stuff.

Searching for something you created or downloaded today or yesterday

I tend to lose things immediately, so first I try to search for files created in the past day or so. Hopefully, one of them is the one that's missing.

In Windows 98:

1. **Choose My Computer from the Look in drop-down list.**

   If you don't do this, the Windows may look only on the desktop for your file. You need to tell the computer to look everywhere, so choose My Computer.

   If you're certain that the file is on drive C, choose Drive C. Or, if you're certain that the file is somewhere in the My Documents folder, choose that folder from the drop-down list. That way, the search doesn't take as long.

2. **Click the Date tab.**

3. **Click to select Find all files.**

4. **Choose Created from the drop-down list.**

5. **Choose during the previous day(s).**

6. **Ensure that a 1 (one) is in the previous days gizmo.**

7. **Click the Find Now button.**

   A list of files fills up the window. That is because Windows is continually creating new files, temporary files, and other whatnot — especially if you've been on the Internet.

   Now you can get even more specific with the results window.

8. **If you know the approximate time you created the file, click the Modified heading.**

   You may have to scroll over to the right to see that heading. When you click it, the files are sorted by date and time, which makes it easier to locate a file you downloaded at, say, 2:10 in the afternoon.

   Likewise, you can sort the results by file size if you have a guess about how large the file is.

I'm assuming that you've found the file. Yippee! You probably want to move it to a better location. You can do that in several ways, though the easiest is simply to drag the file's icon from the Find All Files window out onto the desktop. From there, you can drag the icon into any other folder window — hopefully, where it should belong.

If you don't find the file, consider adjusting the search period from Step 5. Search back two days. If that technique still doesn't find the file, the file simply isn't on your computer.

Be sure to close the Find All Files window when you're done.

In Windows Me:

1. **Choose My Computer from the Look in drop-down list.**

   Or, you can be specific. For example, if you're *certain* that the file is on Drive C, choose it. Or, if you *absolutely* know that the file is somewhere in the My Documents folder (or a subfolder), choose My Documents. The more specific you are, the faster the Find command operates.

2. **Be sure that the Search Options part of the panel is open.**

   It should look like the one shown in Figure 9-2. If not, click the Search Options link.

3. **Click to put a check mark by the Date option.**

   A new part of the Search panel opens, so you may have to scroll down a ways to see the various date and time options.

4. **Choose Files Created from the drop-down list.**

5. **Select the In the last ... days item.**

6. **Ensure that a 1 (one) is in the days gizmo.**

7. **Click the Search Now button.**

   After a few moments, the right side of the window fills with a list of all the files created during the past day (see Figure 9-4). You will see a few of them; Windows is continually creating new files, especially temporary Internet files.

   To best find your file, you need to get specific and sort the list.

8. **If you know the approximate time you created the file, click the Modified heading.**

   This step sorts the list by date and time, so if you know that you down-loaded the file at about 4 p.m., you can easily scan for files created around that time.

   You may have to scroll the file list over to see the Modified column.

   Likewise, if you have a good idea what the file size was, you can sort the list by file size: Click the Size heading.

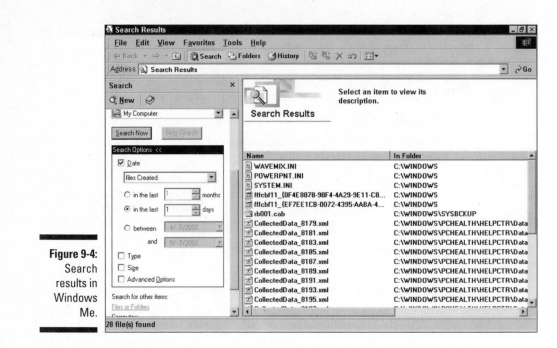

Figure 9-4:
Search
results in
Windows
Me.

If everything goes well, you find the wayward file. Pat yourself on the back. The next step is to move the found file to a more proper location, somewhere that it can't be lost again. (Hmmm. Didn't you think that way the first time? Oh, well.)

Right-click the icon and choose Send To⇨My Documents. This action places the file in the main My Documents folder. From there, you can move the file to another, specific folder, but at least you know exactly where the file is.

If the file didn't turn up, you can change the search time in Step 6 to two or three days. If that technique still doesn't locate the file, assume that it's no longer on your computer.

Be sure to close the Search Results window when you're done messing around.

In Windows XP:

In Windows XP, the Search Companion is your guide to finding files. I'm not very happy with it because it hides many of the useful searching options in the name of being "easy." Poppycock. Let me at them controls!

1. **Choose All files and folders.**

2. **Choose My Computer from the Look in drop-down list.**

   You want to ensure that Windows looks everywhere for your file, though if you're certain that it's in the My Documents folder or on Drive C, choose those options instead; that makes the search go a wee bit faster.

3. **Click the down-pointing chevron by the option When was it modified?**

4. **Choose Specify dates.**

   You must be specific — today or even yesterday!

5. **Choose Created Date from the drop-down list.**

6. **Type yesterday's date in the From field.**

   The date shown is today's date, so modify the day (and month, if needed) to reflect yesterday.

   The To field contains today's date, so it need not be changed.

7. **Click the Search button.**

   Files flow into the window (see Figure 9-5), each one of them created today or yesterday. Hopefully, you don't see too many; Figure 9-5 says that 146 files were found. Golly.

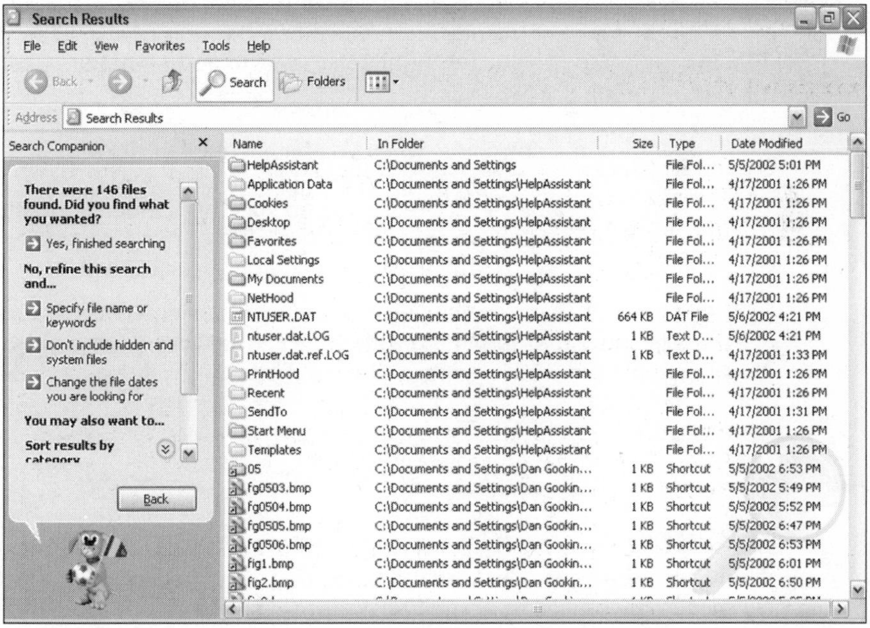

Figure 9-5:
Search results in Windows XP.

8. **If you know the approximate time you created the file, click the Date Modified heading.**

   Scroll through the list to seek out files created during the approximate time you were downloading. That should find you the file you want.

   You can also use the Size column to locate the file if you can remember about how big it was. For some reason, I remember how large download files are (probably because of the time it takes to receive them).

If you found the file, great! Right-click its icon and choose Send To⇨ My Documents from the pop-up menu. That action moves the icon to the My Documents folder — perhaps not the best place for the file, but at least a place where you can see it! Close the Search Results window, and then you can move the file from the My Documents folder to wherever you feel would be a better place for it.

If the search results came up with disappointing results, maybe the file just wasn't saved to disk. That happens. You can try modifying the dates to search: Specify a date earlier than yesterday, for example, and then try again.

Searching for something when you know only the file's contents

The more you know about a file, the easier it is to find. For example, I knew I had an Excel spreadsheet that documented some payments I was making. I forgot the name of the file, but I remembered that it was an Excel spreadsheet and that it had the phrase "but I don't want to go to jail" in it. That certainly makes finding the file easier.

- ✔ Alas, on the downside, when you have Windows search each file for a chunk of text, the searches can last forever. So when you do need to search for a bit of text, please try to specify as much additional information as possible: filename (or part of it), program that created the file or file type, size, or date or approximate date, for example.

- ✔ The Find/Search command can locate documents only by text, not by any other information. Graphics files, for example, cannot be searched, even if the graphics image is a text picture.

- ✔ Be sure to specify the My Documents folder and check to ensure that subfolders are being searched. Rarely is it necessary to search *everywhere* on the hard drive for a document containing a bit of text.

Windows 98

In Windows 98, use the Name & Location tab in the Find All Files dialog box. Specify the bit of text in the Containing text box.

Fill out other options if you know them. For example, if you know which application created the document, click the Advanced tab and choose the application's name from the Of type drop-down list.

Click the Find Now button to locate the file.

Windows Me

The Containing Text box stares right in your face on the Search panel. Just fill in the box with whatever text you want to search for.

Fill in additional options, such as Date or Type or Size if you know them. Remember that the narrower you make the search, the happier you'll be with the results.

Click the Search Now button to locate the file.

Windows XP

As you would expect, Windows XP buries the option for finding text in a document. I suppose that it's in the name of making things easier, but compared to the two *inferior* versions of Windows I just discussed, it just isn't so.

To find a file based on a bit of text, follow these steps:

1. **Choose the Documents (word processing, spreadsheet, etc.) item.**

   Only documents contain text. All the other choices are for system files or files that aren't likely to contain text.

2. **Click the Use advanced search options link.**

   They felt it necessary to hide the text box; clicking the link displays it.

3. **Enter your text into the box labeled A word or phrase in the document.**

4. **Click the Search button.**

   And Windows XP marches off to hunt down the file.

Again, the more options you can specify, the more accurate the results. Below the word or phrase text box are additional refinement options you can use to help narrow the search.

How to find a found file's folder

The folder containing your wayward file is listed along with the other information about the file. If you need to open that folder in Windows Me or Windows XP, right-click the file and choose Open Containing Folder from the pop-up menu.

In Windows 98, click to select the file and then choose File⇨Open Containing Folder from the menu.

Recovering Other Lost Things

Most places that deal with the public have a lost-and-found department. With computers, there must also be a Hopelessly Lost and Never Found department. When the Find or Search command comes up empty, you can try my suggestions from the following sections to see about recovering files in more obtuse and creative ways.

REMEMBER

 ✔ Also see Chapter 4 for information on recovering files from the Recycle Bin — yet another place to look for lost things.

 ✔ In fact, Chapter 4 contains lots of other interesting places to look and things to do for recovering hopelessly lost files.

 ✔ Don't forget the Undo key, Ctrl+Z! If something just disappears, try Ctrl+Z to see whether you can call it back.

 ✔ Sometimes, you just have to accept things: When a file is gone, it's gone. Alas.

The shortcut points to nowhere!

Shortcuts are handy copies of a file, but without all the extra bulk. File lite: Same great taste, but only a few bytes of hard drive space. I probably don't need to justify creating a shortcut here because you already have one and, well, its original file has gone bye-bye.

When you see the Missing Shortcut dialog box, as shown in Figure 9-6, don't panic! Windows begins a minisession of the Find or Search command, trying to locate the wayward original file.

Figure 9-6:
Uh-oh.
Shortcut
points to no
man's land.

> **Missing Shortcut** ☒
>
> Windows is searching for fig40.bmp. To locate the file yourself, click Browse.
>
> [Browse...] [Cancel]

Most of the time, the search is successful. Windows finds the original file and asks whether you want to redirect the shortcut to that file. Sometimes, however, the search results may show similar files, but nothing that really works. In that case, too bad.

Finally, if the original file is truly gone and nothing similar remains, you see a dialog box, as shown in Figure 9-7. Click Yes; the shortcut points nowhere.

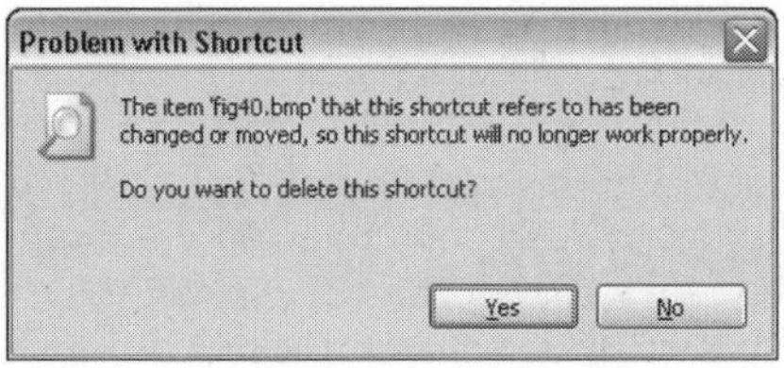

Figure 9-7:
It's time to
give up
finding the
original.

Problem with Shortcut

The item 'fig40.bmp' that this shortcut refers to has been
changed or moved, so this shortcut will no longer work properly.

Do you want to delete this shortcut?

Yes | No

✔ If you renamed or moved the original file, click that Browse button in the Missing Shortcut dialog box (refer to Figure 9-6). Then repoint the short-cut icon back at the original using the Browse dialog box. This advice assumes, of course, that you know where the original was moved.

✔ Windows is smart enough to recognize when you rename or move an original file so that all the shortcuts are updated.

✔ Windows is not smart enough to delete shortcuts when you delete their original files.

✔ Don't forget to look in the Recycle Bin for the original! If you find it, restore the deleted file, and your shortcut works again.

The whatever-submenu on the Start menu is missing!

This problem is an easy one to fix if you have Windows Me. That's because of the frustrating feature called *personalized menus*.

The personalized menus feature, which also appears in Microsoft Office 2000 and Microsoft Office XP, hides rarely used menu items. So if you don't choose the Games menu after a while, it just doesn't show up. Instead, you get "show more" arrows that you can click to display the menu in its entirety. Supposedly, this feature helps make things less cluttered, but it also has the alarming effect of making you think that the menu was deleted! Imagine going to a swanky restaurant where the menu changes like that. "No, madam, we still do have the boiled asparagus, but it's not ordered often, so it slipped off the menu." How annoying.

To see all the menu items in Windows Me, click the down-pointing chevron at the bottom of the menu. Or, to remove the personalized menu feature, follow these steps:

1. **Pop up the Start menu.**

2. **Choose Settings⇨Control Panel.**

3. **Open the Taskbar and Start Menu icon.**

Who knows what evil lurks in the hearts of files? The Shortcut knows!

Shortcut icons remember who owns them. You can discover this information as well, even if the original file has long since left for more digital pastures: Right-click the shortcut icon. Choose the Properties command from the pop-up menu. The shortcut's Properties icon appears, as shown in the following figure. There, you can divine lots of information about the shortcut.

The Target box lists the original file's full pathname. That's where Windows expects to find the original. Don't worry about hunting it down; just click the Find Target button, and that folder is opened for you. This technique doesn't work if the original was deleted; you end up with the same dialog boxes as shown in Figures 9-6 and 9-7. However, it does give you a good idea about where the original file belonged.

fig4.bmp Properties

General Shortcut

fig4.bmp

Target type:

Target location: My Pictures

Target: Gookin\My Documents\My Pictures\fig40.bmp"

Start in: "C:\Documents and Settings\Dan Gookin\My Do

Shortcut key: None

Run: Normal window

Comment:

[Find Target...] [Change Icon...] [Advanced...]

[OK] [Cancel] [Apply]

4. **On the General tab, remove the check mark by the option Use personalized menus.**

5. **Click OK.**

If the menu is missing even after these steps are completed or if you have Windows 98 or Windows XP, the menu could have been moved or deleted. That's because anything on the Start menu can be moved by dragging it with the mouse. So, also check for missing menus elsewhere on the Start menu as well as on the desktop, where the menu would appear as a folder.

✔ If you catch yourself accidentally moving a menu with the mouse, immediately press Ctrl+Z to undo it. Otherwise, you have to look for the menu and carefully drag it back by using the mouse.

✔ If the menu was deleted, look in the Recycle Bin for it.

✔ On rare occasions, you may need to reinstall a Windows component to get a certain menu back. For example, the Games menu may disappear if all the Windows games have been removed. To reinstall the games, use the Add/Remove Programs icon in the Control Panel. See the section in Chapter 4 about bringing back bits of Windows.

✔ To turn off personalized menus in most Office 2000 applications (Word and Excel, for example), choose Tools➪Customize. In the Customize dialog box, click the Options tab. Then remove the check mark next to the option labeled Menus show recently used commands first. Click Close.

✔ For Office XP (Word 2002 and Excel 2002, for example), choose Tools➪Customize to display the Customize dialog box. Click the Options tab and then put a check mark by the item Always show full menus.

Oops! Recovering a menu you accidentally moved off the Start menu

Windows 98 introduced the ability of the mouse to manipulate menu items on the Start menu. You can drag, move, drop, and have all sorts of fun with the menus — to a point. That point is when the mouse slips out of your hand and shoots across the desktop, nailing that picture of you enjoying yourself on the beach in Maui. And the thing you were dragging on the Start menu? It's on the desktop. Panic time!

Of course, pressing Ctrl+Z rescues the missing booger. But if you don't press Ctrl+Z right away, you need to reconstruct your Start menu. The best way to do that is to treat the Start menu like a folder — which is all it is, anyway.

Right-click the Start button and choose Open from the pop-up menu. This action opens the Start menu like a folder, and you can work with the menus (folders) and commands (icons) there just like you can with any other folder in Windows: Copy. Move. Rename. Editing the menus with a folder view is much easier than working with the mouse to drag things.

Suppose that you accidentally drag the Accessories menu down to the Internet menu. Here's how to move it back:

1. **Right-click the Start button.**

2. **Choose Open from the pop-up menu.**

Though Windows XP stores all common Start menu items in the All Users folder, when you make major changes to the menu, they're reflected in only your own account's folder. So you do not choose the Open All Users command in this case.

3. Open the Programs folder.

At this point, your menu editing would be specific to whichever menu you're recovering. Remember that in this example, you would be moving the Accessories menu from the Internet submenu back to the main Programs menu.

4. Open the Internet folder.

And there you see the Accessories folder.

5. Click to select the Accessories folder.

Or click to select whichever folder you want to move.

6. Press Ctrl+X to cut the folder.

7. Click the Back button to return to the main Programs folder.

8. Press Ctrl+V to paste the folder back where it belongs.

And life has returned to normal.

9. Close the Programs window.

Don't be distressed if you still can't find the menu! It's there — it just most likely has been added to the *end* of the list. To move it to the top of the list, you have to — be careful! — drag it up there.

On second thought, maybe it just looks better at the end of the list.

- ✔ You can use the folder technique to customize and hone the way the Programs/All Programs menu looks in Windows. I like to keep my own Start menu brief and logical, so I combine many of the items there into general menus.

- ✔ These steps also apply to the programs (menu items) you may accidentally move from the Start menu or from one menu to another.

Chapter 10

Sounds Like Trouble

● ●

In This Chapter

▶ Troubleshooting the no-sound problem

▶ Setting up your sound scheme

▶ Things too loud!

▶ Things too soft!

▶ F-f-f-fixing the stuttering sound

● ●

*E*arly computers were mute. In fact, the "bell" the computer rang was on the teletype machine, not inside the computer itself. When the micro-computer first came out in the late 1970s, it had a speaker — much cheaper than installing a bell. And the hobbyists of that era soon discovered that the speaker could be programmed to make all sorts of noise.

Sound has evolved to become an indispensable part of computing. The computer talks, sings, plays music, and does a number of other interesting audio things — all of which you miss when the sound system stifles itself. Because sound has evolved in the PC (it was sort of a happenstance thing), the root of the sound problem could lie in a number of places: the CD-ROM drive, sound adapter, speakers, or software, for example. This chapter helps you narrow down the options and get your PC bleeping again.

✔ Refer to Chapter 8 for information on beeps (or no beep) you may hear when the computer first starts.

✔ Indeed, sound has evolved on the PC. The original IBM PC had a speaker that could beep or play simple songs. The Tandy 1000 computer intro-duced an integrated sound card into its PC design in 1986. When CD-ROMs became a part of the PC's hardware inventory, external speakers became the requirement. Then, along came the Web in 1996 or so with *streaming audio*. And in 1999? MP3 files. Sound has come a long way.

✔ The ASCII code for the bell is ^G (Control-G). The ASCII code for page eject is ^L (Control-L). A common college prank of the 1970s had sophomore computer science majors concocting a program that sent an infinite number of ^G^L commands to the system printer, usually at 2 a.m. Ha-ha. On today's computers, you can still hear the bell: Open a DOS prompt window and type **ECHO** and a space and then press Ctrl+G. Press the Enter key.

It Is the Sound of Silence

Sound is so much a part of the computing experience that we miss it when it's gone. So a frantic search begins! There's no specific place to start looking, so obey the steps in the following sections in order and hopefully one of them will lead to a noisy solution.

✔ As with most immediate boo-boos, try restarting Windows to see whether that gets the sound back.

✔ Install any new hardware or software recently? Hmmm? That's often the reason the sound stops.

✔ Windows Me or Windows XP users who have System Restore, or folks with GoBack or similar utilities, should immediately attempt a System Restore to go back to a louder time and see whether that works.

Checking the speakers

The sound trail actually starts at either side of your head, with your ears. Not to make light of excess cerumen build-up, but do ensure that your ears are clear of debris. That's the first step. Next, check your PC's speakers.

Check the speaker connections. Here's that patch of ground where your computer becomes a stereo system. The question: Are your speakers properly plugged in — plugged into the computer; plugged into each other; plugged into a subwoofer; and plugged into the power source? Use Figure 10-1 to help you check things. (If you think that the figure is ugly, wait until you see all the cables behind the PC!)

From the computer, the sound goes out the speaker jack, which may also be labeled Line Out or Phones (as in headphones). This is where the speakers plug in.

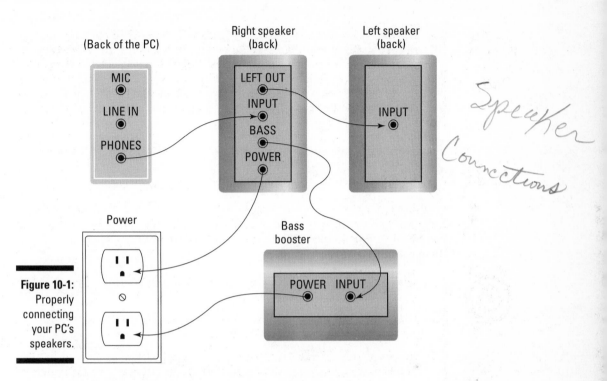

Figure 10-1:
Properly
connecting
your PC's
speakers.

On the back of the speaker, the wire goes into an input jack, though most speakers have this wire permanently attached.

Another wire goes from one speaker to the other. In Figure 10-1, the Left Out wire goes to the input jack on the left speaker.

Finally, speakers need power, so a power cable goes from the main speaker (the one on the right in Figure 10-1) to a power source.

If you have a subwoofer, the nightmare gets worse: Sound must go from the speakers to the subwoofer, and the subwoofer must be powered as well.

  ✔ If your PC has a DVD player, check to see whether it also has a DVD player expansion card. If so, plug your speakers into that card and not into the regular sound jacks! Turn your PC around and look for the DVD expansion card, which should have speaker jacks as well as an S-Video connector (plus other connectors). Plug your speaker into the speaker jack on that card.

  ✔ Make sure that everything is plugged in snugly!

- Subwoofers are also called bass boosters.

- As you're facing the monitor, the "right" speaker is the one that sits on the right side of the monitor. The "left" speaker is the one sitting on the left side. This arrangement can be confusing because when you work on the speakers, you're often working behind your computer, where left and right are backward.

- The speakers plug into the speaker jack.

- The speaker jack may also be labeled with a symbol, one that usually has an arrow pointing away from it.

- Newer systems have color-coded audio jacks. The speaker jack is typically coded lime green.

- Figure 10-1 shows the right speaker as the main one, though the left speaker may be the main one on some makes and models.

- In some situations, the subwoofer is the main speaker, and it connects directly to the PC. Then the left and right speakers connect to the subwoofer.

- Yeah, it's nuts.

- I hate to mention it, but you can often "test" the speakers by touching the input plug — the one that plugs into the computer — to the computer's case. If the speakers are okay, you hear a slight hum as you do that, which is the sound of the speakers picking up the computer's electric field. I'm sure that audiophiles would cringe at the thought, but it works.

Any knobs on the speakers? Some speakers have volume control knobs. Are they up? How about a power knob? Is the speaker on?

Are the speakers getting power? Yes, this is a speaker connection issue, but note that some speakers use batteries as their source of power. Be sure to check the batteries.

Or, to hell with batteries! Go get a power converter for your speakers. They should have a little power plug that the converter can plug into. Listed somewhere on the speaker are its power requirements, which you should note and then go to the electronics store to get the proper converter.

Are the speakers getting enough oomph? If the speakers make noise, but only feebly, check the volume control, which is covered later in this chapter.

If the volume is all the way up, however, what's most likely happening is that the sound is unamplified. Check your PC's rump to see whether it has another hole for the speakers to plug into.

If none of these steps works, try running the speakers through a subwoofer. Or, if they're running through a subwoofer, ensure that the subwoofer is on!

If nothing seems to help, get a new set of speakers.

Checking the master volume control

So the speakers work, huh? Maybe it's the computer itself to blame? Check to see whether Windows has muted the situation:

1. **Click the Start button.**

2. **Choose Run.**

3. **Type** SNDVOL32 **into the box.**

4. **Click OK.**

    This step runs what I call the Master Volume Control program, though depending on your version of Windows, it's called Volume Control or Play Control. Figure 10-2 shows the Windows XP version.

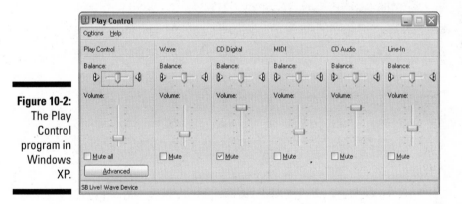

Figure 10-2:
The Play Control program in Windows XP.

So? Is anything muted? Check the Mute options, such as the CD Digital item shown in Figure 10-2.

Is any specific volume turned down? If so, adjust the volume slider higher.

Test-play a sound: Choose Help➪About Volume Control from the menu. An About dialog box appears. Now try to click the Volume Control or Play Control window. The computer should beep when you try to do this because the About window is on top of the other one. That's the easiest way to test the sound.

Close the About dialog box.

Adjust the sound levels as necessary and then close the Volume Control or Play Control dialog box when you're done playing with it.

Last stop: The Device Manager

Now you're getting your elbows dirty. You need to summon the Device Manager and examine the Sound, Video, and Game Controllers option. Follow these steps:

1. **Open the Device Manager.**

   See Appendix A for information on opening the Device Manager.

2. **Open the Sound, video, and game controllers item in the Device Manager window.**

   There, you see a list of anything having to do with sound in your computer, as shown in Figure 10-3.

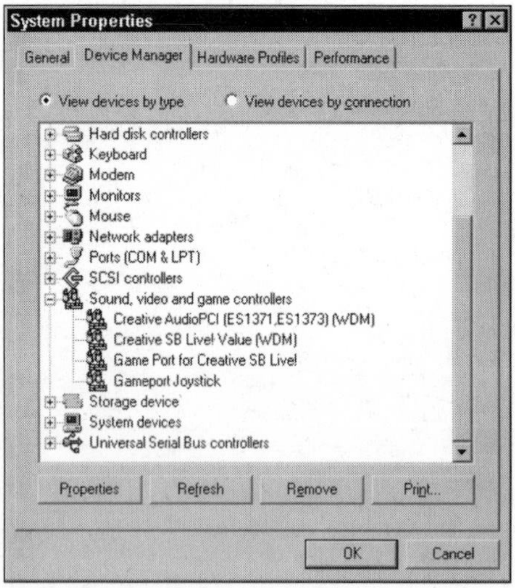

Figure 10-3: The Device Manager in Windows Me.

Figure screenshot: System Properties window, Device Manager tab, showing "View devices by type" selected. List includes: Hard disk controllers, Keyboard, Modem, Monitors, Mouse, Network adapters, Ports (COM & LPT), SCSI controllers, Sound, video and game controllers (expanded to show Creative AudioPCI (ES1371,ES1373) (WDM), Creative SB Live! Value (WDM), Game Port for Creative SB Live!, Gameport Joystick), Storage device, System devices, Universal Serial Bus controllers. Buttons: Properties, Refresh, Remove, Print, OK, Cancel.

If you notice immediately a yellow circle flagging a particular device, something is definitely wrong: Double-click to open the flagged device and follow the information you see in that dialog box.

If the Device Manager's seas are rather calm, you can always poke around.

3. **Select your computer's sound card.**

This is the tricky part; the name isn't that obvious. In Figure 10-3, it's Creative Audio PCI, though a few other entries appear as likely candidates. Don't worry if you get this wrong the first time; you're just poking around.

4. Click the Properties button.

In Windows XP, the Properties button is on the toolbar below the View menu, or you can choose Action➪Properties.

Peruse the Properties dialog box to see whether you can glean any useful information. Note that a Troubleshooter button is in Windows XP.

If you have any conflicts or other problems, they're displayed in the Properties dialog box. Heed those instructions to see how to repair things.

5. Click the Driver tab.

Even if you have no problems, sometimes it works like a charm to replace or update the *driver* — the software that controls your computer's sound system. Clicking the Update Driver button does this, though I recommend choosing that option only if nothing has helped thus far.

The Update Driver button runs a wizard that helps you locate or install a new driver for your sound system. Hopefully, that technique fixes the problem.

6. Close all open windows when you're done troubleshooting.

At this point, you've entirely scanned the computer's sound system, from top to bottom. If the problem hasn't been solved, return to the speakers and start over again.

✔ For solutions to problems with playing a music CD, see the section in Chapter 15 about CD-ROM catastrophes.

✔ If your problem is with playing a specific audio file, consider that the file may be corrupted — or you may not have the proper software to play that file.

Sounds to Scheme Over

Providing that the sound software and hardware are, well, "sound," you can do a variety of things with sounds in Windows. It's all controlled from the Control Panel, though the icon is called a different thing for each version of Windows:

✔ In Windows 98, it's the Sounds icon.

✔ In Windows Me, it's the Sounds and Multimedia icon.

✔ In Windows XP, it's called Sounds and Audio Devices.

Figure 10-4 shows the Sounds tab in the Windows XP Sounds and Audio Devices Properties dialog box. The Sound Property dialog box in Windows 98 and Windows Me looks similar: You see a scrolling list of events to which you can assign sounds in Windows.

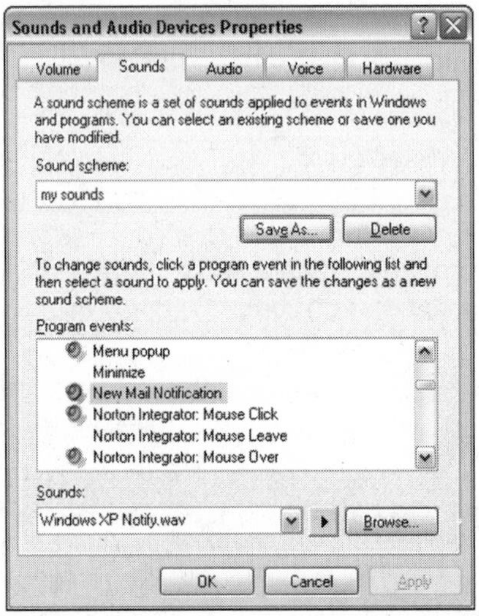

Figure 10-4:
Control-
ling your
computer's
sounds.

For example, to play a specific sound when you get new mail, you scroll through the list and find the New Mail Notification event. Click to select that event, and the selected sound file appears in the dialog box. Click the Play button to hear the sound or use the Browse button to pluck out a new sound.

If you go through the trouble of assigning your own, unique sounds to events, do yourself a favor and save them to disk as a theme:

1. **Click the Save As button.**

2. **Enter a name for your sound scheme.**

   Be Microsofty and call it My Sound Scheme.

3. **Click the OK button.**

   Now that scheme shows up on the list. Your stuff is saved!

If anything ever happens to your sounds, such as they get changed or someone else messes with them, you can instantly restore all of them at one time by choosing your sound scheme from the drop-down list.

✔ If you don't save your sounds as a scheme, you have to individually restore each and every sound on the list.

✔ Check out some of the other available sound schemes, one of which may only require subtle modification to become your own, personal sound scheme.

Other Sound Weirdness

You know what sounds weird? Lots of things! See the sections that follow for some sound weirdness cures and tonics.

Sound gets suddenly loud!

Holy smokes! That was loud!

When the computer suddenly grows thunderous on you, check the usual suspects: the volume control in the system tray/notification area, volume knobs on the speakers, and even the master volume control.

Then, check the program you're running. Some games make their own sounds, which means that the sound setting must be made in that game independently of Windows. See the game's options or settings to see whether you can reset the sound level to something your neighbors would be more comfortable with.

The microphone gets muted

When you use a microphone with a computer, you run into a potential problem: The microphone may pick up the sound coming from the speakers. The result is *feedback,* which can morph from a soft echo to a loud, piercing squeal!

To prevent feedback, you mute the microphone. The problem is that some programs do that for you! The solution, unfortunately, is to use the master volume control — keeping that window open — so that you can unmute the mic when you need it.

✔ You can also write to the software developer and ask them to include a nonmuting or unmute option for future releases of the program.

✔ Another nifty option is a microphone with an on-off switch on it so that you can "hardware-mute" the thing.

✔ See the section "Checking the master volume control," earlier in this chapter, for more information.

Annoying MIDI files play on Web pages

This is my own personal rant: I dislike sudden music coming from Web pages or even e-mail. The music isn't in the form of WAV files. It's in the form of MIDI files, which are files played over the computer's internal synthesizer. I love turning that option off so that the unexpected music doesn't startle me.

To turn off MIDI music for your computer, mute the MIDI column in the master volume control, as shown in Figure 10-2. Or, if you prefer to hear the music, but not as loudly, just slip that volume slider down a tad. There.

✔ The MIDI column may be labeled SW Synth on some computers. That stands for *software synth*esizer, which is essentially the same thing.

✔ If you don't see the MIDI column, choose Options➪Properties in the Master Volume Control window. Scroll through the list to find the MIDI option and check it. Click OK.

✔ MIDI sounds differ from WAV files just as sheet music differs from buying a CD. WAV files are recorded (or generated) sounds. MIDI files just tell the computer's internal synthesizer to play various notes or instruments for certain durations.

✔ And now you know that your computer has an internal synthesizer.

That stuttering sound

This problem is a puzzling one, but one I've experienced myself: The sound playback seems choppy, or the sounds themselves stutter rather than play smoothly. Alas, I have no specific solution, although it is definitely a problem.

On my computer, I discovered that if I move the mouse while sound is playing, the sound gets interrupted. The reason was a conflict between the mouse software and the sound software; the sound "hardware" was really a software emulator that pretended to be hardware. The solution was to upgrade to a "real" sound card and disable the cheap motherboard sound.

If your computer isn't up to speed, the stuttering may be caused by a slow processor. Most games recommend a certain CPU speed. If your computer's microprocessor is too slow, that may cause the stuttering sound.

Another possibility is that the cache size for the CD-ROM may be set too low in Windows 98 and Windows Me. Here's how to check it:

1. **Right-click the My Computer icon on the desktop.**

2. **Choose Properties from the pop-up menu.**

   This step summons the System Properties dialog box.

3. **Click the Performance tab.**

4. **Click the File System button.**

   The File System Properties dialog box appears.

5. **Click the CD-ROM tab.**

   A slider in the dialog box controls the supplemental cache size.

6. **Move the slider all the way over to Large.**

7. **Click OK to close the various dialog boxes.**

   You may be asked to restart Windows. Do so.

This fix may work if your CD-ROM drive was slow and access to it was interfering with the sound playback.

Chapter 11

The Mystery of System Resources (And Memory Leaks)

*F*ew can argue that computers are not technical. They are — very technical! Swirling around any computer is a maelstrom of technical terms and jargon. Windows helps insulate you from such lingo, so you can use your computer all day and never worry about the *stack* or the *heap* or any of several dozen various *buffers*. But one technical term pops up more than others: That's *resource*.

Because there is an error message that goes something like "Resources are low," many people find themselves obsessing over resources. Logically, if resources are low, you must endeavor to fill them up again. And that's when the trouble starts — so much trouble that I've devoted this entire chapter to help you troubleshoot and solve the low-resource quandary.

What Are System Resources?

After boiling the term *system resource* for several hours, venting off all the steam and impurities, what you're left with is plain old memory. RAM. System resources are simply one way your computer uses memory. The resources part is what Windows uses the memory for: windows, icons, fonts, graphics, and other pieces parts.

As you use Windows, it consumes resources. When you have several windows open on the screen, they devour resources. Using lots of fonts? There go the resources!

Some programs are real resource hogs. Microsoft Word is one. When Word runs, it sets aside memory for oodles of resources — whether it needs them or not.

Bottom line: When you run lots of programs, you use lots of resources. When those resources get low, some programs may not be able to run. The quick solution is to simply close a few programs and try again. Or, restarting Windows often flushes out all the resources and lets you run the program.

Displaying resource information

You can display and monitor resource information in Windows in various ways. The first is by using the Resource Meter, which is found in Windows 98 and Windows Me:

1. **Close all open windows and programs.**

   This step isn't required in order to run the Resource Meter. You get better numbers if you close your windows and programs, plus it helps with a demonstration shown in a later step.

2. **Click the Start button.**

3. **Choose Programs⊏⊅Accessories⊏⊅System Tools⊏⊅Resource Meter.**

   A dialog box tells you that the Resource Meter appears as an icon in the system tray.

4. **Click OK.**

5. **Double-click the Resource Meter icon in the system tray.**

   The Resource Meter appears, as shown in Figure 11-1. Here's what it means:

Figure 11-1:
The
notorious
Resource
Meter.

> ≣ **Resource Meter** ☒
>
> System resources: 71% free
> ■■■■■■■■■■■■■■■■■■
>
> User resources: 71% free
> ■■■■■■■■■■■■■■■■■■
>
> GDI resources: 92% free
> ■■■■■■■■■■■■■■■■■■■■■■
>
> OK

- **System resources.** This is the core of Windows, also known as the *kernel*. These resources include memory, disk storage, the clock, ports, and most of the basic, nitty-gritty parts of the PC.

- **User resources.** These resources include all the nongraphical things you use in Windows: fonts, sounds, programs, and the memory required to store those things.

- **GDI resources.** These are all the graphical resources — the memory required to draw a window, icon, or anything you see on the screen.

You can graphically [sic] demonstrate how the GID resources work. Take note of the percentage value you see there (it's "92% free" in Figure 11-1).

6. **Open the My Documents window.**

7. **Open the My Computer window.**

8. **Open the Recycle Bin window.**

9. **Open a program, such as Notepad.**

10. **Switch back to the Resource Meter to see how the GDI number has changed.**

    Click the Resource Meter button on the taskbar to switch back.

    On my computer, GDI resources dropped to 84 percent. The missing 7 percent is now being used by the windows and programs I just opened. That's the essence of how system resources are consumed.

11. **Close the extra windows you opened.**

12. **Click OK to close the Resource Meter.**

13. **Right-click the Resource Meter icon in the system tray.**

14. **Choose Exit from the pop-up menu.**

    This step closes the Resource Meter — which, incidentally, also frees up a few system resources.

Of course, viewing the resources isn't the problem. What happens is that most people see that the figures are less than 100 percent, so they waste time striving for 100 percent, which is impossible. Continue reading in the next section.

Your system will never have 100 percent free resources

To run Windows, you *must* use system resources. Because of that, there will never be a time when you have 100 percent free resources. In fact, the only time you could possibly have 100 percent free is when the computer is turned off. Otherwise, something is always going on in the computer, which consumes the resources.

A better way to monitor your computer's performance

If you really want to see how your computer is performing, you need to use a tool called the System Monitor. It's available only with Windows 98 and Windows Me. System Monitor graphically displays many aspects of the system's performance, as shown in Figure 11-2.

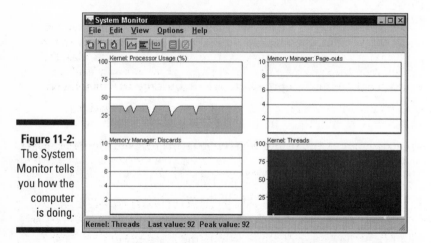

Figure 11-2:
The System Monitor tells you how the computer is doing.

1. **Click the Start button.**

2. **Choose Programs⇨Accessories⇨System Tools⇨System Monitor.**

   The System Monitor appears, looking something like the one shown in Figure 11-2.

   The System Monitor can keep track of a number of things. The most useful things performance-wise are

   • Kernel: Processor usage

   • Kernel: Threads

   • Memory Manager: Discards

   • Memory Manager: Page-outs

   You should add these items to the information the System Monitor displays.

3. **Choose Edit⇨Add Item.**

4. **Choose an item from the Category list first; for example, Kernel.**

5. **Choose an item from the Item list second, such as Processor Usage.**

6. **Click OK.**

7. **Repeat Steps 3 through 6 for each item you want to add.**

   Use the items listed in Step 2 as your guide.

   You can also remove items from the list: Choose Edit⇨Remove item and then use the Remove Item dialog box to pluck out anything you don't want to see monitored, such as anything that's obviously not changing over time.

8. **Observe.**

   Watch what happens with the System Monitor. A high number of discards or page-outs, for example, could indicate a memory leak (a program that is consuming more memory than it really needs). Alas, the System Monitor merely points out such problems; it doesn't tell you which program is causing them or offer suggestions for a resolution.

9. **Close the System Monitor window when you're done gawking.**

What is a memory leak?

I remember a gag letter I wrote in to one of those Q&A computer columns in the newspaper: "I think my computer may have a memory leak. Should I put down a towel?" Ha-ha. And I've heard jokesters telling naïve computer owners to tape over the ports and holes in the back of a PC so that a memory leak won't happen. Ha-ha.

Leak is perhaps the wrong term. A better description is *memory hole,* or a place where memory is poured in and never returns. And the hole grows larger! But, alas, we're stuck with the leak jargon.

A *memory leak* means one of two things. First, it could be a program that is simply dead in memory. Windows cannot remove the program, so it just ropes off that memory so that other programs don't touch it. The memory is "occupied," but not being used; therefore, it's wasted. The solution is to restart the computer to free the dead memory, which is why you should restart after a program crash.

The second type of memory leak is nasty. It happens when a program continues to use memory and cannot be stopped. For example, you close a program, yet some small part of it remains in memory, consuming more memory. Over time, the program uses up all the memory in the computer and everything stops. That's a true memory leak, and you can discover it by observing a dwindling number of resources over time with no apparent cause.

The cure for the memory leak is to kill the program that's consuming memory. Hopefully, that frees up the used memory. If not, the only other cure is not to run that program in the first place.

The two most important things I scrutinize with System Monitor are the kernel and memory. If either the Kernel: Threads or Kernel: Processor Usage items grow over time — and I'm not doing more with the computer — then some program has run amok. Finding out *which* program is the problem, but the two usage charts do tell me that it is some program and not just the computer going wacky.

The memory manager items can also help pinpoint a program gone AWOL. If the values of the items increase over time and you're not increasing the computer's workload, something is going wrong.

The solution for either kernel or memory manager problems is to isolate the program causing the trouble. If you suspect something, run your programs one at a time until you can nail down the perpetrator. Then you can stop that program, hopefully freeing resources. The solution is then to contact the developer and alert them to the problem. (Memory leaks are something you can only identify, not something you can fix yourself.)

Things You Can Do to Improve Resources

Rather than strive to improve your dismal resources situation, you should do some healthy things to improve your computer's overall performance. There is a link between resources and performance: Improving one does improve the other.

Number-one strategy: Add more RAM!

Resources equals memory! Adding more memory to your computer fixes many of the low-resource problems.

✔ One key item that slows down all Windows computers is the virtual memory, or disk storage, used to supplement regular memory. The more "disk swapping" that needs to be done, the slower the PC's performance. The solution: Add more memory.

✔ Windows 98 just swims in 64MB of RAM.

✔ Windows Me is more demanding; I recommend 128MB for it.

✔ Windows XP really needs about 256MB of memory to do well. However, I theorize that 512MB would be ideal. (It's only a theory because I have only a 256MB Windows XP system.)

Remove excess fonts

Sure, you can have 10,000 fonts installed, but that definitely drains on resources and slows things down, to boot. The solution: Install only those fonts you regularly use.

For the rest of the fonts, either keep them on the CD-ROM they came in or create an Excess Fonts folder, which you can store in the My Documents folder. Just move into that folder the fonts you seldom use; move them as you would cut and paste any file.

Do not move system fonts out of the Fonts folder. Windows needs these fonts, and if you copy them out, the computer doesn't display information properly. System fonts are flagged with an *A* icon in the Fonts folder.

✔ You can get to the Fonts folder from the Control Panel; open the Fonts icon.

✔ In Windows 98 and Windows Me, the Fonts folder is located inside the main Windows folder.

✔ The picture in the margin shows what a system font icon looks like.

✔ Also avoid moving the following fonts, which are often used by Web pages:

- Arial
- Comic Sans MS
- Tahoma
- Times New Roman
- Trebuchet
- Verdana

Disable unneeded background programs

Background programs — such as antivirus utilities, disk optimizers, animated desktops, and Active Desktop items — also consume resources. If resources are low, consider disabling or halting such programs.

Refer to the section in Chapter 8 about stopping programs from automatically starting for more information on disabling programs.

Mind what you install; uninstall what you don't use

If you're like me, you occasionally download and install programs from the Internet just to see what they do. If so, great. But be mindful to uninstall the program if you don't use it.

All installed programs use resources. By uninstalling the program, you free up those resources. So occasionally scour your Program Files folder as well as the Add/Remove Programs icon in the Control Panel. Look for programs you no longer intend to use and uninstall them.

Uninstall the programs! Do not succumb to the urge to simply delete them. That strategy is wrong and causes big heaps of trouble later.

I recommend the CleanSweep utility, from the Norton people. It's perhaps the best tool you can use to completely uninstall older programs.

Dealing with Resources in Windows XP

Windows XP is more professional about the way it displays resource information, which is odd given its overall cartoony look. But, like most things, the location is fairly well hidden so that you wouldn't accidentally benefit from the good information stored there.

To deal with Windows XP resources, summon the Task Manager: Press Ctrl+Alt+Delete, and the Task Manager window appears. Resources are used to display information hidden on the Processes and Performance tabs, which are covered in the sections that follow.

✔ You can also run the Task Manager by pressing Win+R to bring up the Run dialog box. Type **TASKMGR** in the box and click the OK button.

✔ A Task Manager of sorts is in Windows 98 and Windows Me, but it lacks the power of the Windows XP version.

Perusing Windows XP Performance

The Task Manager's Performance tab is the home of the Windows graphical monitoring station, as shown in Figure 11-3. Granted, it's not as exciting or as interactive as the System Monitor (refer to Figure 11-2), but it does boil down the performance charts to the bare essentials.

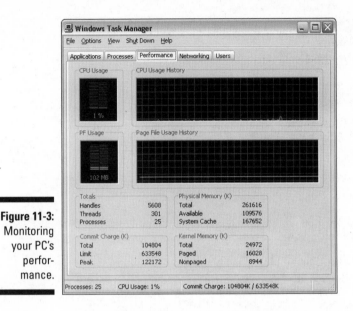

Figure 11-3:
Monitoring
your PC's
perfor-
mance.

The top chart monitors microprocessor (CPU) usage; the busier the computer, the more spikes you see in the graph. The bottom chart shows page file usage, which tells you how often and how much stuff is being written to or read from virtual memory.

Below the two scrolling graphs are four areas of text information that look really impressive, but I have no idea what it could all mean or what's really vital to watch. No, the real solution to the memory leak problem lies on the Task Manager's Processes tab, which is covered in the next section.

- ✔ *Virtual memory* is disk storage used to supplement regular memory, or RAM.

- ✔ If you want to see the CPU usage jump, open a few windows or play a sound.

Tracking down a memory leak in Windows XP

Memory leaks are easily spotted in Windows XP, on the Task Manager's Processes tab. That tab lists not only the major applications, but also every dang doodle program, or process, the computer is running. Figure 11-4 shows a sample.

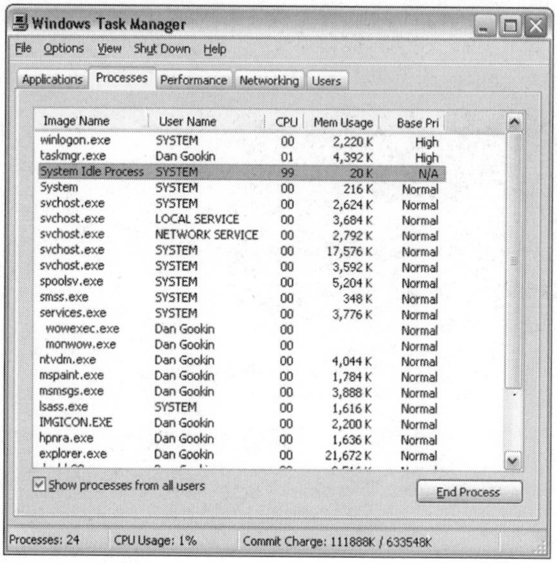

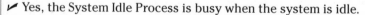

Windows Task Manager

File   Options   View   Shut Down   Help

| Applications | Processes | Performance | Networking | Users |

Image Name	User Name	CPU	Mem Usage	Base Pri
winlogon.exe	SYSTEM	00	2,220 K	High
taskmgr.exe	Dan Gookin	01	4,392 K	High
System Idle Process	SYSTEM	99	20 K	N/A
System	SYSTEM	00	216 K	Normal
svchost.exe	SYSTEM	00	2,624 K	Normal
svchost.exe	LOCAL SERVICE	00	3,684 K	Normal
svchost.exe	NETWORK SERVICE	00	2,792 K	Normal
svchost.exe	SYSTEM	00	17,576 K	Normal
svchost.exe	SYSTEM	00	3,592 K	Normal
spoolsv.exe	SYSTEM	00	5,204 K	Normal
smss.exe	SYSTEM	00	348 K	Normal
services.exe	SYSTEM	00	3,776 K	Normal
wowexec.exe	Dan Gookin	00		Normal
monwow.exe	Dan Gookin	00		Normal
ntvdm.exe	Dan Gookin	00	4,044 K	Normal
mspaint.exe	Dan Gookin	00	1,784 K	Normal
msmsgs.exe	Dan Gookin	00	3,888 K	Normal
lsass.exe	SYSTEM	00	1,616 K	Normal
IMGICON.EXE	Dan Gookin	00	2,200 K	Normal
hpnra.exe	Dan Gookin	00	1,636 K	Normal
explorer.exe	Dan Gookin	00	21,672 K	Normal

☑ Show processes from all users

[End Process]

Processes: 24   CPU Usage: 1%   Commit Charge: 111888K / 633548K

Figure 11-4:
Checking for
leaks of the
memory
kind.

Memory leaks are spotted on the list by noting a program that shows growing values in the CPU or Mem Usage columns. For example, if the Windows Explorer program is crashing, you may notice that the explorer. exe Image Name (program) on the list is using 25 percent CPU time, which suddenly ticks up to 26 and then 27, and yet you're not doing anything on the computer.

To halt a process gone awry, click to select it and then click the End Process button. You're asked to confirm; click the Yes button. Then, when you have control over your system again, restart Windows.

✔ If a program is running intensively, it shows a high value in the CPU column. That's normal. It's only when a program uses more CPU time than seems logical that you have a problem.

✔ Yes, the System Idle Process is busy when the system is idle.

✔ Be sure to reset after ending a process! If you don't, remnants of the process may interfere with the computer's operation and lead to other crashes.

✔ I've caught only one memory leak and fixed it in this manner (which is more a credit to Windows XP than to myself). The computer was being sluggish, so I looked at the processes and noticed one hogging lots of CPU time. Ending that process instantly made the computer peppy again. Still, I did restart Windows just to be sure.

Chapter 12

The Slow PC

- -

In This Chapter

▶ Getting to know slow

▶ Dealing with a slow computer

▶ Tips for improving speed

▶ Some slow computer Q&A

- -

*O*ne of the welcome features in a new computer is its speed; new computers are notably faster than the ones they replace. The speed difference is attributed to technology, of course. Replacing a tired old Pentium II computer with a Pentium 4, for example, makes everything run faster — or at least seem to.

The problem with a slow PC isn't that technology is brushing by. That's more of a fact than a problem. No, the true slow PC is sluggish for a number of reasons, some of which can definitely be helped, as discussed in this chapter.

> ✔ See Chapter 16 for information on improving slow Internet connections.
>
> ✔ I recommend drinking coffee for slow mornings or to help your own brain maintain speed during long meetings. I do not recommend coffee for your computer.

Slow Is Relative

Computers are not designed to be slow. In fact, if you were to peer into a tiny window and observe the microprocessor, you would discover that it spends most of its time waiting. That's because most things the computer does aren't that speed-intensive.

When you word-process, the computer spends electronic eons waiting for you to type the next letter — even if you're a fast typist. And no matter how fast your Internet connection, the computer is literally twiddling its thumbs while waiting for the next byte of data to fly in.

There are intensive operations, of course: Any time you manipulate graphics, you're making the computer do some real work. Even the fastest computers have to wait while images are rendered. And some mathematical calculations cause the microprocessor to fire all its burners. But even then, for the most part, the computer sits and hums.

- ✔ It's because the computer sits and waits that you find things like barking dogs or tap-dancing wizards to amuse you while you type in your word processor.

- ✔ Speed, apparently, is not a true issue when it comes to computer performance. Developers could make software go even faster than it does today, but there is little demand for it. Also, increasing program speed would mean that the programs would take longer to develop, so as long as people don't mind waiting, developers have no incentive to make things faster.

Why things can get slow (and what you can do about it)

Your computer can slow down for a number of reasons, almost too many to mention. Slothfulness boils down to one of the following causes:

Malfunctioning hardware: The hard drive may be going, in which case it has to read and reread information because of errors. That adds overhead.

Corrupted programs: Most sudden slowness is caused by some corrupt program, which may be tainted on the disk or somehow became besmirched in memory. In any event, the program's response time dwindles, which affects overall PC speed.

Viruses: Computer viruses can also slow things down, either by corrupting existing files or consuming resources in memory or on the hard drive, or they may just be designed to slow down your computer.

Most of the time, some corrupt program brings the computer down and crawling on its knees. Fix or eliminate that program, and the problem goes away. Typically, recovering speed is simply as easy as restarting Windows.

Please be patient! Yes, restarting Windows probably fixes the situation. But give the slow computer its due. Obey the rules! Shut down like you normally do, even if it seems to take longer. Give the computer a chance before you impatiently punch the power switch or defiantly unplug the sucker.

✔ Corrupt programs may be spotted by their memory leaks. Refer to Chapter 11.

✔ Refer to Chapter 2 for information on restarting Windows, the penicillin to cure most PC ills.

✔ Sluggish hardware needs to be fixed or replaced. Alas, there is no easy way to spot sluggish hardware, which tends to get slower over time.

✔ Some third-party utilities, such as Norton's, have various disk diagnosing programs that can indicate pending hard drive doom.

✔ Also check with the Microsoft Knowledge Base on the Web to see whether the slowness can be attributed to any known flaws in Windows or other Microsoft products: `http://support.microsoft.com/`.

✔ Little-known fact: A hard drive can misread data on a disk up to three times before it reports an error. The operating system itself can tolerate up to five errors of this type before it reports a problem with the drive.

Any way to speed things up?

The old joke went that you could double your computer's speed by plugging it into a 240-volt socket. I actually got e-mail from a man who believed this to be true and wanted to know where he could get a power adapter. Alas, following through would result in a blown-up power supply.

Computers do some things fast and some things slow. Aside from getting a newer computer, you can do only a handful of legitimate things to improve overall performance:

✔ Eliminate what you don't need. Uninstall programs you don't use.

✔ Review your start-up programs, as covered in Chapter 8. Ensure that utilities you don't need are disabled and not using RAM or disk space.

✔ Install more RAM. Computers can always use more RAM.

✔ Check for viruses.

✔ Keep an eye out for memory leaks.

✔ Defragment (especially good for older drives).

In your applications, try to avoid using lots of fonts or pasting images into a word processor until the text editing is done. Word processors, such as Microsoft Word, really slow down when you add graphics into the mix. Write your text first and then add images.

For image editing as well as other demanding applications, try not to run other programs at the same time. That conserves resources and gives more power to the programs that demand it.

Above all, try to avoid software fixes that claim to speed up your computer. Although some of them may subtly tweak resources and give you better performance, most of the ones I've encountered are shams. These programs seldom perform as promised and end up turning your PC into a billboard for endless advertisements or porn.

- ✔ I do not recommend upgrading the microprocessor as a solution to a slow PC. Older PCs that could theoretically benefit from a newer CPU are typically not compatible with the new microprocessors. And the replacement CPUs you can get often don't give you the same bang for the buck as a better upgrade, such as more RAM or a second hard drive.

- ✔ Also refer to Chapter 11, on system resources. Low resources can also cause a system to run slowly.

- ✔ See Chapter 21 for more information on defragmenting a hard drive.

- ✔ Internally, the computer uses only 12 or 5 volts to run things, so doubling the input voltage from 120 to 240 volts — even if you could — wouldn't improve your speed situation at all.

Some Slow Q&A

Anyone who has used a PC for any length of time has encountered the slow PC. After initial disbelief, you probably act like I do and seriously wonder whether a black hole is nearby, slowing down the entire space-time continuum.

Do you slam your keyboard into the desktop? I've tried it. Doesn't work.

And, yes, a few times I just flipped off the power to the UPS because the computer was taking geological time to restart. I know. Naughty me, but sometimes the stupid device wears my patience paper-thin.

Q: It's suddenly slow and it wasn't like that yesterday!

Sudden slow is good. Sudden slow means that some program has twisted itself into a confusing garden of electronic salad. A simple reset fixes this problem.

If you have Windows XP, try checking the Task Manager's Processes tab to see whether you can find the process hog and kill it off. At least that method tells you which program was running amok, if only for future reference. Refer to Chapter 11.

Q: The computer is just always slow.

Remember that speed is relative. Or, as it was put to me long ago by a friend with a much better computer: You never know how crappy your system is until you sit down at a better one.

Buy more RAM! Consider running fewer programs.

Also consider using a thorough disk drive analysis utility, such as the Norton Utilities, to see whether the hard drive is becoming too error-prone. If so, consider replacing the hard drive.

Q: The computer gets slower the longer I leave it on.

This is definitely a sign of a memory leak. The best way to track this one down is as follows:

- ✔ **First, don't run any software.** Just let the computer sit and stew. Note whether it's getting slow. If so, it's Windows itself that's slow, one of the supersecret start-up programs (refer to Chapter 8), or perhaps a virus that's causing the problem.

- ✔ **Second, run your programs one at a time.** Pause. Note whether that particular program is causing the computer to slow down. If not, restart the computer and run your next program. Run them all one at a time to search for the culprit.

When you find the program that's slowing down the computer, check with the developer to see whether they have any information on causes or fixes. Refer to Chapter 5 for more information on tech support.

Q: The computer has gotten slower and slower in recent weeks.

This problem is probably with the hardware. The first suspect: the hard drive. Check to see whether it's getting full. If so, then you have to either delete some stuff there or buy a second hard drive and move stuff to it instead.

Slowness can also just be a sign of "tired RAM" or an older computer in general. It's time to buy a new one.

Q: The computer's clock is slower than normal time.

Yes. Computers make lousy clocks. The clock in your typical PC will be off anywhere from several seconds to a few minutes at the end of each day, depending on what you do with the computer. This is normal.

You can manually reset your clock, or you can use any of the many "atomic" clock utilities that coordinate your PC's clock with a national time server. Or, if you're on a network, perhaps the network has a time server to keep all the computers on the same time.

In Windows XP, you can configure the computer to automatically set the time: In the Control Panel, open the Date and Time icon to display the Date and Time Properties dialog box. Then click the Internet Time tab to see something that looks like Figure 12-1.

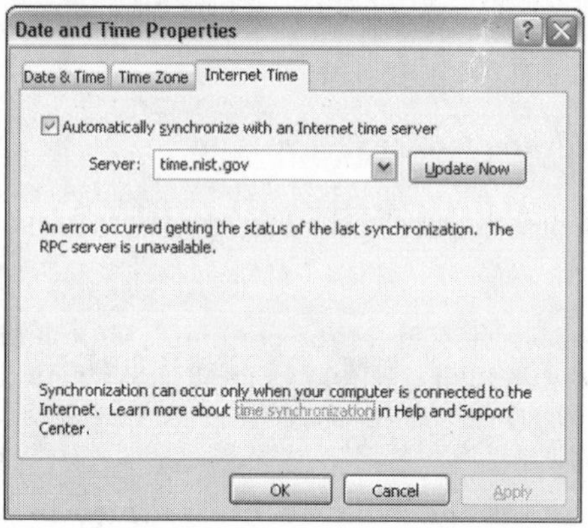

Figure 12-1:
Keeping
the clock
current in
Windows
XP.

To synchronize your PC's clock with a live time server, click the Update Now button. (You must put a check mark by the option Automatically synchronize with an Internet time server for that button to work.) Click OK when you're done.

Similar utilities exist for Windows 98 and Windows Me. You can search on the Internet for *atomic clock* or *Internet time* utilities. One of my favorite sites for software searching is shareware.cnet.com.

✔ The best atomic/Internet clock utilities can be set to automatically dial or connect at specific times every day, keeping the clock very current.

✔ If your computer is on a Local Area Network, check with your network administrator about time servers you can use to keep the PC's clock accurate.

✔ Notice in Figure 12-1 that my system was unable to connect with the time server. That is because of my network's firewall, which is one situation where such a utility doesn't work.

✔ A *firewall* is a program (or sometimes hardware) that protects your PC from unauthorized access. You would think that it would be set up that way automatically, but no.

Chapter 13

Keyboard, Mouse, and Monitor Dilemmas

. . . .

. . . .

*W*hat do the keyboard, monitor, and mouse all have in common? Anyone? Anyone?

Yes! They comprise the PC's basic input and output, the old I/O. Remember those songs you used to sing in computer camp? Well, perhaps not. But in any case, the keyboard is the primary way *you* (the human) communicate with the computer. Supplementing that, of course, is the mouse. And the computer communicates back to you using text or images displayed on the monitor.

Without a keyboard, mouse, or monitor, the computer would have to communicate with you via its flashing lights or beeping speaker. You (the human) could always kick the computer, but that has rarely been an effective communications technique.

Therefore, all three of these devices — keyboard, mouse, and monitor — have similar troubleshooting issues, problems, and resolutions — hence, this combined chapter.

✔ This book does assume that you are human or, if visiting from elsewhere, that you are assuming human form.

✔ In 1978, a divider was installed beneath the table to prevent the world chess champion Anatoly Karpov and the challenger Viktor Korchnoi from kicking each other during the match.

The Best Way to Tell Whose Fault It Is

When it comes to the keyboard, mouse, or monitor, a common question pops up: Is the device itself or the computer to blame? For example, is your mouse itself wacky, or is it the mouse port or the motherboard or mouse software? The easy way to find out is to *swap it out.*

First, turn off the computer.

Second, remove the device that's causing trouble — the keyboard or mouse or monitor. Set it aside.

Third, install a working replacement device. It can be a keyboard, mouse, or monitor from another computer or a friend's computer. Ensure that you know the device is working properly.

Fourth, turn on the computer and see whether the device works. If the swapped-in component works just fine, you've solved your problem: Replace the keyboard, mouse, or monitor with something that works.

✔ Keyboards and mice are relatively inexpensive to replace.

✔ Before replacing, see other sections in this chapter for some potential solutions to keyboard and mouse problems.

✔ You can try having your monitor fixed, especially if it's a high-end model. Most TV repair places can fix computer monitors.

✔ Never try to fix the monitor yourself, even if you have the proper footwear. Monitors and PC power supplies are two things you should never disassemble or otherwise mess with.

✔ Or — what the heck? — toss that old monitor and get yourself a fancy new LCD monitor.

✔ There is no need to turn off the computer if your mouse or keyboard (or even the monitor) is a USB device.

✔ Never plug a mouse or keyboard into the standard mouse or keyboard port when the PC is on. Doing so can damage the keyboard, mouse, or computer.

✔ You can plug a monitor in or out from a working computer. I've done it a few times. But I feel better about turning the thing off whenever I attach or detach any hardware.

Keyboard Kraziness

Keyboards don't have the run-amok potential of other computer peripherals. I think that the reason they stay so well-behaved is that they know how cheap replacement models are. So, unless your hands weigh 75 pounds each, your computer's keyboard will most likely outlive just about anything else on the computer.

✔ A simple reset should cure most keyboard strangeness, such as one key producing another key's character.

✔ Keyboard-mapping and macro programs are available, such as QuickKeys, from CE Software, Inc. (www.cesoft.com/). You can use them to customize keyboard behavior as well as assign lots of text or complex commands to simple key combinations.

The keyboard's Control Panel home

Any messing or adjusting of the keyboard is done in the Control Panel by opening the Keyboard icon, as shown in Figure 13-1. This area is where you adjust things such as the keyboard's repeat delay and repeat rate:

Figure 13-1: The official keyboard-messing location.

✔ The *repeat delay* is how long you have to hold a key down before its character repeats.

✔ The *repeat rate* is how quickly the character repeats.

According to Figure 13-1, pressing and holding the P key down after a short delay quickly prints a bunch of *P*s: pppppppppppppppppppppppppp. (Supposedly, that's how kitty cats do it.)

The language problem

You can configure your keyboard to mimic the behavior of foreign language keyboards. For example, in France, they have keys on the keyboard for the ç and Ç keys. In the United Kingdom, Shift+3 produces the £ character rather than #. And many foreign language keyboard layouts have "dead keys," which are used for diacritical marks, such as ü or á, or are just not used for anything.

 All this foreign language nonsense is controlled through the Control Panel's Keyboard icon in Windows 98 and Windows Me, but through the Regional and Language Options icon in Windows XP. If you suspect that your keyboard is misbehaving in a strange, foreign manner, check its language.

In Windows 98 and Windows Me, open the Control Panel's Keyboard icon. Click the Language tab. (In Windows Me, you then need to click the Change button.) Review the list of installed languages. If you see more than one, consider removing the non-native (English) ones. Or select the keyboard layout you prefer to use and click the Set as Default button.

In Windows XP, open the Control Panel's Regional and Language Options icon. Click the Languages tab, and then click the Details button. Choose the keyboard layout you want to use from the Default input language drop-down list.

Click OK to close the various dialog boxes after you've made your choices.

✔ When you're using another keyboard layout, the language bar indicator appears in the system tray/notification area. It's two letters, such as *EN* for English, enclosed in a black box. That's your tip-off that the keyboard layout has changed.

✔ The keys used to switch languages are usually the left Shift and Alt keys, though they can be changed according to instructions in the dialog box.

Mouse Mayhem

I used to write "You need a mouse to use Windows." Well, you kinda do. I've discovered that many things done with a mouse — especially with regard to clicking menus and buttons — can be done faster with keyboard shortcuts. But that's another story. If the mouse doesn't work, I'll bet that you would rather keep using the mouse as opposed to train yourself how to use keyboard shortcuts, whether they're faster or not.

Give me mouse control!

Most common mouse options (speed, pointer appearance, and special effects, for example) are set from the Mouse icon in the Control Panel. Alas, the options and settings and their locations vary depending on which type of mouse you have, so some poking around in the Mouse Properties dialog box (see Figure 13-2) may be required for you to discover which settings need adjustment.

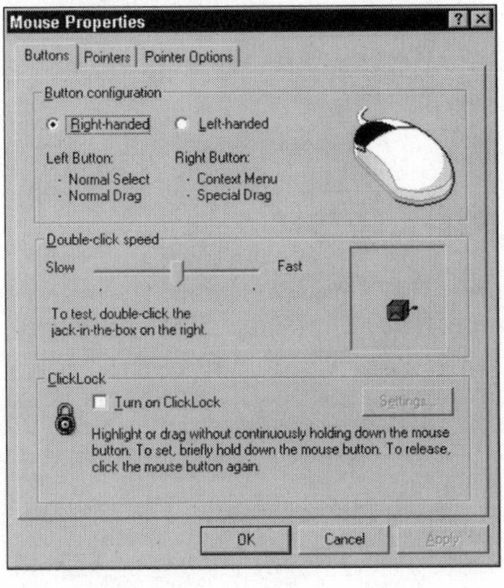

Figure 13-2: The Mouse Properties dialog box.

✔ If you have trouble seeing the mouse, select a new mouse pointer from the Mouse Properties dialog box. The Pointers tab is the place to look.

✔ The mouse can be made left-handed, if you like. Refer to either the Buttons or General tab for the details.

✔ For more mouse configuration information, refer to my book, *PCs For Dummies* (published by Wiley Publishing, Inc.).

Common mouse maladies and cures

Most mouse mishaps can be cured with a simple restart of Windows. Why does the mouse go nuts? I don't know. But whenever my mouse pointer is missing or the mouse freezes or just acts plain weird, restarting Windows solves the problem.

If you have a USB mouse, unplugging the USB connection and plugging it in again sometimes wakes the mouse back up.

If restarting doesn't work, check the Device Manager, which displays any conflicts and offers some fixes or suggestions. That's also the spot where you can reinstall the mouse driver, if need be. Mouse drivers and software updates are at the mouse manufacturer's Web page.

- ✔ Mouse pointer jumping around? Hard to control? See "Cleaning the mouse," later in this chapter.
- ✔ See Appendix A for information on using the Device Manager.
- ✔ You can find software for the various breeds of the Microsoft mouse at the Microsoft download center, at www.microsoft.com/downloads/.
- ✔ Logitech mouse support can be found on the Web at www.logitech. com/cf/support/mouselist.cfm.

Your mouse is getting s-l-o-w

Mice can slow down if they're dirty. Consider cleaning the mouse, as discussed later in this chapter. But a more common cause is simply age. Old mice slow down.

If the mouse is older than about four years (sometimes not even that old) and it's getting frustratingly slow, replace it. Buy a new mouse. That fixes the problem.

Monitor Madness

Monitors are possibly the most peaceful of computer peripherals. Unless, of course, you're watching a science fiction TV show from the 1960s. In that case, the monitor is most likely the thing that explodes whenever the computer becomes confused. But that's mere fiction! Ha-ha.

Monitors don't explode. They implode. That's because the CRT (cathode ray tube) is a vacuum. If you poke a hole in your monitor's glass — *thwoop!* — implosion. I don't feel I need to devote any space here to troubleshooting that problem.

Beyond the rare implosion, your monitor will rarely, if ever, screw up. No, it's the *image* on the screen that bugs you most of the time. Those problems are covered in Chapter 6, in the section about the display being stuck in dumb mode. For now, here's a small assortment of monitor hardware problems:

The monitor buzzes or hums. Monitors buzz and hum naturally. Loud humming can be a problem, however. If the humming distracts you from doing your work, repair or replace the monitor.

Connections get loose. If the image is missing or appears in all one color or "weak," check the monitor cable. Ensure that one end is snugly plugged into the monitor and that the other end is snugly plugged into the PC.

The image is distorted. This could be a sign of interference from some other electronic device. Strong magnetic fields can distort the image on a monitor. If the monitor is exposed for long periods, the magnets damage the monitor permanently. To fix this problem, move the monitor away from whatever is causing the interference.

The image gets fuzzy. Monitors lose their crispness over time. The sure sign of an old monitor is a fuzzy image. If the image doesn't improve the longer the monitor stays on, retire the monitor and get another.

Another way to fix a fuzzy, flickering, or generally frazzled monitor is to adjust the refresh rate. You can use the buttons on the front of the monitor or change the screen's resolution or number of colors.

A Time to Clean

Another thing the keyboard, mouse, and monitor have in common is that they're easy to clean. And — boy! — is that ever necessary. I've been using the same keyboard for almost 12 years now. And although the robust sucker has lasted me through five different computers, it is just filthy! Time to clean:

- ✔ The best way to keep your stuff clean is *not to eat in front of your computer.* I know that's a hard admonishment to keep.

- ✔ Also, if you sneeze, cover your mouth and nose so that nothing ends up on the screen.

✔ And smoking? Bad for the computer. And you.

✔ Keep cats away from computers. Computer mice love cat hair, and it eventually screws up the mice. Cat hair also loves to stick to the monitor.

✔ Yes, I *like* my keyboard. I have another just like it for when this one breaks. It's an IBM keyboard from the early 1990s. Metal. Heavy. Full action. Hearty click noise.

Yes, you can clean your keyboard

They're hard to find, but when you see one of those tiny keyboard vacuum cleaners, get it! It deftly sucks the dirt, crud, hair, and potato chip chunks from the inner crevices of your keyboard.

One good way to clean the keyboard: Flip it over and give it a good, vigorous "You've been naughty" shake. Have a whisk broom and dustpan handy to dispose of the results of this action.

To clean the key caps, use an old toothbrush and some household cleaner, like 409 or Fantastik — if you can stand the smell. Ammonia is perhaps the best key cap cleaner. Put the cleaner on the toothbrush and then brush away at the key caps. Don't use much liquid because it drips into the keyboard's guts.

Finally, you can give your keyboard a bath if it needs it. For example, if you spill orange soda pop into the keyboard, try to save matters by bathing the keyboard. First, turn off the computer. Second, unplug the keyboard. Third, immerse it in some warm, soapy water. Let it sit for a spell. Then remove the keyboard and let it drain. Keep it out overnight so that it's utterly dry when you reconnect it.

Cleaning the mouse

Mice pick up crud from your desktop or mouse pad and, boy, does that really gum up the works!

For a traditional mouse, remove the ball from its belly to clean it. A cover twists off so that you can remove the ball. Rub the ball with a damp cloth, though the real filth is on the rollers that detect the ball's movement.

To carefully clean the rollers, get an X-Acto knife and a pair of tweezers. Carefully scrape the gunk away from the rollers using the X-Acto knife. The gunk generally comes off in large chunks, which you can then extract using the tweezers. Replace the ball when you're done cleaning.

Optical mice get dirty too! To clean them, use a pair of tweezers to pull out the hair and gunk in the optical mouse's "eyehole." In fact, any time an optical mouse gets weird on you, flip it over and clean the eyehole. Chances are that a strand of hair is wreaking havoc with the LED sensor.

✔ While you're at it, clean your mouse pad as well as the mouse. Use a stiff brush to clean the cloth pads. Or, heck, just toss the old pad out and get a new one.

✔ If cleaning doesn't help, get a new mouse.

Cleaning your monitor

The only part of the monitor worthy of cleanliness is the screen — the part where information is displayed. Sure, you could clean the monitor's housing, but rarely have I seen that done, nor is it even necessary (unless you opt to clean off that dandelion-like effect all those yellow sticky notes have).

Start by spraying some window cleaner on a soft cloth. Then use the cloth to gently wipe the sneeze globs and bits of bean dip from the front of the monitor. This works for both glass and LCD monitors, though be especially gentle on LCD monitors because they really do have liquid inside them.

✔ Never spray cleaning solution directly on the screen.

✔ It helps to have a nice, bright yet plain image on the screen while you clean. I open up the Paint program and fill the screen with a nice, white palette so that I can see all the gunk on the monitor.

✔ On the other hand, dust disappears unless you turn the monitor off. So if you're just doing a good dust job, turn the monitor off and you'll see all that "pixel dust."

Chapter 14

Printer Problems

. . . .

. . . .

You think you've got printer problems? Ha! Let me tell you about printer problems: You think printing is trouble in Windows? It's nothing! Nothing, I tell you! Back during DOS, *those* were printer problems. You think DOS knew squat about your printer? It didn't! You had to install printer software for *each and every* program you owned! Talk about printer problems. I've got your printer problems. Right here! *Honk-honk!*

Curse Windows all you like, but one of its most sacred blessings is that printing is handled by Windows itself, not by your applications. As long as the printer is connected, the printer software installed and working, just about any program should be able to print. "Should be able" — if not, well, then you have some handy advice, tips, and troubleshooting information right here in this chapter to help you out.

So Is It the Printer?

You can easily tell whether the problem is with the printer or the software you're using: Does the problem happen when you print from the one program or from all of them?

If every program has the same printer problem, it's a printer problem, with either the printer hardware or the printer software (the driver). If it's only one program that can't print, the problem is with that particular piece of software. Contact that software developer — ignore their vain attempts to shuttle you off to the printer manufacturer — and get the problem solved.

Your best friend, Print Preview

When the printer acts up or the hard copy looks strange, don't blame the printer first! Double-check to see that the printer isn't just blindly obeying your orders by using the application's Print Preview command, File➪Print Preview.

How does the document look in Print Preview? How are the colors? The margins? The fonts?

If the screw-up is visible in the Print Preview window, blame yourself or the application. If Print Preview looks like you intended, blame the printer driver or the printer itself. Read on!

- *Hard copy* is another term for the stuff that comes out of the printer — printed information as opposed to information on the screen.
- The Print Preview command has a companion toolbar button in many applications.
- Not every program has a Print Preview command.
- Graphics applications in particular seem to lack a Print Preview command. That's because the graphics image you see on the screen is supposed to be identical to the one that's printed.

It helps to know this painful information on how printing works

Printing happens in a PC like this: You give the command to print, Ctrl+P. That tells the application to print the document. But it's not the application itself that does the printing. Instead, instructions are passed along to something called the printer driver.

The *printer driver* is a part of the operating system, installed when you first set up Windows. The driver's job is to control the printer, telling it what to print. So although some things — document content, margins, colors, and styles, for example — are controlled by your application, it's the printer driver common to all of Windows that's really in charge of the printing job.

As the printer driver takes over, a wee little "printer guy" icon shows up in the system tray/notification area (on the right end of the taskbar).

The printer driver's job is to talk directly with the printer, sending it the proper instructions that tell the printer to print what you want. Hopefully, if all goes well, your stuff gets put down on paper and you become O So Very Happy with the results.

After the document is printed, the printer driver goes back to sleep and the wee printer guy icon disappears from the system tray/notification area.

Problems? They can occur anywhere along the line. Having a general idea of how the process works, however, can help you pinpoint who or what is to blame.

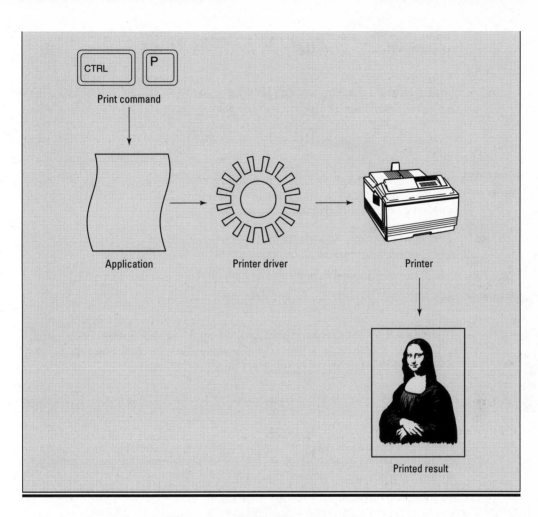

Controlling the printer from your application

The printer, like all hardware, is dumb all by itself. It needs your carefully guided instructions to tell it what and how to print. That's the job of the Print dialog box, but also the Page Setup dialog box in most applications.

Figure 14-1 shows the Page Setup dialog box for the Paint application in Windows XP.

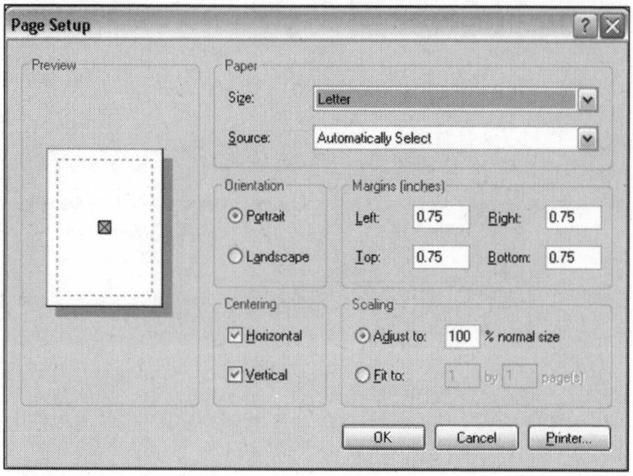

Figure 14-1:
Various printer options in the Page Setup dialog box.

The Page Setup dialog box in other applications contains similar commands, though often more of them and perhaps organized a bit differently. Typically, you can set the following items in the Page Setup dialog box:

- **Margins:** These define the area where printing takes place. Most printers require a minimum half-inch margin inset from the edge of all four sides of the paper.

- **Paper size:** Most often, you print on letter-size paper, but this spot is where you tell both the application and the printer that you're printing on another size of paper, such as legal or envelope.

- **Paper source:** Some printers have different trays for different sizes of paper. Or, if the paper is manually fed into the printer, this is where you set that option.

- **Orientation:** You have only two choices: normal, which is called Portrait orientation, or long-ways, which is called Landscape orientation.

- **Layout options:** These settings can include options for binding, centering the page, scaling the image (larger or smaller), headers, footers, and multiple pages per sheet.

Not every application has a Page Setup dialog box. In some applications, the only control you have over printing is with the Print dialog box, a sample of which is shown in Figure 14-2.

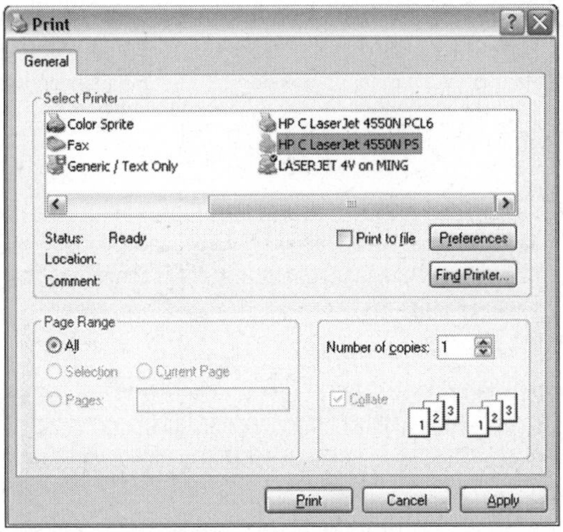

Figure 14-2:
Options in
the Print
dialog box.

Yes, you find additional printing options here:

✔ **Select a printer:** Windows affords you the luxury of using one of any number of computers, either directly connected to your PC or via a network. It's in the Print dialog box that you choose which printer you want to print on.

✔ **Configure the printer:** The Print dialog box is a part of Windows, but it typically contains extra tabs or an Advanced, Properties, or Preferences button (as shown in Figure 14-2) that lets you set custom printing options, such as graphics resolution, color settings, printer language, and other often trivial settings.

✔ **Choose the pages to print:** Normally, you print all the pages, though the Print dialog box lets you select a single page, individual pages, or ranges of pages to print.

✔ **Select the number of copies:** You can also print multiple copies of the same document. When I create my Christmas letter, I specify several dozen copies to print, one for everyone on the list.

✔ **Collation and other options:** Each Print dialog box is different, with different options and settings depending on the printer or application. An option common to many of them is *collation,* which prints multiple copies either one page at a time (seven Page 1s followed by seven Page 2s) or in sets (Pages 1 through 5, and then another set of Pages 1–5). Another option is printing in reverse order, which is nice if the copies come out of the printer face-up.

The Page Setup and Print dialog boxes are two places you can use to configure your printer from your application. Of course, after you click the Print button (in the Print dialog box), control passes to the printer driver. So any problems from that point on are blamed on the driver itself or the printer, as covered in the rest of this chapter.

✔ Setting the page margins is not the same thing as setting paragraph margins inside a word processor. Refer to your word processor's help system for more margin information, or just read the best book on Microsoft Word ever written, my own *Word For Dummies* (published by Wiley Publishing, Inc.).

✔ Yes, many applications switch options between the Print and Page Setup dialog boxes. In some programs, you select paper orientation in the Page Setup dialog box; with other programs, you do that in the Print dialog box.

✔ Selecting a printer other than the *default,* or main, printer may affect the outside margins on a page. If so, you have to print again, returning to the Page Setup dialog box to fix your margins.

✔ Acquaint yourself with some of your printer's more esoteric options. If additional tabs are in the Print dialog box or if you see a Properties or Preferences button there, click it to peruse those extra options.

✔ Be especially observant of the location where you can turn color printing on or off for a color printer. For example, the printer chosen in Figure 14-2 is a color printer, yet the option for printing in color isn't apparent in the dialog box. Therefore, the option must lie elsewhere, such as behind that Preferences button.

✔ Some applications may also have a Document Setup command on the File menu. You can find additional page configuration items in that dialog box.

✔ Which dialog box has priority? The Print dialog box does. Any changes you make there directly affect the printer. Often times, however, some coordination is required between the Page Setup and Print dialog boxes. For example, if you're printing in Landscape mode, you need to tell both the application (via the Page Setup dialog box) and the printer (via the Print dialog box) to print in that mode and on that paper.

Envelope printing tips

The best way to print an envelope is to use a program that's designed to print envelopes! After all, the specialist knows more about their specialty than the jack-of-all-trades. For example, the Envelope printing tool in Microsoft Word is a great way to print envelopes. But printing an envelope on the fly in something like WordPad takes skill and, well, knowledge of the following pointers:

✔ Know that an envelope is merely a specialized type of paper. Specifically, in the USA, envelopes are known as number 10 or Envelope #10. If you choose that type of "paper" in the Page Setup dialog box, your document automatically formats itself to envelope dimensions.

✔ Use the Print Preview command to see how the envelope paper is oriented on the page. You want to ensure that this orientation matches how the envelope is fed into the printer.

✔ Use the program's margin settings (the paragraph margins, not the page margins) to set the locations for the address and return address.

✔ Use Print Preview again to determine that you've placed the address and return address in the proper position and orientation.

✔ Pay special attention to how the printer eats envelopes (which side is "up" and how the text gets positioned, for example).

✔ Print a test envelope first. Better still, mark which end of the envelope went into the printer first and which side of the envelope was "up." That way, you can confirm that the envelope was inserted in the proper orientation.

Where the Printer Stuff Hides in Windows

To properly futz with a printer in Windows, you need to know where these printer things are and what they do:

✔ The Printers folder

✔ Your printer's window

✔ The little printer guy

Each one has something to do with printing, as described in the sections that follow.

Finding the Printers folder

The Printers folder is where Windows stores information about all the printers connected to your computer, either directly or indirectly. This folder is also where you can add new printers, though in Windows XP network printers are added automatically.

To open the Printers folder in Windows 98 and Windows Me, click the Start button and choose Settings➪Printers.

In Windows XP, open the Printers and Faxes folder from the Control Panel. If you're using Category view in the Control Panel, click the Printers and Other Hardware link and then click to open the Printers and Faxes folder. What you see looks similar to Figure 14-3.

Figure 14-3: The Printers and Faxes folder in Windows XP.

You can do several things in the Printers folder as far as troubleshooting is concerned:

- ✔ **Click the Troubleshoot printing link in Windows XP to run a Windows troubleshooter for your printer.** Alas, this is a Windows XP–only thing.

- ✔ **Open your printer's Properties dialog box: Right-click your printer's icon and choose Properties from the pop-up list.** This method is good for adjusting and tweaking the printer. You can also print a test page from the dialog box.

- ✔ **Instantly stop printing by right-clicking your printer icon and choosing Purge Print Documents from the pop-up menu.** This technique works in Windows 98 and Windows Me, but in Windows XP you must choose Pause Printing instead. (See the section "Halting a printer run amok," later in this chapter, for more information.)

- ✔ **Delete and reinstall a printer: Click to select an icon and then choose File⇨Delete from the menu.** That removes the printer. Then, after the printer is gone, use the Add Printer Wizard in Windows 98 and Windows Me or the Add a printer task in Windows XP to reinstall that same printer. Often times, this technique fixes printer driver problems.

✔ **Choose which printer you want to use as your main, or default, printer.** Just click the printer to select it and choose File⇨Set as Default from the menu. The default printer has a white-on-black check mark by its icon, as shown in Figure 14-3.

Your printer's window

When you print, you can open your printer's icon in the Printers window to view the progress of the documents being printed. The documents appear there, in the order you printed them, marching off to the printer one by one while you move on to do something else.

Figure 14-4 shows a printer window, though no documents are listed in it — my printer is too fast to list any. So just pretend.

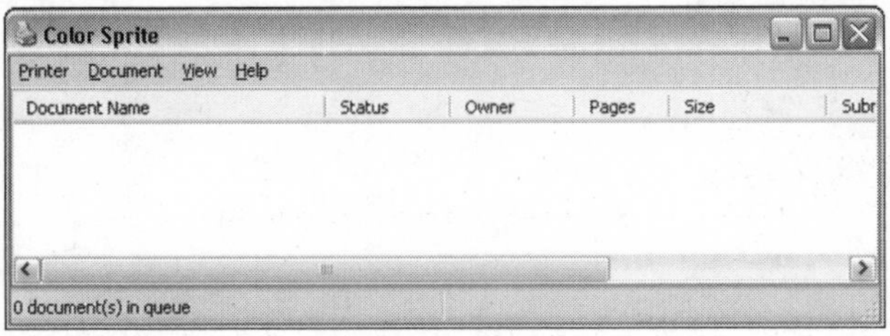

Figure 14-4: The ever-busy printer window.

✔ The items waiting to be printed are called print *jobs*.

✔ The printer's window is primarily a place where you can change the order of the print jobs. Do this by simply dragging one document above another.

✔ You can also remove jobs from the list by selecting the job and choosing Document⇨Cancel from the menu. Also see the section "Halting a printer run amok," later in this chapter.

Little printer guy

You never really need to keep an eye on the Printers folder while you print. Whenever something is printing (or, to be technical, whenever the printer driver is sending information to the printer), a printer icon appears in the system tray/notification area. You can double-click that icon to instantly open your printer's window and review the documents waiting to be printed.

The little printer guy goes away when the last byte of data has been sent to the printer.

And Then the Printer Goes Wacky

Printers are dutiful little creatures, handily going about their work without care or notice . . . until they screw up. Then the printer can become the most hated piece of office equipment in the building. Vile creatures. Cruel and unkind. And stubborn? I don't care how fancy the display is on your computer, when it's acting stupid, it has nothing useful to say.

General troubleshooting advice

The first thing to try when the printer goes haywire is a printing troubleshooter. This is the Microsoft Q&A way to help track down most printer problems.

In Windows 98, follow these steps:

1. **Click the Start button.**
2. **Choose Help from the Start menu.**
3. **Click the Contents tab in the Windows Help window.**
4. **Open the Troubleshooting book.**
5. **Open the Windows 98 Troubleshooters book.**
6. **Click the Print "chapter."**
7. **Work through the troubleshooter on the right side of the window.**

In Windows Me, follow these steps:

1. **Click the Start button.**
2. **Choose the Help command.**
3. **Beneath the "What would you like help with?" title, click Printing, Scanning, and Photos.**
4. **Click Troubleshooting for printers, scanning, & photos.**
5. **Click Printing Troubleshooter.**

   This option is at the lower-left side of the screen, beneath the word *Troubleshooting.* You see the Printing Troubleshooter appear, as shown in Figure 14-5.

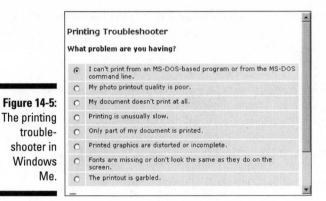

Printing Troubleshooter

What problem are you having?

- ● I can't print from an MS-DOS-based program or from the MS-DOS command line.
- ○ My photo printout quality is poor.
- ○ My document doesn't print at all.
- ○ Printing is unusually slow.
- ○ Only part of my document is printed.
- ○ Printed graphics are distorted or incomplete.
- ○ Fonts are missing or don't look the same as they do on the screen.
- ○ The printout is garbled.

Figure 14-5:
The printing trouble-shooter in Windows Me.

In Windows XP, open the Printers and Faxes icon in the Control Panel, as described earlier in this chapter, in the section "Finding the Printers folder." Click the Troubleshoot printing link in the See Also panel.

✔ If you need to reinstall a printer driver, the easiest way to do that is to delete your printer from the Printers folder and then add it again.

✔ You may want to check with your printer's manufacturer's Web page to see whether it has any updated printer drivers. Refer to Chapter 5 for more information on finding those Web pages.

Things to check when the printer isn't printing

Ah, the usual suspects: Check all the cables. One cable must plug between your computer and the printer — both ends must be snug. The other cable plugs between your printer and the wall socket. Snug. Snug. Snug.

Is the printer turned on?

Is the printer *selected?* Some printers have the ability to be powered up, but deselected or taken offline. You typically push a Select or On-line button to ensure that the printer isn't ignoring the computer. (This option is on high-end computers mostly.)

Do you have a device between your printer and the computer, such as an external disk drive or CD-R or scanner? These printer-port devices must be turned on for the printer to print.

Ensure that you've chosen the proper printer from the list in the Print dialog box. I once sent my wife's printer three copies of a document before I figured out that I had the wrong printer selected and *that* was the reason nothing was printing on my own printer.

Also check the printer's display or panel for errors. Some low-end printers simply blink their lights if they have a paper jam or low-ink problem.

The "weird text atop the page" problem

Printers that print strange text across the top of the first page, or ugly text on every page, have a driver problem. Most likely, the wrong printer driver was installed when the printer was set up.

You can try changing the driver by using the Printer's Properties dialog box: Right-click the printer's icon in the Printers folder window and then choose Properties from the pop-up menu. A Driver tab may be staring you in the face, or you may have to hunt for the Update Driver button somewhere in the dialog box. If so, use it to scour a new driver for the printer.

Or, of course, you can always delete and reinstall the printer in the Printers folder to ensure that the proper driver is installed. If so, be extra sure that you have the proper, *exact* make and model number for your printer.

✔ If the weird text appears only when you print from one application, it's the application's doing and not the printer driver's.

✔ Use the File➪Print Preview command to ensure that it's not the application itself that's producing the weird characters.

✔ If the characters at the top of the page appear to have their heads cut off, your page's top margin is set too high; use the Page Setup dialog box to increase the top margin.

The color is all wrong

Adjusting the color of printer output is an obsession with some people. But this type of error doesn't involve the subtleties between PMS 133 and PMS 140. If the color is wrong, such as too green or not enough red, your printer is probably low on one type of ink.

✔ Alas, unless you have a printer with separate ink cartridges, you have to replace the entire color ink cart when only one color gets low. I know: It's a rip-off. But the printer was cheap, wasn't it?

✔ PMS is an acronym for the Pantone Matching System, a set of numbers matched to specific colors. PMS is used by graphics professionals to ensure that the printed result is exactly the color they want.

✔ You can try checking the Print dialog box for an Advanced, Properties, or Preferences button and see whether you find further controls there for manipulating the color. Most of the time, a discolored image is the sign of low ink.

"My black-and-white image prints dark blue"

Most color printers come with a 3-color ink cartridge and then a single black ink cartridge. Their controls can also switch so that you can use only the black cartridge, which is the case if you're printing a black-and-white or grayscale image. Simply tell the Print dialog box that you want to use only the black ink.

✔ The color doesn't have to be dark blue. It could be dark green or dark red or any tone other than black.

✔ Some older, cheaper inkjet printers lack the black ink cartridge alto-gether. They create "black" the same way little kids do: by mixing all the other colors together. Obviously, with this type of printer, obtaining a true black tone would be fairly impossible.

Halting a printer run amok

I've done this tons of times: You print and then . . . you realize that you want to take it back and stop printing at once! Here's what you do:

1. **Scream "Stop, you jerk!"**

   This step doesn't really help, but it sure *feels* good.

2. **Double-click the little printer icon in the system tray/notification area.**

   This step is the fastest way to open your printer's window and cancel the document being printed.

   If you don't see the little printer guy, all the information has been sent to the printer and is now living inside the printer's memory. Skip to Step 6.

3. **Locate on the list the document you want to halt.**

   It's the one that's "printing."

4. Select the document and choose Document⇨Cancel from the menu.

It's Document⇨Cancel Printing in Windows 98 and Windows Me.

5. Wait until the document disappears from the list.

After it's gone, you notice that the printer is still printing. That's because most printers have internal memory in which to store several pages of a document. And, yes, the printer continues to print. Oh, gads!

6. Turn off the printer.

Yes, this is a mean thing to do. But it works. It stops the printer from printing, and it erases the document in the printer's memory. It does not harm the printer, though it may make some inky spots with some cheap inkjet-style printers.

7. Turn the printer on again.

As long as you purge all the printing documents from your printer's window (refer to Step 4), nothing else prints.

8. Eject the page from the printer.

This step removes the last bit of the document that was printing and prepares the printer to print again.

These steps are your only hope if you run off and print something you want to cancel. Well, that — or you can stop at Step 4 and just wait for the printer to spew out two or three more pages. (I had to halt my printer once when I realized that it was printing 300 pages of random text. Ugh.)

Printer Maintenance Chores

Printers run relatively maintenance free, which is amazing considering how many moving parts are inside.

The only regular maintenance you need to perform on the printer is the routine changing of the ink carts or toner.

If you have a nice inkjet printer, meaning that you paid over $300 for it, I recommend buying brand-name or approved replacement ink cartridges. The reason is that these high-end printers rely on the high-end cartridges to help keep the inkjet nozzles clean.

If you have a cheaper printer, you can save some money by using those ink cart refilling syringes that are advertised on TV and sold in office supply stores. They work just fine and aren't really that messy, but the ink is of a lower quality, so you don't want to use them in a high-end inkjet printer.

For laser printers, you can get a few extra sheets out of the thing by "rocking" the toner cartridge when the first Toner Low warning comes. Simply remove the toner from the machine and rock it from left to right gently in your hands. This technique somehow redistributes the toxic inkstuff so that you can print a while longer before you have to shell out beaucoup bucks for another toner cartridge.

As far as jams go, simply clear them as best you can. Printer jams happen because the paper is damaged, too thin, or too thick.

In my travels, I've discovered few printers that can print on paper stock heavier than 25 pounds. One printer could do it, but it was a laser printer where the paper passed in a straight line from the front to the back of the printer. Other printers, where the paper scrolls up and down and back and forth, cannot handle thick paper stock, which will jam and cause you undue delay and stress.

And we could all use a little less stress.

Chapter 15

Dealing with Disk Disaster

● ●

In This Chapter

▶ How to tell whether a hard drive is in trouble

▶ Dealing with a failing hard drive

▶ Troubleshooting CD-ROM drives

▶ Messing with the AutoPlay feature

▶ Figuring out floppy disk dilemmas

● ●

*P*erhaps nothing else in a computer can toss the thunderbolt of dread better than a disk error. *Disks* are where you store your stuff. Disk errors mean that, potentially, you may lose your stuff. Even when my first PC's feeble 63-watt power supply blew up (blue smoke and all), I was merely surprised. Then I laughed, "Ha! Ha!" I knew that my data was still safe on the hard drive.

Many types of disks are in the typical PC. The most important type is the hard drive, which is where the operating system lives, where your applications live, and where your stuff lives. Obviously, its care is important, but you probably have other disks as well: CDs, DVDs, and floppies. I cover them all here in this rather beefy chapter on dealing with disk disaster.

Note: You should also refer to Part III of this book, which deals with preventive maintenance, backup, and other disk tools.

Smells Like Hard Drive Trouble

Security spinning in the bosom of your typical PC, the hard drive is expected to last anywhere from four to five years. After that time, the hard drive begins to call it a day, errors increase, and things move slower. That's expected. Anything wrong before that is not only unexpected, but unwelcome as well.

Hard drive, hard disk — what's the diff?

The terms hard drive and hard disk are fairly interchangeable, and I'm sure that at nerd cocktails parties they would argue the differences down to the tiniest micron. But that's a moot point.

The hard drive is a chunk of electronics about the size of a thick paperback book (though the size does vary). That unit contains several spinning disks, all stacked on the same spindle and all of which store data on both sides. That whole thing is a hard drive, but for technical reasons, refer to it as a physical drive. Most PCs can have two or more physical drives installed internally and as many external physical drives as you can afford.

As far as the operating system is concerned, a physical hard drive can be one or more *logical*

drives. You can *partition* the physical drive inside your computer into two logical drives: C and D. So one physical disk can be one or more logical disk drives.

You can find lots of technical folderol having to do with disk drives, partitioning, and such, but my point is that when a single physical hard drive goes, it can bring down one or more of the logical drives as well. Conversely, a corrupt file on a logical drive may not affect any other logical drives on the same physical drive.

So, the terms hard drive and hard disk aren't really important. But it does help to know that a physical hard drive can be divided into logical hard drives.

"A hard drive is missing!"

Whoops! How did the hard drive escape?

Your first option, as usual, is to restart the computer to see whether the missing hard drive can be found. That generally fixes the problem.

If the hard drive is an external model, ensure that it's properly connected and getting power. I've noted that some external FireWire drives must be attached directly to the computer's FireWire hub for them to work.

If you're certain that the hard drive is a second physical drive inside the console, turn off the computer and open up the console to see whether it's still properly connected. Or, if that makes you uneasy, consider having your dealer do it.

Sometimes, the hard drive icon may be hidden in the My Computer window; choose View➪List to change the way the drives are displayed. That reveals any icons hiding behind other icons.

If you boot with a floppy disk, you cannot access any high-capacity hard drives, such as the Windows XP 32-bit file system. Alas, no tools seem to allow you to access the drive from a start-up floppy.

- ✔ **External drives must receive power.** Some external drives must be turned on before the computer starts so that they're recognized.

- ✔ A *hub* is a device that expands a FireWire or USB system. The single hub plugs into the computer, but then many devices can plug into the hub.

- ✔ *Daisy-chaining* some types of drives (connecting two or more drives, one after the other) may render the last drive invisible to the operating system.

- ✔ For FireWire or USB drives, note that the device the drive is plugged into must receive power in order for the drive to be recognized.

Hard drive failure warning signs

Rarely does a hard drive go suddenly. No, I take that back. I had a hard drive die on me in only half a second. A brief power outage occurred. The power was back on before I knew it and the computer reset, but somehow it zapped the hard drive. It was only a 90MB hard drive, but back then it cost me $1,000 to replace. (Fortunately, I had a backup.)

Most of the time, hard drives let you know well before they die. If your computer were a novel, the hard drive death scene would go on for pages and pages. That's good news — well, good news about impending bad news.

If the drive is deceased, is its data dead as well?

Sometimes the information on the hard drive goes with the hardware, and sometimes the information on the hard drive is still intact. That is why it's best to copy that stuff from the failing hard drive while you have the chance. If the hard drive does go, however, it's still possible to recover your data. Possible, but *expensive*.

Various outfits in most major cities specialize in disk disaster data recovery. Most of these places can take an old hard drive and, as long as you didn't blast the thing with a shotgun, fully recover all the data, placing it on either a CD-ROM or a new hard drive or printing it all out for you.

Although this sounds like a wonderful service, please recognize that data recover is very expensive. It's primarily used for large companies or the government or other situations where the files are critical and no other backup exists. If your stuff is precious to you, *back up your hard drive,* as covered in Chapter 22. Save the data recovery job for those few places that can afford it.

You may see several signs of impending hard drive doom. They may come in this order, in any order, or all at once, or only one may occur:

First sign: An increasing number of errors and bad sectors occur. As you run your programs, you may see access or read errors on the infamous Blue Screen of Death. Or, when you run ScanDisk or other disk utilities, errors may be reported. At first, they're fixed — which is great. But as time rolls on, the number and frequency of errors increase.

Second sign: Drive performance suffers. Disk access becomes sluggish. Defragmenting the drive doesn't help.

Know your CD-ROM drive letter

If you're going to be working with your CD-ROM, and especially if you end up phoning tech support, you need to know which drive letter belongs to your CD-ROM drive. This PC puzzle is one that most users haven't yet solved.

In most documentation, the CD-ROM drive letter is referred to as Drive D. That's because Drive D is the CD-ROM (or DVD) drive in about 70 percent of the computers sold. Drive C is the one and only hard drive. Drive D, the next letter, belongs to the CD. But that's not always the case.

If you have a hard drive D, the CD-ROM drive letter may be E.

If you're a clever user and have reassigned your CD-ROM drive letter, it could be any letter of the alphabet, up to Z! On two of my computers, the CD-ROM is drive letter R. So how can you tell?

Open the My Computer icon on the desktop. Choose View➪Details from the menu. You see your computer's disk drives organized as shown in the following figure. Look in the Type column for any CD-ROM Disc or Compact Disc entries. That's your CD-ROM drive. Note which letter it is, such as R in the image. (Drive S is a DVD drive, though you cannot tell from the My Computer window.)

```
My Computer                                                    _ □ ×
 File   Edit   View   Favorites   Tools   Help
 ← Back  ▾  →  ▾        Search    Folders   History
 Address    My Computer                                     ▾   Go

                  Name ▴              Type            Total Size   Free Space
    [icon]        3½ Floppy (A:)     3½-Inch Floppy Disk
                  WINDOWS ME (C:)    Local Disk        9.98 GB     7.01 GB
 My Computer      ARCHIVES (D:)      Local Disk        7.98 GB     6.54 GB
                  DOS 622 (E:)       Local Disk        1.00 GB     941 MB
 Select an item   Compact Disc (R:)  Compact Disc
 to view its      Compact Disc (S:)  Compact Disc
 description.      Zip 250 (Z:)       Removable Disk
 Displays the     Control Panel      System Folder
 contents of your
 computer

 See also:
 My Documents
 My Network Places
 Dial-Up Networking

 8 object(s)                                         My Computer
```

Third sign: The drive becomes louder and louder. I caught one recent and rather sudden drive failure because I noticed a clicking sound as the drive was accessing data. The clicking got louder over the next hour, and immediately I backed up the entire drive. Good thing too because the next morning, it was dead.

Other sounds include an increasing whistling or grinding noise that may diminish over time, but still is a sign that the drive may be on its last leg.

✔ The monitor, too, can make a loud, annoying noise when it's starting to go berserk. Refer to Chapter 13 for information on how to tell whether it's the monitor, and not the hard drive, that's hurting your ears.

✔ See Chapter 21 for more information on ScanDisk.

✔ Hard drives also tend to die when you turn the computer on, so if you suspect trouble — by all means! — leave the computer on until you can do a backup.

What to do when you suspect trouble

Whenever you suspect trouble, *immediately* you should back up your data. If you have a backup program, run it now!

If you do not have a backup, but have a second physical hard drive, back up the data to that hard drive; just copy all your important files over to the drive. But it must be a separate physical drive, not another logical drive (or partition) on the same physical drive.

Hands down, you have to replace the defective drive. You're buying, at minimum, your computer a second hard drive. If possible, try to get an internal hard drive. Have your dealer set it up as the main hard drive, and have them reconfigure the existing hard drive as the second hard drive. Then you can copy information from the old hard drive to the new hard drive and eventually dispense with the old one.

✔ Under no circumstances should you expect or accept someone's offer to fix the drive. No, just replace the defective drive. It's not worth the cost or trouble to fix the drive.

✔ See Chapter 22 for information on backing up a hard drive.

✔ It helps to get a second, larger hard drive in any computer. The cost isn't that much.

✔ Yes, you can add a second hard drive yourself, but it's often a real pain. Hard drives must be configured as master and slave, which can be confusing — especially if you get two drives from different manufacturers. No, unless you consider yourself experienced at this sort of thing, have your dealer do it.

CD-ROM Catastrophes!

Since the mid-1990s or so, the CD-ROM drive is a standard feature on every PC. Almost all new software comes on CDs, and with the addition of CD-R/RW and DVD drives, these removable, shiny media are a valued and trusted part of any PC system.

And like anything else in the computer, they can go kaput at the most ugly of times.

The all-purpose, do-or-die, tried-and-true CD-ROM troubleshooter

When the CD drive won't read a disk, play music, or do anything, you can follow these steps to effectively troubleshoot the drive:

1. **Push the eject button on the drive.**

   What should happen: If the tray slides out or the disk spits out (depending on the type of drive), you can be absolutely certain that the drive is getting power.

   If nothing happens: The drive is dead. Two things you can do: First, you can (if you know your screws and nuts) turn off the computer and check the drive connections to see whether they're loose. If they're all snug, you do the second option, which is to replace the drive with one that works.

2. **Insert a music disc.**

   The computer is smart enough to know that you play music discs when they're inserted. Notice that most CD-ROM drives even have a headphone jack and volume control. You use them to hear whether the music CD is playing.

   What should happen: You hear the music play over the headphones. This means that the drive is working and what's missing is the connection between the drive and the motherboard (for data) or the connection between the drive and your PC's sound card (for music).

If nothing happens: The drive is dead or the connections are loose. You can check the connections, and that may fix the problem. If not, replace the drive.

3. **Insert a cleaning disc.**

   Go to Radio Shack or Wal-Mart or wherever and pick up a CD drive cleaning disc. This disc buffs out the laser lens and possibly fixes a CD drive that skips or reads data intermittently.

   What should happen: The drive suddenly works again.

   If nothing happens: It's time to get a new drive.

That's pretty much it for troubleshooting. Generally speaking, only a few things can go wrong with a CD-ROM drive: Its connections become loose, in which case the drive seems to have power, but inserting a disk has no effect; the drive has no power, which generally means that the drive is dead; or the drive intermittently reads data, which means that the lens needs cleaning.

✔ Do not use a CD drive cleaning kit on a CD-R/RW or DVD-R drive. Those drives have self-cleaning laser heads, and using a cleaning disk on them can damage the drive.

✔ Yes, CD-ROM drives do die. Remember that anything with moving parts is more likely to die than something fully electronic.

✔ If the CD-ROM drive ever goes AWOL, consider running the Add New Hardware Wizard (from the Control Panel's Add New Hardware icon) to reinstall it.

✔ If you can't eject a disk, use the "beauty mark" hole on the front of the drive. Stick a straightened paper clip into the hole. Push gently. This action ejects the disk — even when the computer is off or the drive totally lacks power.

Turning AutoPlay on or off

Windows comes configured to automatically play any CD you stick into the CD-ROM drive. This means that music disks should play automatically and that the auto-play programs on most data CDs automatically run a Setup or Install program.

You can turn the auto-play feature on or off. As you would expect, this feature works differently for the various versions of Windows.

In Windows 98 and Windows Me, follow these steps:

1. **Open the Device Manager.**

   See Appendix A for information on how to get to the Device Manager.

2. **Open the CD-ROM item.**

   Click the plus sign [+] by the CD-ROM drive. This step displays the list of CD-ROM drives in your computer. If you have more than one, you have to repeat the following steps for each drive, as shown in Figure 15-1.

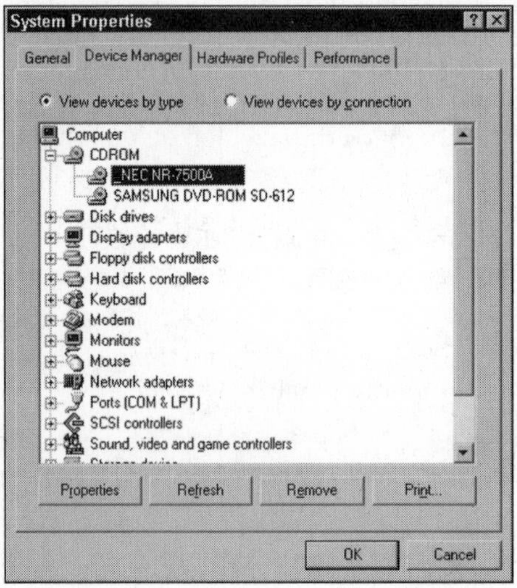

Figure 15-1:
Choosing a CD-ROM drive in Windows Me.

3. **Click to select the CD-ROM drive.**

4. **Click the Properties button.**

   The CD-ROM Properties dialog box appears.

5. **Click the Settings tab.**

6. **Click to add or remove the check mark next to the Auto insert notification option.**

   Putting a check mark there turns on the auto-play feature; removing the check mark disables that feature.

   Also note that in this dialog box you can change the CD-ROM drive letter; use the Reserved drive letters area in the bottom of the dialog box, as shown in Figure 15-2.

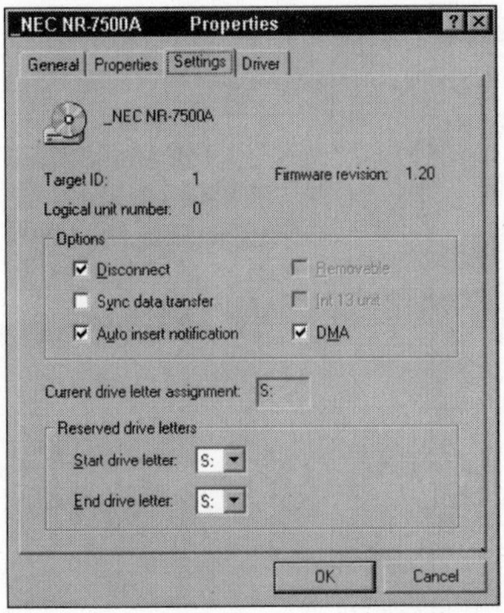

Figure 15-2:
Setting the
Auto insert
notification
item.

7. **Click OK to close the CD-ROM Properties dialog box.**

8. **Close the Device Manager window.**

In Windows XP, follow these steps:

1. **Open the My Computer icon on the desktop.**

2. **Right-click your CD-ROM drive's icon.**

3. **Choose Properties from the pop-up menu.**

   The CD-ROM drive's Properties dialog box appears.

4. **Click the AutoPlay tab.**

   You're presented with a slate of options, as shown in Figure 15-3. Here's what to do:

   • If you want nothing to happen, choose Select an action to perform and select Take no action from the list. That way, the computer ignores you any time you stick in a disk.

   • If you want a music CD to play, choose Music CD from the drop-down list. Then choose Select an action to perform and select the option Play using Windows Media Player from the list.

5. **Click the OK button after you've made your choices.**

6. **Close the My Computer window.**

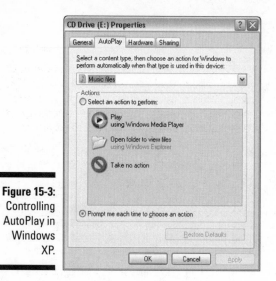

Figure 15-3:
Controlling
AutoPlay in
Windows
XP.

CD-R and CD-RW drive stuff

CD-R and CD-RW drives present other problems in addition to that of the normal CD-ROM drive. That's because, as their name implies, these drives can actually write discs, either the CD-R recordable discs or the CD-RW read-write discs — or both! Here are some thoughts:

✔ My advice is to "burn" data to a CD-R or CD-RW disc in big chunks, and the larger the chunk, the better. Using a CD-R/RW drive like a regular disk drive may result in less usable storage space on the drive; the extra overhead required to keep track of all the small recording sessions does add up over time.

✔ Though it appears that you can delete files on a CD-R or CD-RW drive, the space used by the files isn't recovered. No, the CD-R or CD-RW drive merely "masks" the deleted file. So don't be surprised when you delete 50MB of stuff from a CD-R or CD-RW and don't see an extra 50MB of storage appear on the drive.

✔ CD-R discs fail, just like other types of disks. If the CD-R disc cannot be written to, throw it out. Ditto for CD-RW discs.

✔ The CD-RW drive may appear to be dead, but most likely the disc is full. Try replacing the disc and see whether it still works.

Floppy Disk Woes

Pity the poor floppy disk. My friend Reza from the United Kingdom believes them to be doomed. Alas, they may be underused and ignored on many PCs, but they're still standard equipment. Quite a few smaller programs and utilities still come on floppy disks. They're cheap; easy to mail; easy to transport. But they can cause woe and distress just like any other disk in the system.

"The floppy disk doesn't format!"

All floppy disks need to be formatted before you can use them. Even those preformatted disks should be formatted by your own floppy drive. If they can't be formatted, *toss them out!*

Floppy disks are cheap enough that you shouldn't waste any of your time trying to get one to format.

Why don't some of them format? The answer is alignment.

Floppy drives are not manufactured with the same rigid precision as other disk drives in your PC. Because of that, the alignment from drive to drive varies. A disk formatted in one drive (at the factory, for example) may not work in your own PC's drive. Likewise, you may find that your floppy disks can't be read on other drives because of bad alignment.

Floppy disks are unreliable

Please do not use floppies as your primary form of disk storage. The hard drive is where you're supposed to put all your vital stuff. Floppy disks are for transport or backup use, for that second copy.

The reason you shouldn't rely on floppy disks is that they just aren't as reliable as other disks. The floppy drive read/write head actually rubs the disk media every time you use the disk. Eventually, the head does rub the magnetic material off the disk, rendering the disk useless.

Chapter 16

Internet Connection Mayhem

• •

• •

1 survived! For my research into this chapter, I read the technical description of how the typical PC connects to the Internet. The reading was tough, even dangerous. No pictures. And it wasn't a *For Dummies* book, either. I read lots of jargon about layers and protocols and bits hither, thither, and yon. The process is all so complex that it makes you wonder how it ever happens at all, but you know it does. In a way, I could compare it to the differences between reading about sexual reproduction in biology class versus a backseat experience in a GTO at a drive-in movie, but I think that my publisher would strenuously object.

Fortunately, you don't ever have to learn the ins and outs of what goes on behind the scenes when you make an Internet connection happen. With any luck, it just does. When it doesn't, you can turn to this chapter for some solutions or soothing words of advice.

Just a Sampling of the Zillions of Things That Can Go Wrong with Connecting to the Internet

It's supposed to work like this: You start an Internet program, and your computer automatically connects to the Internet and dishes up whatever data it is you're requesting: a Web page, e-mail, file — whatever.

The sections that follow, presented in a somewhat logical order, are the things that can go wrong or may go wrong, or they're just general questions about connection calamities and losses.

"Windows doesn't remember my password!"

You go to connect to the Internet and, sure enough, you have to reenter your connection password. Again and again. And the Save option is dimmed, meaning that you cannot save the password. What's up?

The problem is that you're not logging in when you first start Windows 98 or Windows Me or that your account doesn't have a password in Windows XP. When you log in properly and provide the Login dialog box with a name and password, Windows activates the *password chain,* which is simply a location where Windows remembers all your various passwords.

The solution? Log in properly to Windows 98 or Windows Me, or give your account a password in Windows XP.

✔ To make the login dialog box reappear in Windows 98 or Windows Me, click the Start button and choose the Log Off command. Click the Yes button to log off. Then, when you see the Logon dialog box, enter a username and password. This action sets up the password chain, allowing you to save your Internet passwords.

✔ The username and password used to log in to Windows is different from the username and password you use on the Internet.

✔ In Windows XP, apply a password to your account by opening the User Accounts icon in the Control Panel. Choose your account from the list. Click the Create a password link.

Automatic-connection dilemmas

People automatically complain about two things in connecting to the Internet: They want it to happen, or they want it not to happen.

For example, if you enjoy automatic connection, when you start an Internet application, such as Internet Explorer, the connection box just pops up and dials into the Internet. That's automatic connection in action.

On the other hand, some people prefer to have the Connect To dialog box pop up and then have to click the Dial button to manually connect to the Internet.

But what if you're always connected?

High-speed, or *broadband,* Internet connections are always on. If you have DSL, cable, or even a T1 type of connection, your computer is always connected to the Internet. In that case, you don't ever see the connection dialog box because the connection is made instantly whenever you turn on your computer. That's the advantage to having a high-speed Internet connection.

If you would rather not connect to the Internet with a high-speed connection, choose File⇨ Work Offline from the menu of whichever Internet application you're using. What this command does is to temporarily suspend the connection for that application; the command makes the program pretend that it's not talking

to the Internet. You see "Working Offline" displayed on the application's title bar.

To reconnect the application, choose File⇨ Work Offline again, and the connection is reestablished. Or, you may see a dialog box asking you to reconnect. It's a mere formality; with a high-speed connection, you're always connected.

(The only way to truly disconnect a high-speed connection is to turn off the DSL or cable modem. Or, if the connection is through some type of Ethernet cable, disconnect the Ethernet cable. That temporarily suspends Internet access both to and from your PC. You rarely have any reason to do this, however.)

Either way is possible, controlled from the Connecting To dialog box, as shown in Figure 16-1 (though this dialog box has subtle variations in all versions of Windows). Look in that dialog box for the Connect automatically option.

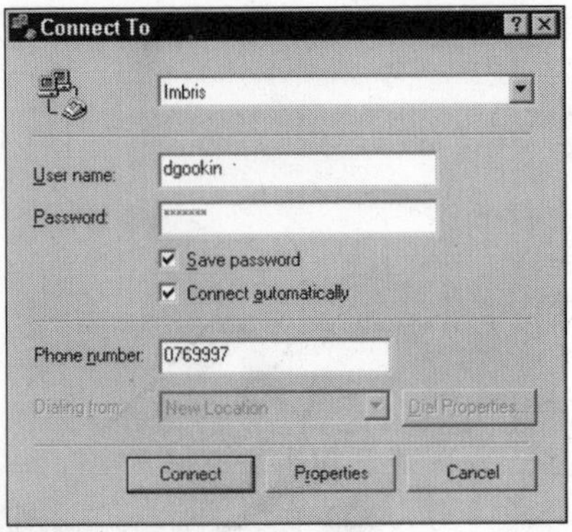

Figure 16-1:
The
Connect To
dialog box.

If you want to connect automatically, put a check mark by Connect automatically, as shown in Figure 16-1.

If you would rather not connect automatically, when you see the dialog box displayed (usually while it's trying to connect), click the Cancel button and remove the check mark by Connect automatically.

 ✔ If you have a cable or DSL modem, see the nearby sidebar "But what if you're always connected?" for more information.

 ✔ Also see the next section, "Where Windows hides the connection information."

Where Windows hides the connection information

All Internet connections are handled in the Internet Properties dialog box:

1. **Open the Control Panel.**

2. **Open the Internet Options icon.**

   In Windows XP Category view, choose Network and Internet Connections and click the Internet Options icon.

3. **Click the Connections tab in the Internet Properties dialog box.**

   The top of the dialog box lists the various ISPs you connect to, as shown in Figure 16-2. You may see only one, or several if you have several accounts — including AOL.

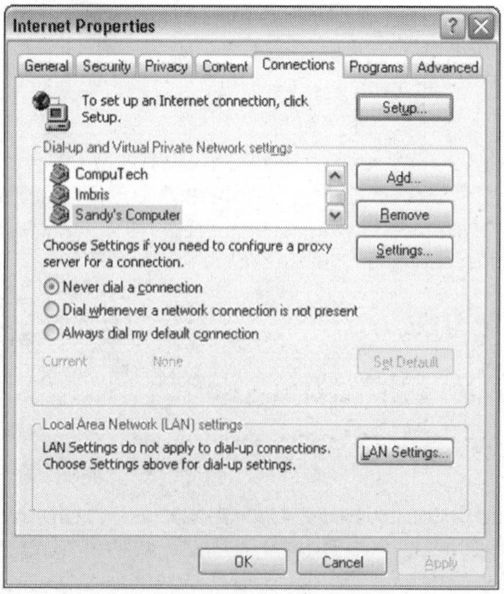

Figure 16-2:
The Internet Properties/ Connections dialog box, Windows XP variation.

As far as connecting is concerned, you have three options, as shown in the middle of the dialog box. Here's what they mean:

Never dial a connection: Windows doesn't automatically connect to the Internet when you open Internet Explorer. Windows may, however, connect automatically for other applications, especially if you've clicked to select Connect automatically in the Connect to dialog box (refer to the preceding section.)

Dial whenever a network connection is not present: This option is the one that most people with traditional modems should select. It tells Windows to connect to the Internet whenever you open an Internet program.

Always dial my default connection: This option is puzzling because it sounds like the one you should check, but you should check the preceding option instead.

4. **Make whatever settings or changes are necessary.**

5. **Click OK to close the Internet Properties dialog box.**

6. **Close the Control Panel window.**

Most people get into trouble in the Internet Properties/Connections dialog box when they choose Always dial my default connection rather than Dial whenever a network connection is not present.

✔ You can still connect to the Internet if you choose the Never dial a connection option. You must summon the Connect To dialog box, from either the Dial-Up Networking window or the Network Connections window.

✔ If you have a DSL, cable, or other broadband Internet connection, you should choose Never dial a connection from the Internet Properties/Connections dialog box. That's right — you don't need to "dial" anything; you're always connected.

✔ The default connection is your preferred connection if you have more than one. You can always select another connection, from either the drop-down list in the Connect To dialog box (refer to Figure 16-1) or the Internet Properties/Connections dialog box.

The PC dials into the Internet at seemingly random times

In many instances, your computer attempts for some reason to dial into the Internet. It seems random because you may not be doing anything directly related to the Internet at the time. Or, it may happen when you start the computer. Is the computer possessed? Call the digital exorcist!

Obviously, *something* in your computer is trying to connect. What it could be is anyone's guess. The way I deal with the problem is to turn off the automatic connection feature, as described earlier in this chapter. That way, when I see the Connecting To dialog box, I click the Cancel button and the computer stops dialing into the Internet.

✔ Some start-up programs may connect to the Internet because they confuse your Local Area Network (LAN) address with the Internet. So rather than try to connect directly with some other computer local to you, the computer dials the Internet, looking for that computer. It's dumb, but it happens.

✔ The same type of situation may happen if you print to a networked printer; your computer may attempt to dial up the Internet to try and find the printer.

✔ Also consider contacting the printer manufacturer or software developer to see whether anyone there has any information on the product dialing into the Internet. Refer to Chapter 5 for tech support information.

✔ Consult with your network administrator if you suspect that your computer is dialing the Internet to find a local computer. Consider changing the local IPs to the 10.0.0.*x* range of addresses. Again, the network person knows how to do this.

Connection mysteries in Outlook Express

Two mysteries must be unraveled regarding Outlook Express and your Internet connection: The first is when Outlook Express (OE) fails to automatically connect (which may or may not be wanted), and the second is when OE immediately disconnects after picking up your mail, which is mostly unwanted.

Whatever the case, you need to wander off to the Options dialog box in OE: Choose Tools⇨Options. This command displays the Options dialog box. Ensure that the General tab is selected, as shown in Figure 16-3. (The figure shows OE Version 6 in Windows Me, though it's similar to the other editions of OE for other versions of Windows.)

The main thing you need to notice is the drop-down list near the middle of the dialog box. It's titled If my computer is not connected at this time, and three options are on the list:

✔ Do not connect.

✔ Connect only when not working offline.

✔ Connect even when working offline.

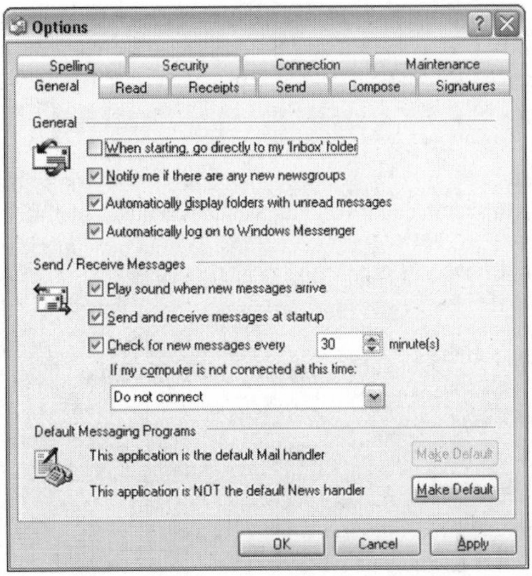

Figure 16-3:
Setting
the OE
connection
options,
Part I.

The first item is obvious: if you start OE and don't want to dial into the
Internet, choose that option. OE should (and I'm sorry, but this is a "should"
situation) not dial into the Internet. Sometimes it does, specifically if you
also have checked the option labeled Send and receive messages at startup.
Better uncheck that item too if you really don't want to connect.

Another way to avoid connecting — even if you have a broadband connection — is to choose File⇨Work Offline. This command tells OE to pretend that
it's not connected to the Internet, even if it is. When you choose that option,
the second two items in the drop-down list come into play, and OE connects
or not depending on which option you've chosen.

Confused? If so, and if you really don't want OE to connect, remove the check
mark by Send and receive messages at startup and choose Do not connect
from the drop-down list.

✔ Be careful to note the commands on the drop-down list. One says "If my
computer is not connected at this time." That means that if the computer *is* connected, the instructions on that list are ignored — unless
you choose File⇨Work Offline, in which case OE pretends that it's not
connected anyway.

✔ And Pooh said, "Oh, bother!"

✔ If you use Windows XP and detest that the Windows Messenger program
always starts up when you run OE, uncheck the item Automatically log
on to Windows Messenger.

TIP

Disabling the annoying call waiting

Windows can be taught to automatically switch off the call waiting feature so that you don't get accidentally disconnected by it when you're on the Internet. You do that by opening the Modems icon in the Control Panel.

In Windows 98 or Windows Me, click the Dialing Properties button in the Modem Properties dialog box. In the middle of the Dialing Properties dialog box, you notice a setting labeled "To disable call waiting, dial" followed by a drop-down list. Click to select that option and enter the numbers or buttons you punch to disable call waiting in your area. Click OK and then close the Modem Properties dialog box.

In Windows XP, open the Phone and Modems icon in the Control Panel. In the Phone and Modem Options dialog box, click the Dialing Rules tab. If locations are entered, select the current location and click the Edit button. Otherwise, click the New button to create a new location. Click the item "To disable call waiting, dial" and select the proper key sequence for your area to disable call waiting. Click OK to close the Phone and Modem Options dialog box.

After you make these adjustments, Windows automatically disables call waiting for each call the modem makes.

Disconnection mysteries in Outlook Express

One frustrating option in Outlook Express (OE) is found on the Connection tab of the Options dialog box, as shown in Figure 16-4. It's the Hang up after sending and receiving option.

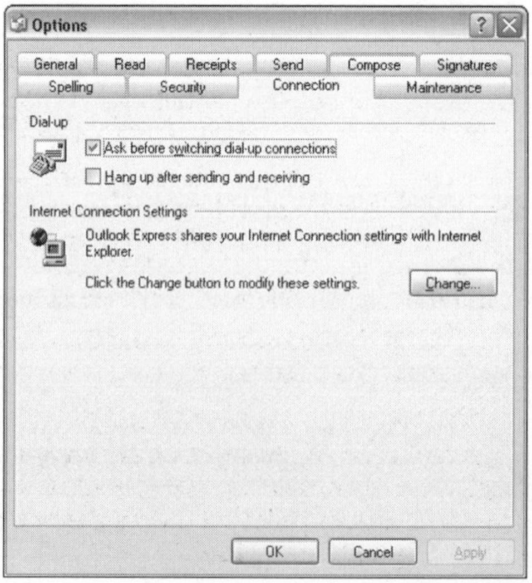

Figure 16-4:
The
Connection
tab in the
OE Options
dialog box.

If you choose that option, OE itself kills your Internet connection, no matter what else is going on.

I've had readers who are happily surfing on the Web discover that they've been disconnected simply because OE has automatically picked up some new e-mail *and then disconnected*. It can be a frustrating thing, especially if you don't know where to look for turning it off. Now you know.

Losing the Connection

Internet connections drop for a gazillion reasons — anything from squirrels on the line (I kid you not) to someone else in the house picking up the extension. The phone connection is a delicate thing, and just about anything short of wishful thinking can bring it down.

✔ Do you suspect your phone lines to be to blame? If so, you can have your phone company test the wires all the way up to your house for reliability. The wires inside your house, however, must be tested by an electrician. See whether your ISP can recommend an electrician familiar with digital communications.

✔ By the way, the phone company can do nothing to improve slow service. It only guarantees a certain speed over its phone wires — nothing faster. (You have to see what the speed is for your area, which depends on the age of the equipment and, well, how lazy your particular phone company is.)

✔ Sometimes the connection works better at night. Radio interference from the sun (that big, bright thing in the sky during the day) can wreak havoc with communications.

✔ At two times during the year, satellite modems get interference from the sun: during the fall and vernal equinoxes. It typically happens about noon or so, when the satellite passes between the earth and the sun.

✔ Call waiting can sure knock you off the Internet. See your phone book or features manual for information on disabling call waiting in your area. See the nearby sidebar "Disabling the annoying call waiting."

✔ The connection can drop because of inactivity (see the next section).

✔ Sometimes, your ISP may drop the connection, especially during a busy time of day. AOL doesn't admit to it, but that doesn't mean that it never happens.

✔ The modem may get hot and drop the connection because of the heat. In this type of situation, you can connect for only about 20 to 30 minutes before getting disconnected. Ensure that your PC's fan is working and that the computer is in a well-ventilated place.

Adjusting the Connection Time-Outs

To ensure that you don't waste precious Internet connect-time, Windows has built in a connection time-out system to disconnect your modem after a period of inactivity. You can adjust this value up or down, or even turn it off, which is nice. The un-nice thing, of course, is that these time-out settings are made in *two* places in Windows. To make the situation worse, the location of these places changes with each version of Windows. Ugh.

- ✔ Obviously, if you have a broadband connection, you don't need to worry about time-out values; you're connected all the time anyway. Nya! Nya! Nya!

- ✔ The following sections also discuss where to set the Automatic Disconnect option, which is a handy tool to use when you have a dial-up Internet connection.

The first secret time-out location in Windows 98 and Windows Me

The first secret time-out location is the same for both Windows 98 and Windows Me. It's the time-out or idle value as set in the Modem Properties dialog box:

1. **Click the Start button.**

2. **Choose Settings⇨Control Panel.**

   The Control Panel window appears.

 3. **Open the Modems icon.**

   The Modem Properties dialog box appears.

4. **Click the Properties button.**

   Almost there!

5. **Click the Connection tab.**

   Finally! You see a dialog box that contains some call preferences. The last item is Disconnect a call if idle for more than [blank] mins. That's the first place Windows looks for disconnecting a call; see Figure 16-5.

6. **Enter a new disconnect value.**

   Or, to keep online forever, uncheck the Disconnect a call item.

7. **Click OK to close your modem's Properties dialog box.**

8. **Close the Modem Properties dialog box.**

   Go ahead and leave the Control Panel open for the next set of steps.

Remember that these steps differ for both Windows 98 and Windows Me, each of which is covered in separate sections that follow.

The second place to look for time-out settings in Windows 98

If you're reading this entire section, you've just told the modem to disconnect a call if you're idle. What is *idle?* It can mean that you're reading or walking to get another cup of coffee or on the phone, but basically not clicking a link with the mouse or typing anything on a Web page. You can check one more place for this idle thing.

These steps continue from the preceding section:

9. **Open the Internet Options icon in the Control Panel.**

10. **Click the Connections tab.**

11. **Highlight your ISP on the list.**

    Or, you may see just one ISP listed.

12. **Click the Settings button.**

    Your ISP's Settings dialog box appears.

13. **Click the Advanced button.**

14. **There, in the Advanced Dial-Up dialog box, is the second idle time-out warning.**

    This one is called Disconnect if idle for [blank] minutes. You can enter a new time-out value or uncheck the item to be online for as long as your bleary little eyes can stand it.

15. **Make your time-out/idle adjustments.**

    At the bottom of the Advanced Dial-Up dialog box you should notice the handy Disconnect when a connection may not be needed option. Check that item if you want Windows to display the Disconnect dialog box after you close the last open window from an Internet application.

16. **Click OK to close the Advanced Dial-Up dialog box.**

17. **Click OK to close your ISP's Settings dialog box.**

18. **Click OK to close the Internet Properties dialog box.**

19. **Close the Control Panel too.**

Now, is that insane or what? I'm not certain of the exact differences between the two. All I know is that it pays to check *both* time-out values and set them identically.

The second place to look for idle disconnect options in Windows Me

The Windows Me instructions differ only subtly from the instructions just given for Windows 98 — but they're subtle enough to warrant fresh information.

These steps continue from the section "The first secret time-out location in Windows 98 and Windows Me," a couple of sections back. I assume that the Control Panel window is open on your screen.

9. **Open the Dial-Up Networking icon in the Control Panel.**

10. **Right-click your ISP's icon in the window.**

    If you have multiple ISPs listed, you have to repeat these steps for each one.

11. Choose Properties from the pop-up menu.

A dialog box for your ISP appears.

12. Click the Dialing tab.

A whole big, juicy section on "idle disconnect" appears near the bottom of the dialog box, as shown in Figure 16-6.

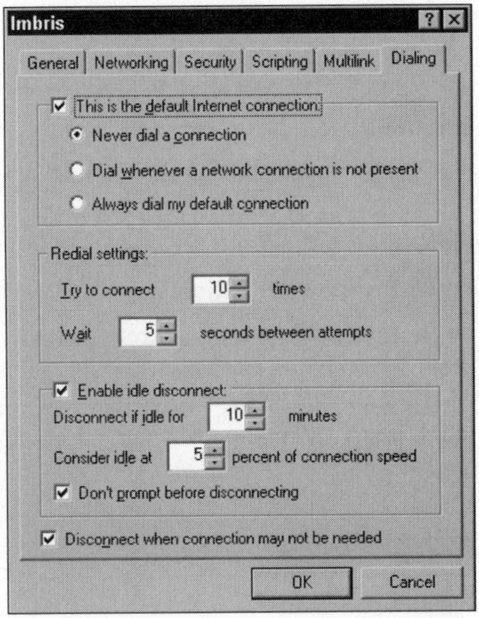

Figure 16-6: Even more idle disconnect options for Windows Me.

13. Remove the check mark by Enable idle disconnect to turn off the feature entirely.

Or, you can keep the check mark, as shown in Figure 16-6, and fill in the information as needed.

Notice that handy option labeled Disconnect when a connection may not be needed. That's the option that directs Windows to display the Disconnect dialog box when you close the last window of the last open Internet application.

14. Click OK after changing or reviewing your settings.

15. Close the Dial-Up Networking window while you're at it.

I'm not sure which option, either this one or the one set from the Modem's Properties dialog box, truly controls the disconnect or time-out. It's gotta be one of them. I just play it safe and set both dialog boxes to the same values.

The secret locations in Windows XP

As with Windows 98 and Windows Me, in two locations in Windows XP you can set the time-out or idle values for an Internet-over-the-modem connection. Start with the modem time-out:

1. **Open the Control Panel's Phone and Modem Options icon.**

   In Category view, open the Printers and Other Hardware link, click to open the Phone and Modem Options icon.

2. **Click the Modems tab in the Phone and Modem Options dialog box.**

3. **Click the Properties button.**

   Another Properties dialog box opens, one specific to your brand of modem.

4. **Click the Advanced tab.**

5. **Click the Change Default Preferences button.**

   Finally, you hit pay dirt in the modem's Default Preferences dialog box, as shown in Figure 16-7.

   To set an automatic disconnect, put a check mark by Disconnect a call if idle for more than [blank] mins. Then enter the amount of minutes to wait for a disconnect.

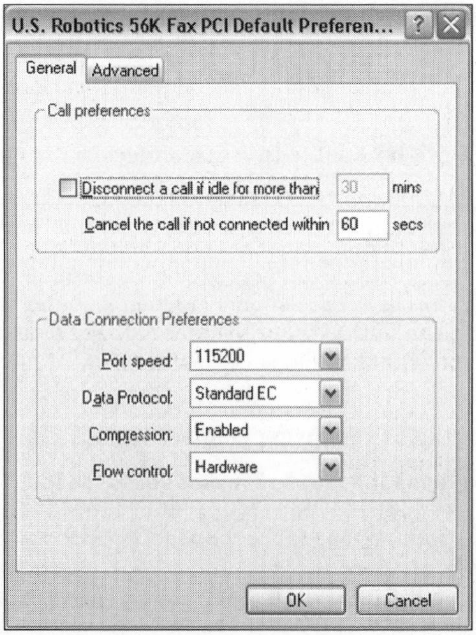

Figure 16-7:
The modem time-out setting is buried way down here.

U.S. Robotics 56K Fax PCI Default Preferen...

General | Advanced

Call preferences

☐ Disconnect a call if idle for more than | 30 | mins

Cancel the call if not connected within | 60 | secs

Data Connection Preferences

Port speed: 115200

Data Protocol: Standard EC

Compression: Enabled

Flow control: Hardware

OK | Cancel

6. **Make the settings your heart desires.**

7. **Click OK to close the Default Preferences dialog box.**

8. **Click OK to close the modem's Properties dialog box.**

9. **Click OK to close the Phone and Modem Options dialog box.**

   Okay! Okay! Okay!

   That's just the first location, and they hid it most effectively, don't you think? The next location deals with your IPS's connection information, which you can get to from the Internet Options icon, also located in the Control Panel:

10. **Open the Internet Options icon in the Control Panel.**

    In Category view, choose Network and Internet Connections and then open the Internet Options icon.

11. **Click the Connections tab in the Internet Properties dialog box.**

12. **If necessary, choose your ISP from the list.**

    If you have only one ISP, it's already selected for you.

13. **Click the Settings button.**

    And a dialog box for your ISP's Settings appears. Believe it or not, you can check in *two* places for time-out values.

14. **Click the Properties button.**

15. **Click the Options tab in your ISP's Properties dialog box.**

    There, in the Redialing options area, is the first idle time before hanging up item. It may be specific to redialing, but why take chances? Set the idle time-out value to a specific number of minutes or to Never to not hang up automatically.

16. **Make your adjustments to the idle time value.**

17. **Click OK.**

    Now comes the second, more serious, time-out value setting for your ISP.

18. **Click the Advanced button.**

    Ah, the Advanced Dial-Up dialog box is just chock-full of time-out and idle values, as shown in Figure 16-8.

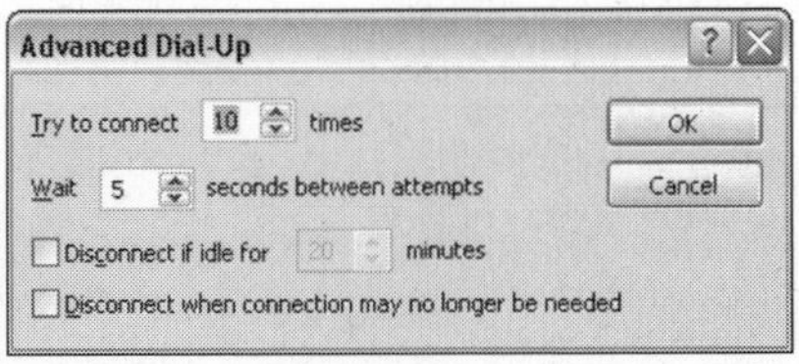

Figure 16-8:
Even more
time-out
options for
Windows
XP!

To disable the idle disconnect, uncheck the Disconnect if idle for [blank] minutes item, as shown in Figure 16-8. Or check that item and enter the number of minutes of inactivity after which the computer should disconnect.

In this dialog box, you also find the handy Disconnect when connection may no longer be needed item. That's the item that tells Windows to automatically display the Disconnect dialog box when you close your last Internet application's window — a handy item to turn on.

19. **Make the necessary settings and adjustments.**

20. **Click OK to close the Advanced Dial-Up dialog box.**

21. **Click OK to close your ISP's Settings dialog box.**

22. **Click OK to close the Internet Properties dialog box.**

23. **Close the Control Panel window while you're at it.**

And be sure to bring in the trash cans before the neighbor's dogs get into them!

Improving Your Internet Connection Speed

You can do little to improve your Internet connection speed. I know that many products out there claim to improve download times and connect speeds and many Web pages and magazine articles give you lists of things to tweak and adjust. But the time savings made, if any, are minute.

The ugly fact is that connection speed is a hardware thing. Unless you get faster connection hardware, the speed will be roughly the same all the time. So, honestly, this isn't even a troubleshooting issue.

✔ Even a fast Internet connection can meet with a slow Internet from time to time. When major parts of the Internet go down or servers are turned off for backup or upgrades, the overall speed of the Internet does drop. Again, you can do little about it.

✔ Some "tips" have you delete temporary Internet files, check your proxies, reset the modem, reboot the computer, and do a host of other chants and genuflections. Do they help? I'm not sure. But if such actions make you feel better, by all means continue.

✔ If the Internet connection gets slower over time, you can try to disconnect, reset the modem, and start over again.

✔ To reset an internal modem, simply restart Windows. You reset an external modem by turning it off and on again. Be sure to wait before turning the modem on again; you want to avoid a fast off-on flip of the switch, which may not have any effect on the hardware.

✔ Cable modems do slow down the more people are on the circuit. So if you're on the Internet and then all the neighbor kids come home from school, that would explain a drop in connection speed.

Chapter 17

Web Weirdness with Internet Explorer

*I*nternet Explorer gets lots of the blame for things that aren't really its fault. You see, a Web browser is merely a window through which you can view information on the World Wide Web. So if a Web page screws up — which happens often — you really have to blame the Web page itself and not Internet Explorer for merely passing on the bad news.

Yea, verily, even though you can pass blame off onto the Web, Internet Explorer does have enough quirks and oddities that warrant its own chapter in this troubleshooting book.

Note: Throughout this chapter, I use the abbreviation IE to refer to Internet Explorer.

Maintaining and Configuring Internet Explorer

Internet Explorer is a relatively easy program to use and configure. It has only a few areas where it tends to frustrate people. I've listed the more popular frustrations and solutions in the sections that follow.

Changing the home page

The *home page* can be anything you want to see when you first start Internet Explorer. Here's how to set the home page to something special or to nothing at all:

1. **Start IE.**

2. **Visit the Web page you want as your home page.**

   For example, visit Yahoo! or my own Web page, `www.wambooli.com/`. Displaying that Web page now makes choosing it as your home page much easier.

3. **Choose Tools⇨Internet Options.**

   You set the home page in the Internet Options dialog box, in the top part of the General tab, as shown in Figure 17-1.

Figure 17-1:
Selecting a home page.

You have three choices:

- **Use Current:** Choose the current page as the home page. You notice that the current page's address appears in the box.

- **Use Default:** This choice would be the Microsoft preference, which is now the MSN home page.

- **Use Blank:** This option tells IE to start with a blank page — an item popular with many folks.

4. **Select whichever option you want.**

   For example, to switch to the page you were viewing, click the Use Current button.

5. **Click OK.**

   Now that page is the first thing you see when you start IE.

You may be redirected to the Internet Explorer update page when a new version of IE becomes available. That's normal; annoying, but normal.

Sometimes, changing the home page may not be possible. These times include any of the following circumstances:

- Your computer has been infected by a virus that disables your home page selection. The solution is to run antivirus software to remove the problem and regain control.

- You've installed software that changes the home page for you, either on purpose or against your wishes. The page may be a feature of a "Web enhancement" program. The solution here is to remove that program.

- IE has been customized to prevent you from changing or using a home page. It happens at large companies or other large institutions where the system administrator restricts your computer's features for security purposes — or just to be mean.

Adjusting the temporary file size

IE stores megabytes and megabytes of temporary files on disk. Officially, this area is known as the *cache* (say "cash"). By storing images, sounds, text, and other information on your computer's hard drive, you make those Web pages you visit frequently load faster. After all, it takes less time to load an image from the temporary file cache than it would to squeeze that same image through the wires connecting you to the Internet.

The problem? The temporary file size can get huge! The bigger it is, the longer it takes IE to search through it, so cutting down on the size may actually improve your Web browsing performance.

Here's how to view or adjust the temporary file size for IE:

1. **Choose Tools⇨Internet Options.**

   The Internet Options dialog box appears. The center part of the General tab deals exclusively with temporary Internet files.

2. **Click the Settings button.**

   Various settings litter the Settings dialog box, as you would expect and as shown in Figure 17-2. The key setting to adjust here is the amount of disk space used for storing the temporary files. That adjustment is made by using the slider in the center of the dialog box or by manually entering a new size in the MB (megabytes) box.

Figure 17-2:
Temporary
Internet file
control.

3. **Adjust the size as needed.**

   Normally, the file size is set to about 1.5 percent of your hard drive's total capacity. You can adjust this to 1 percent, for example, and see how that number affects things; just move the slider left or enter a new value into the MB box.

   Another item to change is the first one. I would select Every visit to the page to keep IE from wandering off to look for new copies of stored stuff.

   If you select Never from the list, which effectively disables the cache, you must use the Refresh command (or press the F5 key) to load in a new version of a Web page. It's definitely an option *not* worth selecting.

4. **Click OK.**

Some folks say to delete the temporary files as another way to speed up Web performance. I'm not certain whether that method works, though it does increase disk space.

If you do want to delete the files, simply click the Delete Files button in the Internet Options dialog box.

Common Puzzles and Solutions

Here are a few of my favorite and most common Web browsing puzzles and their solutions. Consider this the short list; the full list would consume many more pages — perhaps an entire book in itself!

"The text is too small to read!"

I don't know why some Web page designers seem hell-bent to make us old folks squint at the computer monitor. Unless it's that text that says *Copyright* way down at the bottom of the Web page, then — dernit! — I want to read it!

Fortunately, IE has a solution for any Web page where you may find the text too teeny to interpret: Choose View⇨Text Size⇨Larger.

If that doesn't work, try View⇨Text Size⇨Largest.

What that command does is to temporarily boost the size of the text you see on the screen. (Graphic images are not affected, so if the text is really a graphic, the size doesn't change.) Then you can read at your leisure.

Note that this command is a page-only thing and that IE doesn't remember the next time around which pages you magnified.

Pop-up porn puzzles

Nothing is more shocking or irritating than a pop-up parade of porn windows Or, they can be any advertisements, but most often it's shocking pornography — not just once, but as many as 64 different windows all hogging up the screen. Closing the windows is like pounding down a lump in the carpet.

I've known many people who just shut down Windows when the porn pop-up parade begins. Sadly, that's all you can do.

The problem? IE lacks a Quit command. It has no File⇨Exit command whereby you can shut down the program and instantly close all its windows. That's because Microsoft believes that Windows and IE are actually one and the same program. (At least that's how they've explained it to the U.S. government.) Therefore, without a proper Quit command, you're forced to do one of two things to stop the pop-up porn puzzle:

First, you can restart Windows.

Second, you can use another Web browser, something other than IE. Specifically, you would want a Web browser that allows you to disable something called *JavaScript*. One such Web browser is the Opera browser, available for a free test run at `www.opera.com/`.

✔ The pop-up windows appear because you either try to close a Web page window or you attempt to visit another Web page. One sneaky way around this problem is to use the Back button instead (or press the Backspace key), which often backs you out of that porn site without triggering any pop-up windows.

✔ Another way to fight porn is to get antiporn software for IE. I recommend either NetNanny or CyberSitter:

```
www.netnanny.com/
www.cybersitter.com/
```

✔ Please don't bother with the IE Content Advisor. I explain more later in this chapter.

✔ *JavaScript* is a programming language used to automate Web pages. It's responsible for displaying those pop-up windows, usually when you close a window or switch to another Web page.

✔ Only by turning off JavaScript can you utterly disable all the pop-up Windows. Alas, IE lacks such a feature. But other Web browsers, such as Opera, do have that feature, which can effectively shut down all pop-up ads on the Internet. Also see the section "JavaScript errors," a couple of sections down, for more information.

Where did the download go?

Saved a file to disk, didja? And now you can't find the file. It happens. Mostly, it happens because folks are so eager to save to disk that they forget *where* they saved to disk. But it's an easy solution: Use the Search or Find command in Windows to locate any file recently created. Refer to Chapter 9 for more information.

✔ When you download a file, be sure to choose the option that *saves* the file to disk. Do not choose the option that *runs* or *opens* the file.

✔ Sometimes, it's necessary to right-click the file's link and choose the Save Link to Disk option.

✔ Some types of files cannot be downloaded to disk. Certain MP3, Real Audio, and other media file formats can only be played over the Internet. Any attempt to download them results in a tiny file, which is merely an Internet shortcut back to the original file's location on the Internet.

JavaScript errors

JavaScript is a programming language used to automate certain things on a Web page. One of its features is that it can open new windows, which is how you get those annoying pop-up window advertisements (or "infestations"). JavaScript does good things too, such as display rollover buttons and change graphic images on a Web page — stuff you normally wouldn't care about until you get a JavaScript error message.

Figure 17-3 illustrates a typical JavaScript error. How can you tell that it's JavaScript? Well, *you* can't! But that's what it is. (I'm paid to know, plus I program JavaScript, so I'm familiar with what the errors look like.)

Figure 17-3:
An error
message
of the
JavaScript
type
(in Windows
Me).

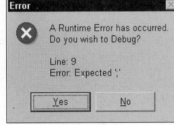

You can't fix the error, mostly because you didn't create it! IE is just reporting it to you. All you can do it tell IE *not* to report the errors in the future. You do that via the following steps — which, remarkably, work for all versions of Windows:

1. **Choose Tools⇨Internet Options to display the Internet Options dialog box.**

2. **Click the Advanced tab.**

3. **Put a check mark by the item Disable script debugging.**

4. **Click OK.**

    You never see the error messages again.

These steps do not disable JavaScript! They merely turn off the error message display, so it's just one less thing to be annoyed by.

✔ JavaScript is not the same thing as Java. No, Java is a programming language that creates programs you can run on the Internet, such as Yahoo! games or MSN games.

✔ Don't bother reporting the JavaScript error to the Web master. I mean, well, you can *try*. But it has been my experience that such reports go unnoticed.

Content Advisor Woes

Internet Explorer has a feature called the Content Advisor. Its role is to control what you see on the Internet, helping to restrict access to sites that have what you may consider to be offensive content — like that Kathie Lee Christmas Web site.

I do not recommend activating the Content Advisor. Instead, I suggest using third-party programs, such as NetNanny and Cybersitter, which I cover in "Pop-up porn puzzles," earlier in this chapter. Just leave the Content Advisor alone!

The main problem with the Content Advisor is that it's password-protected. So if you make some settings and go overboard with them — but you forget your password — you're screwed. You have no way to change password-protected Content Advisor settings. Microsoft can't help. I can't help. No one can help. So rather than risk using Content Advisor and getting stuck, I feel that it's better just to avoid the issue in the first place and *never* enable the Content Advisor.

If you can remember the password, you can disable the Content Advisor:

1. **Choose Tools⇨Internet Options from the IE menu.**

2. **In the Internet Options dialog box, click the Content tab.**

3. **Click the Disable button.**

4. **Type your password (which you remember).**

5. **Click OK.**

   A dialog box appears, to tell you what you just did.

6. **Click OK to get rid of the dialog box that tells you what you just did.**

I don't go into the details of the Content Advisor, mostly because I seldom get any troubleshooting questions on the subject. If you do set up restrictions, however, you may occasionally see a message that tells you something like "Sorry! Content Advisor will not allow you to see this site." Oh, well.

Dealing with Cookies

So it comes down to this! Cookies, huh? What do you think that this chapter should end with — dessert? You are gravely mistaken! Cookies are nothing you eat. On the Internet, they're simply a bad name for a controversial Web browsing feature.

What is a cookie?

A *cookie* is merely information a Web page saves to disk — and it isn't even that much information; it's more like random notes. The information is stored on your computer in a special Cookies folder.

When you go to visit the same Web page again, it can open the cookie it saved. That way, for example, Eddie Bauer remembers your pants size and that you enjoy seersucker. Or Amazon.com says "Hello, Dan Gookin! Welcome back! Boy, have we got some books for you!" Personally, I find that handy.

Some people, however, find the whole cookie thing annoying. They would prefer *not* to have a Web page save anything. And that's fine because you can delete cookies, disable them, turn them off, and stomp them into cookie dust! This information is all covered in the sections that follow.

✔ Web pages can open only the cookies they saved. Cookies saved from other Web pages cannot be opened. (Even if they could, the content is usually so specific that no critical information would be compromised.)

✔ All cookies expire. Some are automatically deleted when you close IE. Some are deleted in several hours or in a day or so. Some last for up to six months. But they all have expiration dates, and they are, with few exceptions, automatically deleted on those dates.

✔ My Web site, www.wambooli.com/, plants a cookie on your computer's hard drive. The cookie is used with my pop-up advertisement for my free weekly newsletter. The cookie tells the Wambooli home page that you've seen the pop-up ad so that — and this is good news — it doesn't display the pop-up ad again. Well, not for eight days or so. I consider that an example of a good cookie.

The official way of deleting cookies

If you're in for the cookies, you can delete them, swiping them from your hard drive like some frenzied couch potato urgently starting a crash diet:

1. **Choose Tools⇨Internet Options from the IE menu.**

   The Internet Options dialog box appears, with the General tab selected (refer to Figure 17-1).

2. **Click the Delete Cookies button.**

   An annoying confirmation dialog box shows up.

3. **Click OK in the annoying confirmation dialog box.**

   Lo, all your cookies have been smote.

Note that this cookie-deleting feature is available only on IE Version 6.0 and later. If you have Windows 98 or Windows Me with IE 5.0 or 5.5, you have no cookie-deleting button; you have to read the following section, on the manual way of expunging cookies.

An unofficial (yet effective) way to delete cookies

Though I admonish my readers *never* to delete any file they didn't create themselves, sometimes you can delete a file you didn't intentionally create. One of those instances happens to be with Internet cookies, which you kinda created, but not directly.

Yes, you can zap any or all your cookies to kingdom come. First job: Find the cookies.

For Windows 98 or Windows Me, you find the cookies located in the same jar: c:\Windows\Cookies:

1. **Open the Windows folder.**

   If you can't see any content, click the link on the left side of the window that displays the files in the Windows folder.

2. **Open the Cookies folder.**

   To set up for the next series of steps, display the files in Details view.

3. **Choose View⇨Details from the menu.**

   Skip down to Step 6.

In Windows XP, each user has his or her own set of cookies for each user's account. So you need to find your own account's cookie jar, which can be done this way:

1. **Open the My Computer icon on the desktop.**

2. **Open the drive C icon.**

3. **Open the Documents and Settings folder.**

4. **Open your account's folder.**

   On my computer, the folder is named Dan Gookin, which coincidentally happens to be my name.

5. **Open the Cookies folder.**

   Second job: Delete the cookies. There's nothing simpler:

6. **Select one or all of the cookie icons in the folder.**

7. **Press the Delete key on your keyboard.**

   They're gone.

A-ha! A trick: I prefer to delete ancient cookies myself. So, with Details view on the screen, I click the Modified column header to sort the cookies by date. Then I drag the mouse to delete any old, ancient cookie on the list — anything older than three months.

Close the Cookies window when you're done killing.

- ✔ The keyboard shortcut for selecting all the files in a window? Ctrl+A.

- ✔ Yes, cookies are simple text files. Most of them are only a handful of bytes long.

- ✔ The cookie is given your computer's or your account's name, followed by an at sign (@) and then the Web page domain name. Note that some Web pages save several cookies.

> ✔ You can delete an INDEX.DAT file along with the cookies. Don't worry about this file; IE can rebuild the DAT file the next time it runs.

Preventing cookies in the first place

Why bother with cookies and deleting them? If they really bug you, turn them off. You have different ways to do this, depending on your version of IE.

For IE 5.0 and IE 5.5, follow these steps:

1. **Open the Control Panel's Internet Options icon.**

   Or choose Tools➪Internet Options from the IE menu.

2. **Click the Security tab in the Internet Options dialog box.**

3. **Click the Custom Level button.**

   The Security Settings dialog box shows up, which you can see in Figure 17-4.

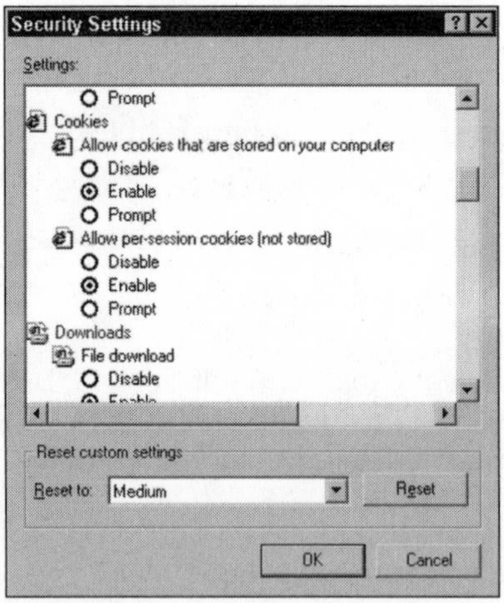

Figure 17-4:
Death to all
cookies!

4. **Scroll down to the Cookies heading, as shown in the figure.**

5. **Click Disable beneath the item labeled Allow cookies that are stored on your computer.**

6. **Click Disable beneath the option labeled Allow per-session cookies (not stored).**

7. **Click OK to close the Security Settings dialog box.**

8. **Click OK to close the Internet Properties dialog box.**

Things have changed slightly with IE 6.0. Here are the steps to take:

1. **Open the Control Panel's Internet Options icon.**

2. **Click the Privacy tab.**

   Yes, cookies are a matter of privacy, not really of security.

3. **Click the Advanced button.**

   The Advanced Privacy Settings dialog box appears (Figure 17-5), but it should really be called the Cookie dialog box.

Figure 17-5:
Death to all
cookies
(Part 2)!

4. **Click to put a check mark by Override automatic cookie handling.**

   You must do this step to enable the other options in the dialog box.

5. **Choose Block for both options in the dialog box.**

   That pretty much shuts down cookies.

6. **Click OK to close the Advanced Privacy Settings dialog box.**

7. **Close the Internet Properties dialog box.**

No more cookies!

- ✔ Cookies that are "stored on your computer" are any cookies that any Web page wants to save. These do not, however, include the per-session cookies.

- ✔ *Per-session* cookies are deleted when you close the IE window.

- ✔ *First-party* cookies are cookies owned by the Web page you're viewing.

- ✔ *Third-party* cookies are cookies saved by the advertisements on the Web page you're viewing.

Chapter 18

E-Mail Calamities with Outlook Express

Some people just live for e-mail. Therefore, you could understand that not getting e-mail or having trouble with an e-mail program (chiefly, Outlook Express) can be the cause of much teeth gnashing and anguish. Nay, even hair-pulling can accompany the many frustrations that mix with the joys of Internet e-mail.

This chapter concentrates on e-mail as the Windows Outlook Express program delivers it (or not, as the case may be). I am aware that lots of people have frustrations with Hotmail and questions about Yahoo! Mail or perhaps problems with other e-mail programs in general. But Outlook Express is the one program that ships with Windows, so to keep this chapter short, poignant, and beautiful, I concentrate only on its own troubles.

> ✔ The abbreviation OE is used in this chapter to refer to Outlook Express.
>
> ✔ There is a difference between OE and the Outlook program that ships with Microsoft Office. The programs do similar things, but they're both different programs. This book covers only OE.

General Nonsense

E-mail is such a simple thing, yet your e-mail program is perhaps the most complex application you'll ever use. I could pack an entire book full of OE tips and tricks, and not a single one of them would be considered advanced or obtuse. That's just the nature of the e-mail beast.

So, it was a tough task, but I was able to pinpoint a few key nonsensical issues with OE and stuff these and their solutions into the sections that follow.

"The Contacts panel is missing!"

Outlook Express divides its screen into several panels, as shown in Figure 18-1. These panels are customizable and utterly controllable by you, though most folks prefer to keep things set up as shown in the figure.

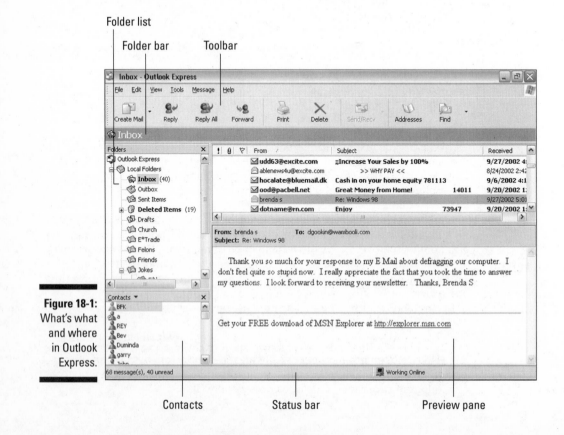

Figure 18-1: What's what and where in Outlook Express.

The problem? The Contacts list (in the lower-left corner) as well as the Folders list (just above Contacts) have X close buttons on them. So it's possible to accidentally close those panels and then freak out at their absence.

To get the missing panels back, choose View➪Layout. This command displays the Window Layout Properties dialog box, as shown in Figure 18-2. You can restore any or all or even more of the OE window by choosing the proper items from the dialog box.

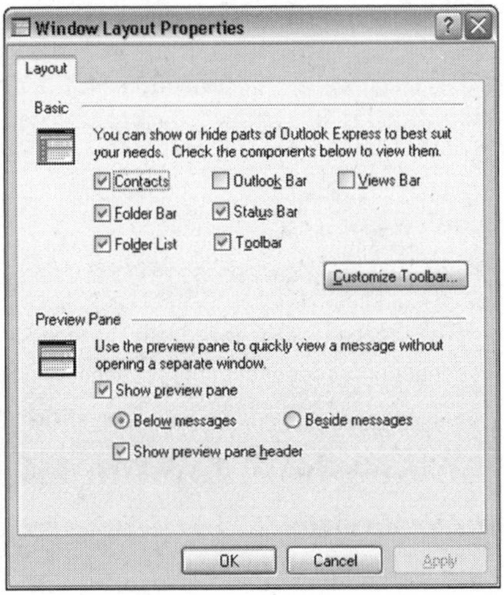

Figure 18-2:
The secret location where stuff is restored.

For example, to restore the Contacts list, put a check mark by Contacts and then click OK.

✔ You can also turn the Preview Pane on or off by using the Window Layout Properties dialog box.

✔ Because OE appears behind the Window Layout Properties dialog box, you can experiment with various views and arrangements. Just click to add or remove a check mark and click the Apply button to see how the OE window is affected.

Unable to spell-check

Outlook Express does not have its own spell checker. Though spell-checking is a feature in OE, it must come from another Microsoft product; either Works or Word or Office must be installed for spell-checking to work in OE.

The spell checker is a *shared* Microsoft file, which must be provided by another Microsoft program. Without that shared file, you cannot spell-check in OE.

Receiving duplicate messages

If your ISP is sending you two copies of every message, you should check with them first for reasons that it may be happening. It could be a problem on their end.

If you have OE Versions 5.0 or 5.5, the problem could lie in a file called POP3UIDL.DBX. You need to disable that file to fix the duplicate mail issue. Here's how:

1. **Quit Outlook Express if you're using it.**

2. **Search for the file POP3UIDL.DBX on your computer.**

   Refer to Chapter 9 for file-finding instructions. This file should be on drive C somewhere.

   When you find the file, it's listed in the Search Results window.

3. **Right-click the POP3UIDL.DBX file icon in the Search Results window.**

4. **Choose Rename from the pop-up menu.**

5. **Change the DBX part of the name to BAK.**

   So the file is renamed to POP3UIDL.BAK.

6. **Press the Enter key to lock in the name change.**

7. **Close the Search Results window.**

8. **Start Outlook Express.**

   OE should rebuild the POP3UIDL.DBX file when it restarts, which fixes the problem.

If the problem isn't fixed, you can check another place (isn't that always true?):

1. **Choose Tools⇨Accounts from the OE menu.**

2. **Click the Mail tab.**

3. **Select your mail account from the list.**

   Or, it may be the only account on the list.

4. **Click the Properties button.**

   Your e-mail account's Properties dialog box appears.

5. Click the Advanced tab.

In the bottom of the dialog box is a Delivery option, as shown in Figure 18-3. If the option Leave a copy of messages on server is checked, that explains your duplicate pick-up.

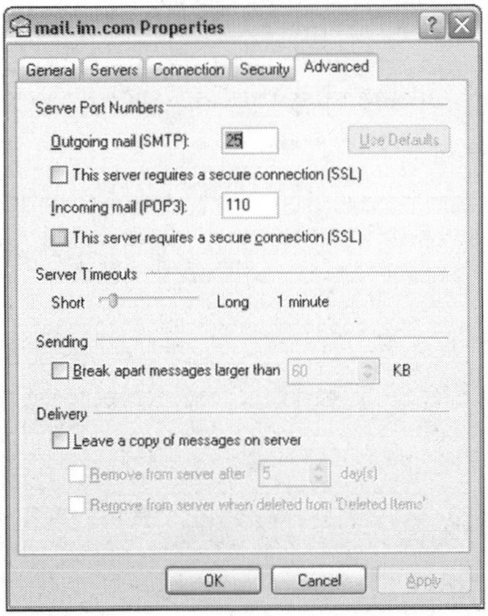

Figure 18-3:
Checking for that nasty Leave mail on server option.

6. Uncheck the box by Leave a copy of messages on server.

That fixes it.

For other versions of OE, or if neither of these tricks works, you need to contact your ISP for a fix.

Displaying the BCC field

The problem? OE doesn't normally display the BCC field when you go to create a new message. BCC, the Blind Carbon Copy field, is used to send e-mail to people secretly; e-mail addresses put in the BCC field don't appear when the final message is received. This stealth nature makes the BCC field ideal for sending to a batch of people and not having each of them see the whole list of e-mail addresses — very tidy.

The solution: Choose View➪All Headers from the New Message window. That command displays the BCC header, and away you go.

For more information on the BCC header, refer to my book *PCs For Dummies* (published by Wiley Publishing, Inc.).

Fragmenting large messages

Another obscure option that OE has is to split large messages into separate chunks. I assume that this feature has some pressing, possibly historical, purpose. But most of the time what happens is that your recipient complains that rather than get that MPEG movie of you at Niagara Falls, they get 50 smaller junk files from you that make no sense.

Here's how to prevent OE from splitting up a long message:

1. **Choose Tools⇨Accounts.**

2. **Click the Mail tab.**

3. **If your e-mail account isn't selected, click it on the list.**

4. **Click the Properties button.**

5. **Click the Advanced tab.**

   Yes, it's the same dialog box shown in Figure 18-3. This time, note the Sending area. Is that item checked?

6. **Uncheck the Break apart messages larger than [blank] KB item.**

   This step tells OE *not* to split apart large messages.

People complain that you send them unreadable messages

Outlook Express sends e-mail using the Web page formatting language, HTML. That way, you can add pictures, formatted text, and other fun things to your e-mail, making it more exciting than plain text.

The problem is that not everyone uses OE. Some people use e-mail programs that cannot properly interpret the HTML-formatted e-mail that OE sends. For those cases, you need to send those folks plain, or *unformatted,* e-mail.

To switch over to plain text in a New Message window, choose Format⇨Plain Text. You may see a warning dialog box, but it's just telling you what you need to know; click OK.

To send out all your e-mail as plain text, follow these steps:

1. **Choose Tools⇨Options in the OE main window.**

   The Options dialog box appears.

    2. Click the Send tab.

    3. Choose Plain text from the Mail Sending Format area.

    4. Click OK.

I consider the sending of plain text to be a courtesy to other, non-Windows users on the Internet. People do forget that fancy formatting and colored text may look good on your computer, but may appear too small or even invisible on someone else's screen.

    ✔ When you choose plain-text formatting, the formatting toolbar in the New Message window disappears.

    ✔ To get an idea of how your message may look in an e-mail program that doesn't support HTML messages, click the Source tab in the New Message window. Yuck. (This trick works only in OE Versions 6.0 and later.)

Folder Folderol

Folders are a great way to organize your e-mail — and I'm talking about folders beyond just the basic Inbox, Outbox, Sent Items, and Deleted Items folders. As you can see from Figure 18-1, I have many folders that I play with for stashing and hoarding my e-mail. You should too — but this isn't the place to lecture you about folders. Instead, let me just get to the two key OE folder issues I often get quizzed about.

The mystery of the Drafts folder

The Drafts folder should really be called the I'm-not-quite-ready-to-send folder. But it's too late to change that now! Instead, the Drafts folder merely poses a puzzle to those who often find their e-mail in there.

How does a message get into the Drafts folder? The Drafts folder is the Outlook Express dead-letter office. It holds e-mail you don't want to send. Rather than click the Send button for a message, you instead closed the messages window. OE asked whether you wanted to save the message, and you said yes. So OE stuck the message in the Drafts folder, where it lingers until you're ready to try to send it again.

How does one get a message out of the Drafts folder? Open the message, edit it if you will, and click the Send button. That sends the message off.

✔ Newer versions of OE *tell* you that the message is being saved in the Drafts folder. Most of the Drafts folder questions I get via e-mail are from users of older versions of OE, where it didn't explain how the messages got into the Drafts folder.

✔ You can also drag a message out of the Drafts folder and into any other folder. Or, if you find that dragging doesn't work, select the message and choose Edit⇨Move to Folder from the menu. Then choose the destination folder from the Move dialog box.

Copying an e-mail folder to a "real" folder

E-mail folders aren't the same thing as real folders in Windows. They're *fake* folders. In fact, an e-mail folder is nothing more than a very large text file hidden somewhere on your PC's hard drive. It only looks like a folder in Outlook Express.

This folder puzzle brings up an interesting issue: How would someone save all the messages in a folder to a real folder out there on the hard drive? The answer is: with much time and patience.

Although you can save any individual message to disk (choose File⇨Save As), you cannot save groups of them to disk at a time. So you're stuck with going through the folder and individually saving each message into a "real" folder on the hard drive.

✔ An e-mail folder in OE is basically a long text file. OE itself splits up the text file so that it appears that there are separate messages — but what you're really looking at is simply a very long text file.

✔ The location of the mail folder/text file is kept secret in Windows; Microsoft really doesn't want you messing with the files.

✔ They're not *exactly* text files. But they contain enough text that you can open them in NotePad or WordPad and be able to read some of the mail.

✔ If you want to search for the file's location, use the Search or Find command, as described in Chapter 9, and look for a file named INBOX.DBX. That's the official name of your e-mail Inbox folder and file.

Any way to undelete a message?

When you delete a message in OE, the message is put into the Deleted Items folder, so it's not really deleted. To undelete the message, open the Deleted Items folder and right-click the message you want to undelete. Then choose Move to Folder from the pop-up menu. That command allows you to recover the so-called deleted message to a specific folder.

Unfortunately, if you empty the Deleted Items folder, the e-mail is gone for good and cannot be recovered. Alas.

✔ No, not even the Norton Utilities or any other unerase program can recover e-mail deleted from the Deleted Items folder.

✔ To empty the Deleted Items folder, choose Edit➪Empty 'Deleted Items' folder. (This command is available only if messages are in the Deleted Items folder.)

✔ You can also have OE automatically dump out the Deleted Items folder every time you quit OE: Choose Tools➪Options and in the Options dialog box, click the Maintenance tab. Put a check mark by Empty messages from the 'Deleted Items' folder on exit. Click OK.

Attachment Adversity

Along with e-mail comes . . . attachments! What a remarkable invention. Attachments make boring old e-mail all the more exciting. You can see pictures of the grandkids. Get a silly tune from Uncle Chet. Or have Aunt Ruth forward you *another* e-mail virus. It's a thrill-a-minute with e-mail attachments!

Here are some attachment highlights for troubleshooting. If you want more detailed information on attachments in general, you should see my book *PCs For Dummies* (published by Wiley Publishing, Inc.), which goes into all sorts of painless e-mail attachment detail.

You just cannot open this attachment!

Try as you can, the attachment doesn't open. Either you have no option to open it or, when you open it, Windows presents you with an Open With What? dialog box and no apparently obvious or useful choice is available. What to do? What to do?

My advice: Give up. I'm serious. If your computer cannot open the attachment, Windows simply lacks the necessary software. Other than rush out and buy that software (and remember that you don't exactly know which software it is), there's nothing you can do.

In this situation, I respond to the message by telling the sender that I cannot open the attachment and asking whether they can resend it in a more common format. For pictures, JPEG or JPG is the most common format. For documents, HTML, RTF, and PDF are common.

- Those PSS files are PowerPoint Slide Show files, which people often e-mail to others without considering that not all of us have the PowerPoint program. (You can, however, pick up a free PowerPoint viewer from `www.microsoft.com`; follow the links for Microsoft Office downloads.)

- PSD files are Photoshop images. Have the sender resend the image in JPG format.

- WPD and WPS files are WordPerfect files: Attention, WordPerfect users: Save your documents as either plain-text (TXT) or RTF files. Thank you.

- MPG, MOV, and AVI are movie files. They represent three different movie file formats. Your computer is guaranteed to play at least two of them, and the third format is the one that everyone always e-mails to you.

But my Macintosh friend swears it's a real JPG image!

The Macintosh, as well as other computers, uses a different method to identify files on disk. In Windows, the last few characters of a file's name (following a period) indicate which type of file you have. So MONALISA.JPG is a JPG file — a graphics image. But MONALISA.TXT is a TXT file, which is a text file.

File extensions — the .JPG part of a file that lets a Windows computer know that you have a JPG image — are not required on a Macintosh. So if some Mac dweeb sends you a file named MONALISA, your PC will have a tough time figuring out what type of file it is.

If the Mac dweeb swears that it's a JPG file, rename the file to MONALISA.JPG (or whatever the file's first name is, followed by JPG).

You just can't go around randomly naming files. If someone sends you a file SOMETHING, ask what type of file it is. That way, you can properly rename the file so that Windows recognizes it.

- Text files end in TXT.

- Graphics files can end in GIF, BMP, TIFF, JPG, and a host of other *file-name extensions*. You must check with whoever sent you the file to see which type it is.

Beware of AOL .ART files

AOL uses a proprietary graphics format named ART. These files appear as graphical images when AOL users e-mail them to each other or view them on their own computers. But ART files are utterly incompatible with computers that don't have AOL installed. (You _must_ use AOL to view an ART file.)

If you're an AOL user and want to send graphics, ensure that the image isn't an ART file. Likewise, if you receive an ART image from an AOL user, understand that you cannot view it.

The solution lies on the AOL user's side. In the Web Graphics section of the Preferences, choose setting B, Never compress graphics. That action fixes the ART problem and makes your images more compatible with other software and other people on the Internet.

The attachment never got there!

For a number of reasons, a file attachment may not make it to its recipient:

✔ An attachment may be too large and get rejected (based on its size) by either your own ISP or the recipient's ISP.

✔ If the recipient is using AOL, AOL doesn't accept certain types of file attachments.

✔ Antivirus or firewall software can prevent an attachment from arriving.

✔ The recipient may be using an e-mail program that doesn't allow or understand attachments.

✔ The recipient may not notice or may ignore the attachment.

In most cases, you can try sending the attachment again. If that fails, you have to use a floppy disk, Zip disk, or CD-R and mail it through the regular postal mail.

Printing an e-mail attachment

OE has no method to print an e-mail attachment. Sure, you can print e-mail, but if you just want to print the attachment, you have to save the attachment to disk, open a program to view the attachment, and print from within that program.

Vain Efforts to Filter Spam

Congratulations if you're one of the few who has figured out how to use the message rules or Blocked Senders list in OE to help cut down on that filthy, unwanted e-mail known popularly as *spam*.

I would love to get into the whole message-rules creation stuff here, but that's not the point of this book. Instead, here are a few sections on various problems that come up when you get too resolutely bold with your spam-fighting efforts.

Reviewing your message rules

Alas, I don't have the space to get into creating message rules here, though I can help guide you with fixing them:

1. **Choose Tools➪Message Rules➪Mail.**

   This step displays the Message Rules/Mail Rules window, as shown in Figure 18-4.

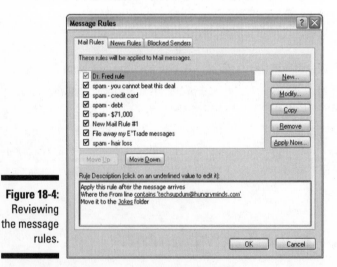

Figure 18-4: Reviewing the message rules.

2. **Review each rule: Click a rule to select it.**

   Read through the rule description. Fortunately, the descriptions are English-like, so they do make sense. Watch out for rules that delete mail. Ensure that the proper mail is getting deleted and that the rule cannot be misinterpreted.

If you're concerned about deleting mail, change the various mail-deleting rules so that the mail goes instead to a specific folder where you can review it later.

3. **Select and review the next rule.**

   And so on, until you've reviewed them all.

4. **Close the Message Rules window.**

   Click OK.

Be careful with rules! I once made an overly aggressive rule that deleted *all* my incoming mail. Oops! So before you assume that it's a light mail day, double-check your rules!

Unblocking accidentally blocked senders

Rather than create rules, many people simply choose Message⇨Block Sender, which instantly deletes any new mail from a specific person. It's a handy trick to use because most of your unwanted e-mail does come from the same idiots most of the time.

Occasionally, you may add someone unintentionally to the Blocked Senders list. If so, you can easily remove them and unblock their e-mail:

1. **Choose Tools⇨Message Rules⇨Blocked Senders List.**

   You see a dialog box listing all the blocked senders.

2. **Scroll though the list for the person you accidentally added.**

3. **Highlight the name you want to unblock.**

4. **Click the Remove button.**

   This step puts the person back to unblocked status — and restores peace in the family if they just happened to be a relative.

Chapter 19

General Windows Disruption (Or, "Is This PC Possessed?")

Any time you have a visual operating system, such as Windows, you see weird stuff on the screen. Perhaps it's not weird, but more like unexpected or unwelcome. It's like the computer is possessed at times. You may be in the driver's seat, but something else is definitely steering!

I don't need to lead everyone down the fearful path of superstition and panic. Although everyone definitely goes through PC rituals (I like pressing and holding the Enter key when I save a file), most of the weird or common disruptions can be blamed on logical, explainable things. Granted, there are probably lots of them, but I tried to limit this chapter's coverage to the most common, interesting, and, well, plain weird.

"That Looks Stupid"

Sure, it looks stupid! And calling something stupid is quite offensive. But you know what? Stupid is easy to recognize. I know stupid when I see it. The following sections cover some of the most stupid-looking things in all of Windows.

Dealing with two desktop images (wallpaper)

This problem happens specifically in Windows 98 and Windows Me. With those versions of Windows, you can have two separate wallpapers, or desktop backgrounds.

The first is what I call the traditional background. It's a BMP (Windows Paint) program you've chosen using the Display Properties dialog box.

The second, however, is a newfangled background — typically, a GIF or JPEG image that was chosen by using the Active Desktop feature. That second image overlays the first image, creating two desktops — and sometimes even obscuring icons and other goodies.

The solution is to eliminate the second wallpaper:

1. **Right-click the desktop.**

2. **Choose Properties from the pop-up menu.**

   This step quickly summons the Display Properties dialog box.

3. **Click the Web tab.**

4. **Uncheck the item View my Active Desktop as a web page.**

5. **Click OK.**

The problem now is that you're stuck with the old BMP wallpaper and perhaps you still want the newer JPG or GIF image instead. To make that happen, you should convert the image from JPG or GIF to BMP: Use the Paint program to open the JPG or GIF image. Then use File➪Save as to save it as a BMP image.

In the Save As dialog box, choose 24-bit Bitmap from the Save as type drop-down list, as shown in Figure 19-1. That converts the image for use as standard wallpaper, which eliminates the duplicate wallpaper weirdness.

✔ Windows XP doesn't have this problem.

✔ This problem is a sneaky weird thing because you're not really certain about what you've done; you've just chosen a JPG or GIF graphics as the background wallpaper image. The consequences of that aren't apparent — until you see the second image, usually as Windows first starts up or as it shuts down.

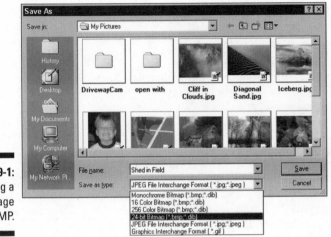

Figure 19-1:
Saving a
JPG image
as a BMP.

Screwy colors

Perhaps you intended that bright red-and-pink theme for Windows? Certainly, the colors are striking. No? Not you? Then your 4-year-old, perhaps? The dark purple and black-on-black makes such a statement. Obviously, the kid has talent!

Colors can grow screwy in two ways. The first is the most definite way, which is when you go nuts inside the Display Properties dialog box, on the Appearance tab in Windows 98 or Windows Me, as shown in Figure 19-2. Windows really doesn't care about your taste, so you can choose some really odd combinations there — and live to regret it later.

How to undo the nonsense? If you can *see* the screen just fine, follow these steps as written. If you're having trouble seeing things, start the computer in Safe mode; see Appendix B for more information.

1. **Right-click the desktop.**

2. **Choose Properties from the pop-up menu.**

3. **Click the Appearance tab.**

4. **Choose Windows Standard from the Scheme drop-down list.**

5. **Click OK.**

   That should fix it.

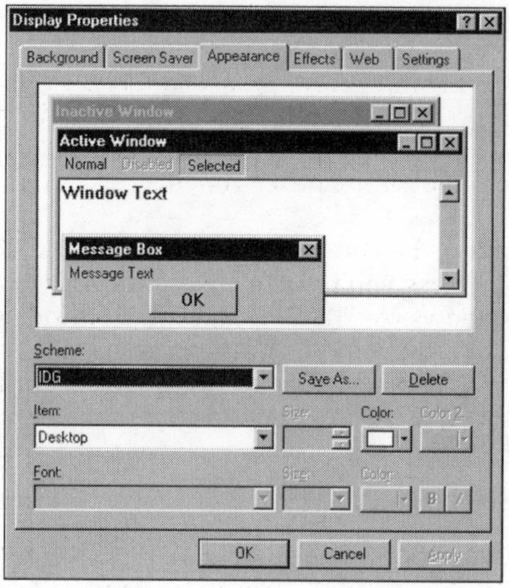

Figure 19-2:
Don't go
nuts in
this-here
dialog box.

If you can't see the screen and would rather fix it quickly using the keyboard, follow these in-the-dark steps:

1. **Right-click the desktop.**

2. **Press the R key.**

   This step chooses Properties from the pop-up menu.

3. **Press Ctrl+Tab.**

   This step selects the Screen Saver tab in the Display Properties dialog box.

4. **Press Ctrl+Tab again.**

   This step selects the Appearance tab.

5. **Press Alt+S.**

   This step selects the Scheme drop-down list.

6. **Press W.**

   This step selects the Wheat scheme.

7. **Press the down-arrow key.**

   This step selects the Windows Standard scheme.

8. **Press Enter.**

   And that step locks in the display, returning to the Windows Standard scheme.

Both these sets of steps restore the Windows Standard scheme, which is what Windows 98 and Windows Me ship with. If you have your own set of custom colors defined, I recommend saving that set to disk as its own scheme: On the Display Properties/Appearance tab, set up your colors as you like them, just so. Click the Save As button. Give your scheme a name and click OK. That way, you can restore your favorite colors whenever you like.

✔ Windows XP doesn't allow the colors to be messed with as Windows 98 or Windows Me did — unless you're running Windows XP to make it look like Windows 98 or Windows Me. To do that, visit the Windows XP Display Properties dialog box. On the Appearance tab, choose Windows Classic style from the Windows and buttons drop-down list. You can then use the Advanced button in the same dialog box to adjust the colors.

✔ For handling problems with the screen's resolution, refer to Chapter 6.

✔ Another instance of color weirdness happens when the colors of icons, and especially the Start button, seem to flash or rapidly change — like the transporter effect from *Star Trek*. That's the sign of a bad or corrupted video driver. Refer to Chapter 6 for information on upgrading or restoring your video driver.

Jiggling icons

The infamous jiggly icon weird thing happens like this: You go to point the mouse at an icon, and the icon moves away from the mouse. You try again, and the same thing happens. It's like the icons are afraid of the mouse. Annoying? Or could it be amusing?

You see, this jiggly icon thing is someone's idea of a joke. Or, more seriously, it's a *virus*. The virus exists as an e-mail attachment that's probably hanging on some message in the Outlook Express Inbox.

The quick solution: Go through your Inbox and remove every message. Just empty the Deleted Items folder: Choose Edit⇨Empty 'Deleted Items' Folder. That fixes it in a drastic way.

If you want to be less drastic, just go through your Inbox looking for any e-mail with an attachment. Graphics attachments are okay, but anything else is suspect as the cause of the virus. Delete 'em.

Of course, buying and using antivirus software would prevent this and other viruses from happening in the first place.

Getting more stuff on the screen

You can't make the screen bigger. I wish you could! But no such thing as a screen-stretcher exists; a 17-inch monitor can display only so much information. If you want more stuff on the screen, the solution is to increase the screen's resolution.

Chapter 6 contains information on setting the screen's resolution. Look there for more information.

Resetting the screen's resolution to something higher does make things look smaller on the screen. You can do two things:

First, in your applications, you can take advantage of the Zoom command, usually found on the View menu. The Zoom command magnifies the contents of the window so that everything is easier to read.

Second, you can make Windows own icons appear larger:

1. **Right-click the desktop.**

2. **Choose Properties from the pop-up menu.**

    This step conjures up the Display Properties dialog box.

3a. **In Windows 98 or Windows Me, click the Effects tab.**

3b. **In Windows XP, click the Appearance tab and click the Effects button.**

4. **Put a check mark by the Use large icons item.**

5. **Close the various dialog boxes.**

    When the last one is closed, you see the new, larger icons on the screen.

You can also use a command to change the icon size on the Start button's menus, though these are already set to Large in most configurations. To check the icon size on the Start button menu, follow the next set of steps that apply to your version of Windows.

In Windows 98 or Windows Me:

1. **Right-click the taskbar.**

    Click a blank area on the taskbar, not on a button. If you can't seem to find a blank area, right-click the time display on the far right side of the taskbar.

2. **Choose Properties from the pop-up menu.**

    The Taskbar Properties dialog box appears.

3. **Look for the item Show small icons in Start menu.**

Leaving this item unchecked keeps the icons big. If the box is checked and you want larger icons, uncheck it.

4. **Close the dialog box.**

In Windows XP:

1. **Right-click the Start button.**

2. **Choose Properties from the pop-up menu.**

3. **Click the Customize button.**

   You see two Customize buttons. Click the top one, next to the Start menu item.

   The Customize Start Menu dialog box appears. The icon size item is right there on top on the General tab.

4. **Choose Large icons (if it's not chosen already).**

5. **Click OK and then OK again.**

Your screen saver seizes the system

People used to have lots of issues about screen savers as well as "sleeping" the monitor to save power. For example, in many early Windows 95 and a few Windows 98 systems, sleeping the monitor would result in the whole computer going comatose. Today, however, these problems are rare.

If you notice that the computer seems to die whenever the screen saver kicks in, disable the screen saver or simply choose another screen saver. Especially if you downloaded the screen saver from the Internet, consider that the screen saver itself is causing the problem and not anything else in the computer.

✔ You choose the screen saver on the Screen Saver tab in the Display Properties dialog box.

✔ If the computer seems to have trouble with sleep mode or any other power-saving feature, check with the computer manufacturer or your dealer to see whether it's a known problem and whether a fix is available. Often, you can find this information by visiting the computer manufacturer's Web site. Refer to Chapter 5 for more information.

The window has slid off the screen

Moving a window on the screen is so easy that few beginning Windows books even bother to explain it in any detail: You use the mouse to *drag* the window around. Simple. But it's not so simple when you can't pinch the top part of the window by using the mouse. In fact, I've known some folks who get so desperate to get the window back that they just end up reinstalling Windows. Bad move!

The trick to getting any window to move when it's off the screen is the same trick you use to move a window when the mouse is broken: Use the keyboard!

These steps assume that a window you want to move is on the screen. Click that window to make it "on top" and selected.

1. **Press Alt+Spacebar.**

   This command activates the window's Control menu.

2. **Press M for *move*.**

   Now you can use the keyboard's arrow keys to move the window.

3. **Press the left, right, up, or down arrow to move the window in that direction.**

4. **When you're done moving the window, press the Enter key.**

The window is too large for the screen

Resizing a large window is next to impossible when you can't grab its edges with the mouse. The solution here is to use the keyboard to help resize the window:

1. **Ensure that the window isn't maximized.**

   You cannot resize a maximized window; click the Restore button (the middle button in the window's upper-right corner) to unmaximize the window.

2. **Press Alt+Spacebar.**

   This keyboard command drops down the window's Control menu.

3. **Press S for *size*.**

   You can now move each of the window's four sides in or out. You do that by first choosing a side and moving the side in or out.

4. **Press the left, right, up, or down arrow to move that side of the window.**

   For example, press the left-arrow key to choose the left side of the window.

5. **Use the left–right or up–down arrow keys to move the window's edge.**

For example, if you chose the left side of the window, press the left or right arrow keys to move that side of the window.

6. **Press Enter when you're done resizing that edge.**

7. **Repeat Steps 2–6 to resize another edge of the window.**

For example, to resize the bottom edge of the window, press Alt+Spacebar, S, and then the down-arrow key to select the bottom edge. Then use the up or down keys to move that edge in or out.

These steps may seem confusing, but if you work through them and actually mess with the window's size, they make sense. Just be thankful that such an alternative window-resizing technique exists.

The window is too tiny

Windows remembers the size and position of any window you open on the screen. When you return to a program or open a folder again, Windows sticks the window back in the spot in which it originally existed and at the same size as when you last used the window.

The problem is that sometimes Windows restores a window that you've resized to be very tiny. Most people just maximize the window at this point, but the problem is that Windows doesn't remember maximized windows. No, instead, the window is opened again at its tiny size.

The solution is to resize the window *without* maximizing it: Use the mouse to drag out the window's edges (top, bottom, right, left) to the size and position you prefer on the screen. With the window larger — but not maximized — you can close it. Then, when that window is reopened, it opens to the larger size.

The taskbar has moved

On my long sheet of Windows regrets is the inability to move the taskbar. I'm certain that someone at Microsoft thought it would be handy to have a taskbar on the left, right, or top of the computer screen. In practice, in my experience? I've *never* seen a taskbar anywhere but the bottom of the screen. Even so, the ability to move the taskbar exists, and many people do accidentally move it — and then desperately want it back on the bottom.

You can move the taskbar just as you can move any window on the screen: Drag it with the mouse. The key, however, is to *close all open windows* so that you can easily grab the taskbar with the mouse.

To move the taskbar back to the bottom of the screen, follow these steps:

1. **Point the mouse at the taskbar (on a spot that has no buttons).**

2. **Press the mouse button.**

3. **Drag the mouse pointer to the bottom of the screen.**

If these steps don't work, you can try using the keyboard and mouse together:

1. **Click the taskbar once.**

   Click a blank spot that has no buttons.

2. **Press Alt+Spacebar.**

   This step pops up a menu. If not, start over again with Step 1.

3. **Press M for *m*ove.**

4. **Press and hold the down arrow key until the mouse pointer is close to the bottom of the screen.**

   If this step doesn't move the taskbar, press the left-arrow key and hold it down. If that doesn't work, press the right-arrow key and hold it down.

5. **Click the mouse when you're done.**

The object is to use the keyboard to move the mouse pointer to where you want the taskbar. Use all four arrow keys — left, right, up, and down — to move the taskbar.

- ✔ Yes, you can accidentally move the taskbar. It happens all the time.

- ✔ Also, mean people move or hide the taskbar. They call it a practical joke, though there's nothing practical about it, nor is it funny.

- ✔ If the moving taskbar frustrates you, I highly recommend that you get used to moving it about. The easier it is for you to move the taskbar through practice, the easier it is to restore it later when it does accidentally jump around.

- ✔ In Windows XP, you can blissfully *lock down* the taskbar: Right-click the Start button and choose Properties from the pop-up menu. Click the Taskbar tab and put a check mark by Lock the taskbar. Click OK.

The taskbar has disappeared

The taskbar cannot disappear, but it can hide. It can also grow so thin as to seem invisible, although it's still there.

First, make sure that you're not using a program in full-screen mode, which would hide the taskbar. Most full-screen programs keep one button or menu item available to allow you to de-full-screen the program. Or, you can try pressing the F10 key to summon the menu bar and try to restore the screen. In Internet Explorer, press the F11 key to unzoom from full-screen mode.

Second, see whether the taskbar is simply too skinny to see. Check each edge of the screen for a thin, gray strip. If you find it, you've found the taskbar: Point the mouse at the strip, and it changes into an up-down pointing arrow (or a left-right pointing arrow if the taskbar is on the side of the screen). Press the mouse button and *drag* the mouse in toward the center of the screen. As you drag, the taskbar grows fatter. Release the mouse button when the taskbar is the proper size.

Third, the taskbar may be automatically hidden, which is an option. To check, point the mouse where the taskbar normally lives and wait. The taskbar should pop right up. (If not, try pointing at the other three edges of the screen to see whether some joker moved *and hid* the taskbar.)

If the taskbar pops up, you can switch off its auto-hide feature:

1. **Summon the Taskbar Properties dialog box.**

   In Windows 98 or Windows Me, right-click the taskbar and choose Properties from the pop-up menu.

   In Windows XP, right-click the Start button and choose Properties from the pop-up menu. Then click the Taskbar tab in the Taskbar and Start Menu Properties dialog box.

2. **Remove the check mark by the Auto hide or Auto-hide the taskbar item.**

   Note the Lock the taskbar item in Windows XP. Click to select it if you don't want the taskbar messed with again.

3. **While you're at it, click to select the Always on top or Keep the taskbar on top of other windows item.**

   Putting a check mark by that item also helps keep the taskbar from hiding.

4. **Click OK.**

You Open the File and You Get Crap

It's supposed to work like this: You choose File⇨Open and pluck out a file, and there it sits on the screen, all happy and eager to be edited or otherwise messed with. But what *really* happens is this: You choose File⇨Open, or you double-click some icon to open it, and you get . . . crap! Not the content, but visually: junky text. It's definitely not what you saved. What happened?

First, it's not *your* fault. (You may remember that from Chapter 1.)

Second, you may be using the wrong format to open the file, which is a common screw-up in most Open dialog boxes.

Suppose that you try to open a file in Word just to recover text. If so, you choose the option Recover Text from Any File (*.*) from the Files of type drop-down list in Word's Open dialog box, as shown in Figure 19-3. So you open the file and mess around and you're happenin'.

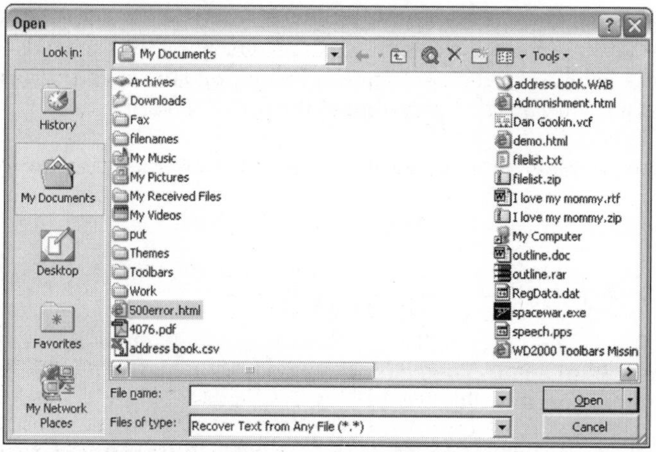

Figure 19-3: Beware the Files of type drop-down list!

Then you go to open the document you've been working on and . . . you get crap! Okay, maybe it's not pure ugliness, but you may notice that your formatting is gone or perhaps that random characters have infiltrated the text. Or, in a graphics program, the colors may be all screwed up.

Relax! What happened is that you misused the Open dialog box and opened a file of one type as another. For example, if you open a Word document but choose Recover Text from Any File (*.*) from the Files of type drop-down list in Word's Open dialog box, you see plain text on the screen — not a formatted Word document.

The solution is to close the document. Do not save any changes! Then reopen the document by first selecting the proper document type from the Files of type drop-down list in the Open dialog box.

✔ This error is quite common, particularly with Microsoft Word.

✔ Sometimes files do get corrupted. If the file still opens as garbage, it probably is garbage. That happens, usually because of some type of disk error. Run Scandisk on your hard drive to check for errors; see Chapter 21.

Uninstalling Uninstalled Programs

You never delete a program from Windows. No, you're supposed to *uninstall* it instead. You use the Add/Remove Programs icon in the Control Panel, and you uninstall the program.

The uninstall routine has worked very well for recent editions of Windows and those recent applications that thoroughly obey the uninstall concept. Many problems occurred back in the Windows 95 days with programs that didn't exactly uninstall. Today, uninstalling isn't a big issue.

Okay. Maybe that's a lie. Uninstalling still involves problems, but you also have solutions.

Use CleanSweep, my boy!

My first solution suggestion is to buy the Norton CleanSweep program. CleanSweep does a much, *much* better job of analyzing a program's installation so that uninstalling the same program with CleanSweep yields fewer problems. Plus, CleanSweep archives uninstalled programs so that you can reinstall bits and pieces of it later if that proves necessary. I highly recommend this product, though you should be aware that it works best on applications installed *after* CleanSweep is installed.

For more information on CleanSweep, see www.symantec.com/.

Giving up and deleting the damn programs

This suggestion is rather sneaky: You may notice that after you attempt to uninstall a program the "real" way, remnants of the program still litter your hard drive. In this case, my advice is simple: Delete the remnants. Specifically, delete any files left in the application's main folder.

Suppose that you do away with a program named Northern Hemisphere On-line (NHO). You've resigned from the service. You've uninstalled the program.

Yet, you notice that you still have an NHO folder with plenty of files installed. In that case, feel free to delete that folder and its contents.

This action may have adverse side effects, so be prepared to undelete the folder if necessary. Or, better, just rename the folder and see whether it affects anything. Rename the NHO folder to NHO.KILL, for example. If this trick doesn't seem to bother the rest of Windows, feel free to delete the folder and its contents.

✔ I recommend that you don't delete any program you didn't create yourself. However, if a program doesn't fully uninstall and you need the disk space, you can delete remnants of the program from its old folder.

✔ Do not delete any program remnants saved in the Windows folder or any of the subfolders beneath the Windows folder.

✔ Sometimes, the remnants are left around in the hope that you may reinstall the program later. For example, I uninstalled a game, but noticed that it kept personal data — saved missions and high scores — in the folder.

✔ You can freely delete remnants such as shortcut icons: Right-click any shortcut icon and choose Delete from the pop-up menu to rid yourself of that icon. You can do that on the desktop as well as on the Start menu.

✔ Also consider checking the System Configuration utility (MSCONFIG) and its Startup tab to see whether bits and pieces of the program are still being started there. (NHO is notorious for this.) See Appendix A for more information on the System Configuration utility.

The uninstalled program remains on the stupid Add/Remove Programs list

Here's a pain in the arse: You do everything properly and go about uninstalling a program the way Lord Gates intended, yet the stupid program name still appears on the list of installed programs in the Add or Remove Program dialog box. How maddening! How rude! How wrong!

The solution is surgical:

1. **Carefully note the name of the program as listed in the Add/Remove Programs dialog box.**

2. **Close the Add/Remove Programs dialog box.**

3. **Choose Run from the Start menu.**

4. **Type** REGEDIT **into the box.**

5. **Click OK.**

   This step runs the Registry Editor.

6. **Open the following folders:**

   HKEY_LOCAL_MACHINE

   Software

   Microsoft

   Windows

   CurrentVersion

   Uninstall

   This location is where Windows keeps the installed program list for the Add/Remove Programs dialog box.

7. **Look for your program on the list.**

8. **Select your program's entry.**

9. **Press the Delete key on the keyboard.**

10. **Click the Yes button when you're asked to confirm.**

    The item is now gone from the list.

The Big, Scary Question of Reinstalling Windows

At some point, reinstalling Windows became acceptable. And I'll be honest: Reinstalling Windows works. It absolutely restores your computer to the way it was when you first got it or when Windows was last upgraded. It's a guaranteed fix, but it's a cheat.

It's a cheat because you usually have a simpler, easier way to fix the problem than to resort to reinstalling Windows. For example, consider going to the doctor for an irregular heartbeat and they recommend a heart transplant. Or go to a mechanic because your engine knocks and they recommend replacing the entire engine. Reinstalling Windows is the same overblown, waste-of-time solution.

Fundamentally, an operating system should never need to be reinstalled. Just quiz a Unix wizard on how many times he has to reinstall Unix, and you get this puzzled, insane look. Even in the days of DOS, reinstalling DOS was never considered a solution. But with 15-minute time limits on tech support phone calls (refer to Chapter 5), suddenly reinstalling Windows is not only a potential solution, most often it's *the* solution.

Poppycock!

- Reinstalling Windows is a solution only when the system has become so corrupted that no other solution exists. For example, if your computer is attacked by a virus or somehow major portions of Windows are destroyed or deleted, reinstalling Windows is an option.

- Reinstalling Windows is also necessary to recover from a botched operating system upgrade.

- Yes, often, reinstalling Windows does fix the problem. But it has also been my experience that it has caused more problems than it has solved. I feel that tech support people who recommend it should be held personally and legally responsible for the consequences of such a drastic recommendation.

- No, reinstalling Windows is not the same thing as rebuilding the kernel in Unix. The kernel is one file, similar to Windows own KERNEL32.DLL file. In fact, you can reinstall single files in Windows, which is one way to avoid reinstalling *every* file.

Are there any benefits to reinstalling Windows?

I've been to various Web sites that tout the virtues of reinstalling Windows. It's almost a religious experience for them. And the sites remind me of reading those ancient alchemy, or "medical," documents that heartily recommend drinking mercury to cure a fever.

Argument 1: Reinstalling Windows removes much of the junk that doesn't get uninstalled when you remove programs. So (blah, blah, blah) you end up with a cleaner system.

Rebuttal 1: The problem is that you also need to reinstall your applications, which reintroduces all the junk right back into the system.

Argument 2: Reinstalling Windows results in a faster system.

Rebuttal 2: No argument there. But the reason that it's faster is that reinstalling has the marvelous effect of also defragmenting the entire hard drive, especially nonmovable clusters. So, like, *duh!* The system is faster — for a time. Fragmentation eventually does creep back in.

Rebuttal 2 1/2: Also don't forget the time wasted reinstalling Windows. Count your computer system down for at least half a day.

Argument 3: Reinstalling Windows fixes a number of problems.

Rebuttal 3: You can fix problems without reinstalling Windows.

I could go on. And I would love to, but I've run out of arguments in favor of reinstalling Windows. If you hear of any, please e-mail them to me for this book's next edition: dgookin@wambooli.com. Thanks!

What about reformatting the hard drive?

Reformatting the hard drive is another evil activity that's foisted on the computing public as a necessary thing. It's not. In fact, you should never, *ever,* have to reformat your computer's hard drive. It's something they do at the factory. It's something a computer technician does. It's no longer anything a computer user has to do.

As with reinstalling Windows, in only one circumstance do I suggest reformatting a hard drive: when a virus has attacked the computer so thoroughly that the only solution to rid it of the virus is to reformat the hard drive. And that's a pretty rare thing; an ugly thing; a thing I hope never happens to you.

Chapter 20

Shutdown Constipation

· ·

In This Chapter

▶ Diagnosing shutdown problems

▶ Using Safe mode

▶ Disabling device drivers

▶ Changing the power button's function

· ·

*1*t is the height of good manners to know when it's time to leave. Alas, Windows has no manners, so it's up to you to shut 'er down when you're done. But even though you go through those proper procedures, something in the box *refuses* to shut down. Good-bye already!

So you sit and wait and wait and wait. "Shutting down Windows," it says. Yeah, right. And the check is in the mail, and the government is here to help you, and so on. What's to believe? With any luck, you can find the cure for your PC's shutdown constipation in the text that follows.

What to Do When Your Computer Doesn't Shut Down

Give the computer about two or three minutes before you're certain that it's stuck. Then just turn the sucker off. I know that's "bad," but what else can you do?

Well, yeah: You can get the situation fixed. Windows is supposed to shut down and, in many cases, turn off the computer all by itself. When it doesn't work that way, you need to fix things.

✔ If the power button doesn't turn the computer off, press and hold that button for about three seconds. That usually works.

✔ If the power button still doesn't turn the computer off, unplug it. Or, if your computer is connected to a UPS (uninterruptible power supply), turn off the UPS.

"Why doesn't it shut down?"

Windows refuses to shut down for the very same reason that some guests refuse to leave a party: rude behavior. Inside the computer, usually some stubborn program has been given the signal to shut down, but — like the guest who doesn't leave despite your walking around in your pajamas and bathrobe — it refuses to leave.

Get a hint, will ya?

The solution is finding that stubborn program and either forcing it to quit before you shut down or just not running the program in the first place. As luck would have it, the list of programs that could possibly not get the hint to quit is quite long.

✔ Some older versions of antivirus software were usually to blame for not letting the computer shut down all the way. The programs would monitor the shutdown to ensure that no viruses were installed, but then they would "forget" to quit themselves.

✔ In fact, if you're looking for anything to blame, older software is generally your number-one suspect. Though Windows is supposed to shut down all open programs before it quits, you probably should manually close older programs before you give Windows the command to shut down.

Common things that stop up shutdown

Of course, it's not always Windows fault. Any of the following situations can also lead to shutdown constipation:

✔ Older, out-of-date, or conflicting device drivers may also hang a computer on shutdown.

✔ Any devices flagged as nonfunctioning by the Device Manager can also be causing the problem. See Appendix A for information on the Device Manager.

✔ If your computer plays a sound file when it shuts down and the sound file is corrupted or damaged, that could also cause the system to hang; Windows just sits there and waits for the sound file to "fix itself."

If the shutdown problem is new, consider what you've installed or updated recently. Odds are that the new software or hardware may be causing the conflict that's preventing the system from shutting down: In Windows Me or Windows XP, do a System Restore. In Windows 98, try uninstalling the software or hardware to see whether that resolves the issue.

To fix the sound problem, try these steps:

1. **Open the Control panel.**

2a. **In Windows 98, open the Sounds icon in the Control Panel.**

2b. **In Windows Me, open the Sounds and Multimedia icon.**

2c. **In Windows XP, open the Sounds and Audio Devices icon and click on the Sounds tab.**

3. **Scroll through the list of events until you find the Exit Windows item.**

   If no sound is listed there — and no icon is by the Exit Windows event name — you're okay. Skip to Step 6.

4. **Click the Play button.**

   This step tests the sound to see whether it's working, though it's no guarantee that the sound isn't the thing that's hanging the computer on shutdown.

5. **Choose (None) from the drop-down list of sounds.**

   By choosing no sound, you effectively disable the sound playing at shutdown.

6. **Click OK.**

If the computer continues to hang when it's shut down, you know that the problem lies elsewhere. Continue reading in the next section.

One quick thing to try

If you're having trouble getting Windows to shut down, follow these steps:

1. **Start Windows as you normally would.**

   Then, after Windows is up and running, complete Step 2.

2. **Shut down Windows.**

If Windows shuts down all normal without any hang-ups, you're assured that it's probably some other program you're running and not Windows itself to blame. The job then becomes one of elimination to see which program is hanging the system.

Of course, this technique doesn't disable the many other start-up programs that are not a part of Windows. Keep reading for more information on those.

Try shutting down in Safe mode

One trick you can try is to start the computer in Safe mode. After you're there, try shutting down. If the computer shuts down successfully, it's not a hardware problem and not a problem with the basic Windows setup. The problem is either a device driver or a third-party program that's not shutting down properly.

See Appendix B for more information on Safe mode.

Disabling the video controller

To see whether the video driver is causing the problem in Windows 98 or Windows Me, follow these steps:

1. **Click the Start button.**

2. **Choose Run from the Start thing menu.**

3. **Type** MSCONFIG **into the box.**

4. **Click OK.**

   This step runs the System Configuration utility, which is covered in Appendix A.

5. **On the General tab, click the Advanced button.**

   You see the Advanced Troubleshooting Settings window, as shown in Figure 20-1.

6. **Click to select VGA 640 x 480 x 16.**

   Yes, this step runs the computer in "dumb" display mode, but by doing so, you're also disabling the video driver to see whether it's to blame.

7. **Click OK to close the Advanced Troubleshooting Settings window.**

8. **Close the System Configuration Utility window.**

   You're asked whether you want to restart Windows. You do.

9. **Click the Yes button to restart Windows.**

   Or, if you're not prompted, just restart Windows as you normally would. Granted, it may not be restarting — which is the core of the problem here. If so, just unplug the computer or do whatever is necessary to restart the sucker.

   When Windows comes back on the screen, it's in dumb display mode. Don't fret — you're troubleshooting!

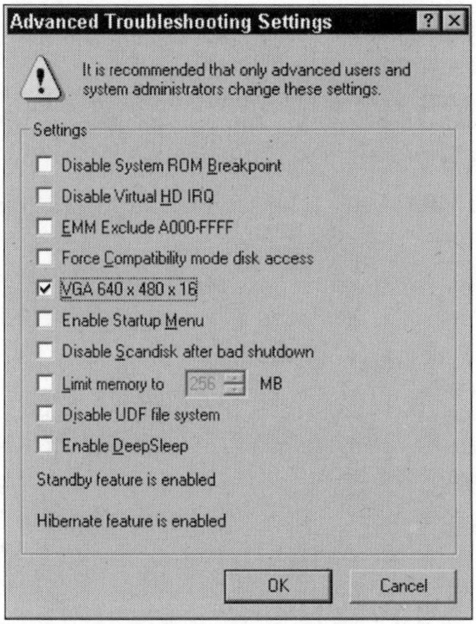

Advanced Troubleshooting Settings   ? X

⚠ It is recommended that only advanced users and system administrators change these settings.

Settings

☐ Disable System ROM Breakpoint
☐ Disable Virtual HD IRQ
☐ EMM Exclude A000-FFFF
☐ Force Compatibility mode disk access
☑ VGA 640 x 480 x 16
☐ Enable Startup Menu
☐ Disable Scandisk after bad shutdown
☐ Limit memory to [256 ⬍] MB
☐ Disable UDF file system
☐ Enable DeepSleep

Standby feature is enabled

Hibernate feature is enabled

[OK]   [Cancel]

Figure 20-1:
Disabling
the video
software.

10. **After Windows comes back up, shut it down again.**

You're testing to see whether shutdown works with the video driver disabled.

If the system shuts down just fine, you need to update or upgrade your video driver. Refer to Chapter 6, the section about updating your graphics device driver, for more information.

If the system still refuses to shut down, the problem is *not* the video system.

11. **Undo the 640 x 480 x 16 testing mode.**

Repeat Steps 1 through 9, but this time remove the check mark by VGA 640 x 480 x 16.

Disabling power management

Turn off that power-management stuff and see whether that's the cause of your shutdown woe. Open the Control Panel's Power Management or Power Options icon. Set everything to Never. Shut down Windows (as best you can). Then restart and try shutting down again. Often, the power-management feature may be stopping you up.

✔ Also, access your PC's Startup program and see about disabling power management there.

✔ Check with the Device Manager to see whether you have a problem with power management. See Appendix A for more information on the Device Manager.

✔ If power management is the root of the problem, consider contacting your PC's manufacturer for a possible fix.

Disabling other device drivers

Just as you did with the video driver, you should attempt to disable other drivers, shut down and restart the computer, and then shut down again to see whether you still have the problem.

Two sets of drivers are suspect:

✔ Sound, video, and game controllers

✔ Network adapters

You have to disable each of these individually, shut down, restart, and then shut down again to see whether they're causing the problem. I know — it's lots of work, but that's how it must be done.

To disable a driver, heed these steps:

1. **Open the Device Manager (see Appendix A).**

2. **Open one of the categories I just listed, such as Network Adapters.**

3. **Select an individual piece of hardware.**

   An example is your network adapter, which appears by name or model number beneath the Network adapters header. Click to select it.

4. **Click the Properties button.**

   Or, just double-click the entry to open it.

5. **Click to select Disable in this hardware profile.**

   In Windows XP, choose Do not use this device from the drop-down list at the bottom of the General tab.

   This step effectively removes the device drivers for the hardware.

6. **Click OK.**

7. **Close the Device Manager.**

TECHNICAL STUFF

I don't tell you how, but tech support might

One additional option available to you, though it's one I'm reluctant to document in this book (because it's a beginner's book and all), is the Selective Startup option. You can find it in the front of the System Configuration Utility (MSCONFIG) window. What it does is to stop certain processes from starting with Windows, and one of those processes could be the source of your shutdown woes.

I don't go into detail on Selective Startup because, honestly, I don't know what it will do to your computer and I can't personally help you troubleshoot any problems that may happen. Therefore, leave the Selective Startup issue alone unless a tech support person tells you to disable or reenable one of the items there.

You may be prompted to reset; do so. If not, restart Windows as best you can. Then, when Windows is up again and the device driver is disabled, try shutting down.

If you can shut down, you've located the problem; repeat these steps to enable the device again, but this time in the device's dialog box, click the Driver tab to update the device's software. (Or, check with the developer's Web page for a newer version, and so on — you know the drill by now.)

If you cannot shut down, you've just eliminated yet another possibility: Reenable the device and try again by disabling another device from the list.

- ✔ Yes, this process takes time — but the good news is that it may yield the solution.

- ✔ Refer to Chapter 5 for more information on finding support on the Web.

- ✔ Also refer to the section in Chapter 8 about stopping programs from automatically starting. There, you find information on halting some of the mystery start-up programs, some of which may be causing your computer to hang on shutdown.

One final thing to try

Microsoft is aware of all the various problems Windows has with shutting down. If you still have the shutdown problem, I recommend going to the Microsoft Knowledge Base Web site and searching for your problem:

```
support.microsoft.com/
```

Be sure to select your version of Windows from the pop-up list and type a brief description of the problem. Include the word *shutdown.* Click the Search button and see what the Knowledge Base comes up with.

You may also try using the online Windows troubleshooter, which covers much of what I've already mentioned but may be of more help to you:

```
support.micorosoft.com/support/windows/tshoot
```

Controlling the Power Button's Behavior

In the old days — and I'm talking pre-1990 here — computers all came with an On-Off button. And that button did exactly what you would expect: On was on. Off was off. Today, with all the emphasis on power management and energy efficiency, the computer's On-Off button has become the on-*whatever* button.

On all computers, the On-Off button most definitely turns the computer on. Good.

On some computer models, the button definitely turns the sucker off. But on other computers, the button can have any of a number of functions. That's why the button is no longer named On-Off, but rather the *power button.* Sounds a bit too important. . . .

You can change the power button's function. Follow these steps:

1. **Open the Control Panel.**

2. **Open the Power Options icon.**

   In Windows 98, it's called Power Management.

3. **Click the Advanced tab.**

   If your PC's power button can be changed, you see a Power buttons area in the dialog box, as shown in Figure 20-2. If you don't see the area, your computer lacks this feature.

4. **Choose a new function for the power button from the drop-down list.**

   For example, if you really want the power button to turn off the computer, choose Power Off. Some computers have a variety of functions available — even some that pop up a menu on the screen whenever you punch the power button.

5. **Click OK after making your choice.**

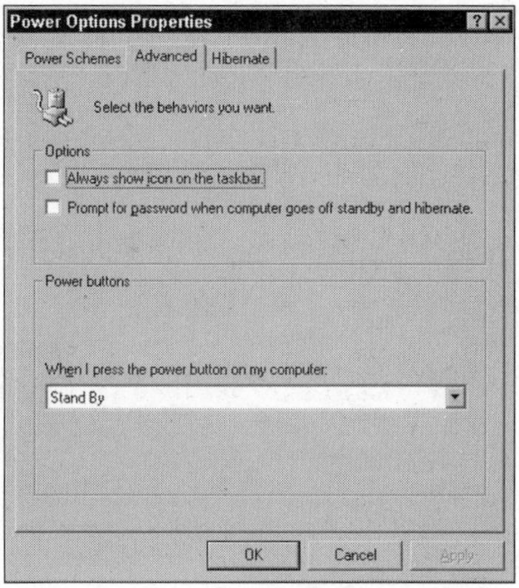

Power Options Properties

Power Schemes | Advanced | Hibernate

Select the behaviors you want.

Options

☐ Always show icon on the taskbar

☐ Prompt for password when computer goes off standby and hibernate.

Power buttons

When I press the power button on my computer:

Stand By

OK Cancel Apply

Figure 20-2:
Change the
power
button's
function
here.

Even though you can change the function of the power button, you still need to shut down Windows properly (or as best you can) whenever you're done working on the computer.

✔ If you see a Shutdown option for the power button, pressing that button does, in fact, shut down Windows and turn off the computer.

✔ In many cases, the power button turns off the computer if you press and hold the button for a few seconds.

✔ If you set the power button to Do nothing, the only way to turn off the computer is to properly shut down Windows. If that doesn't work, you have to unplug the sucker.

Part III
Preventive Maintenance

The 5th Wave   By Rich Tennant

JAWS OF LIFE

"Here's a little tip on disassembly that you won't find in the manual."

In this part . . .

I know only a few people who truly practice the art of preventive maintenance. They're the ones who read their car's manual and who stick to the oil- and filter-changing schedule. They read the handbook for the new washer-dryer and actually perform the few recommended maintenance checks. They clean the coils on their refrigerator every three months. They wash out the lawn mower. Call them diligent. Call them anal-retentive. But you can't call them desperate because when it comes to troubleshooting, they really don't need any.

There is such value to preventive maintenance. It's that confidence you would expect from Dad in a 1950s sitcom: "Oh, darn!," says Dad, driving the family's Buick on a 2-lane highway in the middle of nowhere. "There goes that tire! Fortunately, I just filled the spare with air, not to mention that little Timmy and I spent all last week practicing how to change a flat tire. We'll be on the road again in minutes." You too can experience such self-assurance, as long as you practice a few bits and pieces of preventive PC maintenance.

Chapter 21

Maintaining Your Disk Drives

· ·

· ·

Disk drives hold more importance for your computer because they contain all your stuff — not only the operating system (important) and your applications (more important), but also all the documents and data you create and rely on every day (most important). So, although you can be a whiz-bang at troubleshooting common hard drive burps and glitches, and perhaps you can install a new hard drive in less than 30 seconds, what would work best for you is an ounce of preventive disk drive maintenance. That will save some agony and hair-pulling later.

Improving Disk Performance

Windows gives you two tools for maintaining your hard drive and helping its performance: ScanDisk and Defrag.

✔ ScanDisk and Defrag aren't the best tools for maintaining your hard drive. You can find better versions of these tools in third-party utilities, such as Norton Utilities.

✔ Especially if you're using Windows 98 or Windows Me and you notice that ScanDisk or Defrag seems to poop out on you, consider buying and using Norton Utilities instead.

✔ Hard disk performance decreases as the amount of stuff on your hard drive increases. You can't do anything about this; it's just a simple truth. It takes longer to access and sift through more information than it does for little information.

✔ Other third-party utilities are available for optimizing disk performance and stuff like that. Visit your local Software-O-Rama for more information.

Accessing the disk tools

Windows keeps all its handy disk tools near to the bosom of your PC's hard drives. Here's how to get at this common tool chest:

1. **Open the My Computer icon on the desktop.**

2. **Right-click the icon for hard drive C.**

   Or, you can open any hard drive's icon, such as Drive D if you want to use the tools on that hard drive instead.

3. **Choose Properties from the pop-up menu.**

4. **Click the Tools tab.**

   You see a list of the three common disk maintenance tools, as shown in Figure 21-1. The error-checking tool is ScanDisk. The defragmenting tool is Defrag. And then you see a button for backup, if your PC has backup software installed.

Figure 21-1: Where Windows hides the disk tools.

The remainder of this chapter uses the tools found on the Tools tab in the disk drive Properties dialog box.

✔ You can also find the Defrag and Backup commands on the Start menu: Choose Programs (or All Programs) and then Accessories⇨System Tools, and then look for the program name.

✔ Windows Me doesn't come with a Backup program installed. Windows XP Home doesn't come with a backup program at all.

✔ The dialog box in Windows 98 and Windows Me tells you how many days it has been since you last used each of the maintenance tools. Talk about guilt!

✔ Some third-party utilities may install buttons or options on the Tools tab. Figure 21-1 shows the standard Windows configuration, so if you see anything extra, it's specific to your computer and not a part of Windows in general.

Doing the ScanDisk thing

The ScanDisk program is designed to check for and repair common errors on a hard drive. It's not really a performance-enhancing tool.

On most systems, ScanDisk is run automatically, thanks to a maintenance robot that Windows runs every few days (via the Task Scheduler). But you can always run ScanDisk manually — and you should, especially if you don't leave your computer on all the time and the maintenance robot doesn't have time to run.

Follow these steps to run ScanDisk:

1. **Don't do anything else.**

   This isn't a rule — it's just good advice: ScanDisk prefers to have the computer all to itself while it runs. Doing something else, especially something involving disk activity, may cause ScanDisk to stubbornly restart, which wastes time.

2. **Start ScanDisk from the Tools tab in the disk drive Properties dialog box.**

   (Refer to the steps in the preceding section.)

3. **Click the Check Now button.**

   The Check Disk dialog box opens.

   The standard options that are displayed, such as those for Windows XP, as shown in Figure 21-2, are usually good enough. I do, however, recommend checking the Automatically fix file system errors box.

4. **Click the Start button to check your disk drive.**

   ScanDisk checks a few things — but not everything — just to ensure that the hard drive is in order.

   After ScanDisk is complete, a summary is displayed in Windows 98 and Windows Me. In Windows XP, a simple "I'm done" dialog box appears: Close that dialog box.

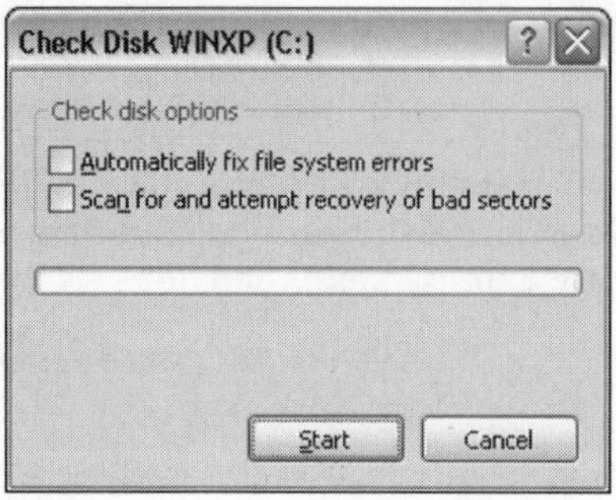

Figure 21-2:
Starting a
ScanDisk
(or Check
Disk)
operation in
Windows
XP.

Check Disk WINXP (C:)   ? X

┌─ Check disk options ─────────────────────────────┐
│   │
│ ☐ Automatically fix file system errors   │
│ ☐ Scan for and attempt recovery of bad sectors   │
│   │
│ ┌───┐ │
│ └───┘ │
│   │
│   │
│   [Start   ]   [Cancel]   │
└───┘

Does ScanDisk increase performance? No. It fixes errors. So, if the errors are stopping up performance, ScanDisk improves things. For the most part, running ScanDisk doesn't make anything run faster.

- ✔ In Windows 98 and Windows Me, you can select either the Standard or Thorough option. Use Standard. Thorough is good if you suspect disk trouble and want to check for bad sectors — a growing number of which provide an early signal to a hard drive's eventual demise. Note that the Thorough option does take time. (The larger your hard drive, the longer ScanDisk takes, up to several hours for huge hard drives.)

- ✔ Don't let the summary information shown by Windows 98 or Windows Me dismay you. Bad sectors aren't a bad thing — unless their number is growing. Bad sectors should be flagged. That way, the computer won't use those sectors and files won't be lost.

- ✔ Sometimes, ScanDisk runs automatically when the computer first starts up, especially if the computer was suddenly, unexpectedly, or improperly shut down. This is a good thing.

- ✔ ScanDisk isn't really called ScanDisk in Windows XP. No, it's Check Disk, which was the old DOS program's name (called CHKDSK).

Defragging a drive

Running the Defrag utility most definitely improves your hard drive's performance. By eliminating most fragmented files and reshuffling popular files to the beginning of the disk (like the head of the line), you see a modest performance improvement.

To run Defrag, visit the Tools panel in your disk drive's Properties dialog box (refer to Figure 21-1). Click the Defragment Now button to run Defrag on the indicated hard drive.

In Windows 98 and Windows Me, Defrag starts right up. But in Windows XP, you can click the Analyze button to see how badly the disk is fragmented before you tune-up. Then you're given a recommendation about whether to continue.

Because Defrag does more for improving performance, I recommend running it at least once a week. In fact, the more often you run it, the less time it takes to do its job.

- ✔ The Norton version of Defrag does an even better job of defragmentation and disk optimization. I highly recommend it.

- ✔ Defragmenting does take time! Be sure to set aside several minutes to a few hours for your hard drive to fully defragment.

- ✔ If Defrag poops out on you, just get Norton Utilities and use its better version of Defrag instead, especially for Windows 98 or Windows Me.

- ✔ Defrag runs best when it's the only program running. Other programs may interfere with Defrag, slowing it down or sometimes causing it to start over.

- ✔ Fragmented files are *not* bad things. Windows tries to make the best use of disk storage, so it must split larger files into smaller pieces, called *fragments*. The operating system keeps track of all the pieces, so you never really can tell which files are fragmented and how badly.

How can these tools run automatically?

The Task Scheduler in Windows is typically set up to run disk utilities once every moon. If not, you can use the Task Scheduler to arrange for ScanDisk and Defrag to be run automatically according to your own schedule.

To use the Task Scheduler, refer to your favorite Windows book, or you can work through the Task Scheduler tutorial on my Wambooli Web page:

```
www.wambooli.com/help/Windows/Generic/task_sched/
```

That Web page explains how to set up the Task Scheduler to run programs at certain times. You can use it to set up ScanDisk and Defrag to run automatically on your PC.

- ✔ The name of the ScanDisk program is SCANDISK in Windows 98 and Windows Me.

- ✔ In Windows XP, you cannot schedule ScanDisk to run because ScanDisk doesn't officially exist in Windows XP. (Complain to Microsoft, not to me!)

- ✔ In Windows 98 and Windows Me, the DEFRAG command runs the Defrag program.

- ✔ In Windows XP, you run Defrag with the command DFRG.MSC.

Increasing Disk Storage

Another potential problem with a hard drive is that disk space suddenly runs dry! At first, this situation is suspect with me because today's hard drives hold lots of information and it would take a busy person to fill things up quickly. But with popular graphics files, videos, and music, you can see the free space dwindle on a 20GB hard drive like watching ice melt in the sun.

First, a few suggestions

If you're collecting more than one type of a specific file, such as graphics, video, or music files, consider putting all that stuff on CD-R discs. Archiving is the name of the game! Just wait until you have a collection of enough files (more than 500MB, for example), and then burn 'em all on a CD-R.

If you absolutely must have all that stuff on a hard drive, however, consider getting a second hard drive for your computer. They're relatively cheap and easy to install — a valuable addition, especially when space is scarce.

Finally, *do not* use disk compression on your hard drive to get more space. Windows 98 and Windows Me offer the DriveSpace program, and Windows XP uses what I call "blue file compression." Don't bother with it. Compressed files on hard drives are something I never want to troubleshoot. Please use one of the preceding suggestions or any of the other disk cleaning advice in this chapter before you even think about disk compression.

- ✔ After you burn your stuff to a CD-R, you can freely delete it from the hard drive, saving yourself oodles of space.

- ✔ The most common disk compression troubleshooting question I get is "I need to uncompress 13GB of data from my 8GB drive. How can I do that?" My answer is "Only by getting a second, larger hard drive" — which, incidentally, is one of my earlier suggestions. That would have saved some time.

- ✔ Okay, I'm changing my mind: The file compression in Windows XP is okay because it's on a file-level basis and you're not compressing the entire hard drive, as you're doing with Windows 98 and Windows Me. Therefore, "blue" file compression is okay in Windows XP.

- ✔ See your favorite Windows XP book for more information on blue file compression. (All my favorite Windows XP books are written by Dan Gookin.)

Running Disk Cleanup

Your greatest weapon in the hard drive space battle is the Disk Cleanup tool. It puts several handy features in one place, allowing you to instantly reclaim lots of hard drive space in one easy step. Here you go:

1. **Click the Start button thing.**

2. **Choose Programs or All Programs.**

3. **Choose Accessories⇨System Tools⇨Disk Cleanup.**

   Windows modestly asks which drive you want to clean. This drive should be C, the busy drive. (Clean other drives on your own.)

4. **Click OK to select Drive C.**

   A brief analysis is made. Sit and hum.

   Eventually, results are posted in a dialog box, as shown in Figure 21-3. Note the items you can select *plus* how much disk space is freed by selecting them. In Figure 21-3, you see that half a megabyte of crap is sitting in the Recycle Bin. Wow!

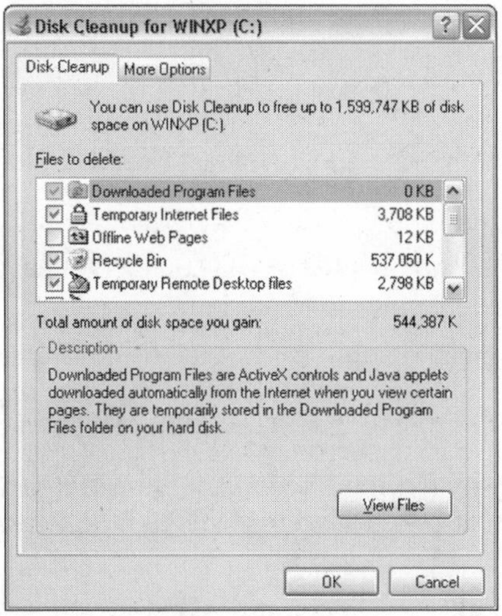

Figure 21-3:
A few of the many things needing cleaning.

![Disk Cleanup for WINXP (C:) dialog box. Tabs: Disk Cleanup, More Options. "You can use Disk Cleanup to free up to 1,599,747 KB of disk space on WINXP (C:)." Files to delete: Downloaded Program Files 0 KB, Temporary Internet Files 3,708 KB, Offline Web Pages 12 KB, Recycle Bin 537,050 K, Temporary Remote Desktop files 2,798 KB. Total amount of disk space you gain: 544,387 K. Description: Downloaded Program Files are ActiveX controls and Java applets downloaded automatically from the Internet when you view certain pages. They are temporarily stored in the Downloaded Program Files folder on your hard disk. View Files button. OK, Cancel buttons.]

Note the Compress old files option in Windows XP — a great way to save space. (Remember that file compression is okay in Windows XP; it's not the same as disk compression in Windows 98 and Windows Me.)

5. **Click and check the clean options you yearn for.**

   Wait! You're not done! There's even more!

6. **Click the More Options tab.**

A few more items to remove are Windows components and installed programs. For example, if you never use MSN Explorer in Windows XP, you
can save some 13MB of disk space by deleting it. Removing those desktop themes in Windows 98 saves a whopping 30MB of space!

Clicking the Clean Up button by Windows Components takes you to the
Windows Setup tab in the Add/Remove Programs dialog box — or the
Windows Component Wizard in Windows XP. There, you can select vari-
ous pieces parts of Windows to uninstall.

Clicking the Clean Up button by the Install program option takes you to
the Add/Remove Programs dialog box, where you can uninstall any software you seldom use and save even more space.

In Windows XP, you can also click the Clean Up button by System
Restore to remove old restore point data from the system and save,
well, even more space.

7. **Make your selections on the More Options tab.**

8. **When you're ready to free disk space, click the OK button.**

9. **Click Yes when you're asked whether you're sure.**

You're sure.

The Disk Cleanup program goes to work for you.

The program ends with no fanfare; it just quits. But your hard drive is much
slimmer! (My Windows 98 system crashed when I last ran Disk Cleanup. Yes,
it happens to everyone.)

✔ No, you can't run Disk Cleanup on a CD or DVD disc; the files on those
discs are read-only, and you cannot delete them.

✔ Note that selecting some cleaning options causes an additional button to
be displayed in the dialog box. Clicking that button displays more options
or allows you to refine your choices, if you're a refined type of person.

✔ The Downloaded Programs option refers to internal upgrades (add-ons
or plug-ins) for Internet Explorer. The option doesn't refer to any share-
ware or other utility you have downloaded.

Other things to try

Please, O please, don't sit and stew over your disk space usage. The disk is
there for you to use, and Windows works fine with either a full or empty hard

drive. In fact, if space gets too low, Windows lets you know. For most people, your computer will most likely die before you get a chance to fill up its hard drive.

Even so, and even with Disk Cleanup and all that, you can try a few more things to keep disk space usage low.

Decrease the size of the Internet cache. Set the Internet cache, or temporary file, allocation to a small size. Refer to Chapter 17 for the details.

Decrease the space used by the Recycle Bin. Here's how you can change the disk space allocation for your deleted files:

1. **Right-click the Recycle Bin icon on the desktop.**

2. **Choose Properties from the shortcut menu.**

   The Recycle Bin Properties dialog box is displayed, as shown in Figure 21-4. The Global tab sets the usage for all drives. Other tabs set drive usage individually, but only if you choose the Configure drives independently option.

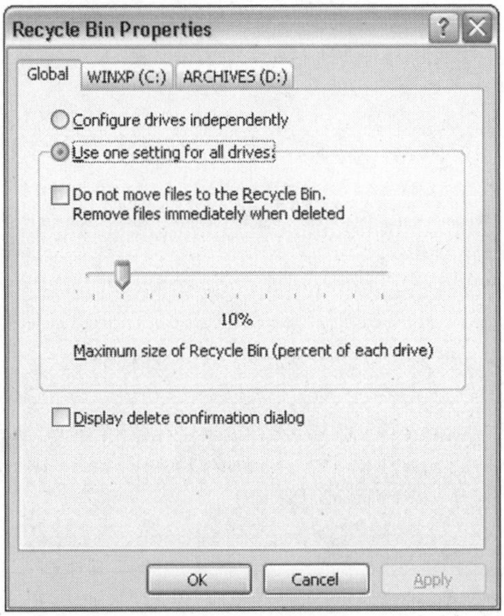

Figure 21-4:
Setting the Recycle Bin's allocation.

3. **Adjust the slider to the left.**

   Sliding the gizmo to the left means that less disk space is used by the Recycle Bin. You can then use more disk space for your own junk.

Or — if you want to risk it — you can click to select the Do not move files to the option labeled Recycle Bin, Remove files immediately when deleted. Choosing that option means that there is no chance of file recovery, but you do get more disk space that way. (No, I don't recommend it.)

4. Click OK after making your adjustments.

Remove the Online Services folder. Many new computers come with a folder named Online Services. It may be on the desktop directly, or it may be a folder in the Program Files folder. Wherever — it's something you can freely delete.

The Online Services folder contains program stubs that let you sign on to various online services, such as AOL, Prodigy, CompuServe, and whatever else is out there. If you don't plan on using those services, zap that folder.

If you get a warning about deleting program files, it's okay. Those programs install only larger programs that you don't plan on using anyway. Yes, you have my permission to delete them — despite my constant admonition never to delete any file you didn't create yourself.

Chapter 22

The Benefits of Backup

*B*ackup is drudgery only if you've never, ever, had a disk problem at any time in your entire life, and maybe even before then. Otherwise, those who use Backup and have benefited from its goodness sing the Daily Praises of Backup song every doo-dah day:

> *O Sing we now of old Backup*
>
> *That good utility;*
>
> *Our data's safe, no disk blow-up*
>
> *Will cause anxiety*

So I won't sit here and debate myself while you read. Instead, if you're wise, you'll heed my backup advice. If you're foolish, you'll rip these pages from this book's binding and make yourself a most excellent paper hat.

What to Back Up, What Not to Back Up

A *backup* is nothing more than a safety copy — a duplicate — of your files, data, and important stuff. It exists "just in case." So, if anything happens to the original, you can always rely on the good old trusty backup. Sounds kind of wholesome, doesn't it?

The main problem with backing up is that performing the operation is time-consuming. (In the old days, backing up to floppy disk was labor-consuming as well because you had to continually exchange floppy disks.) Backing up is time-consuming because it must create a fresh copy of all the information on your hard drive. But does it need to be *all* the information?

Various backup terms

Backup programs may use some interesting terminology. Sometimes, the backup manual explains the terms; sometimes, it doesn't. If not, here are my own handy definitions of various backup terms.

Full backup: This term refers to a complete backup of the entire hard drive. All the files backed up are marked "backed up" by the computer. That way, you can easily spot new files created after the backup.

Specific backup: Only those files that are selected are backed up.

Incremental backup: This term refers to a backup of only those files created or modified since the last full backup.

Differential backup: This type is the same as an Incremental backup in that only files modified since the last backup are archived. However, unlike an incremental backup, the files backed up are *not* marked as having been backed up (a rare option to select).

Copy: Files are backed up, but they are not marked as having been backed up, as they would be for a full backup.

Back up everything! Purists will argue that a full hard drive backup is the only way to fully restore your computer. After all, if a virus infects a slew of files, the easiest way to restore those files is from a full backup.

Back up just your stuff! On the other hand, why back up files that you can easily copy from an installation CD? If the worst happens, you can reinstall Windows and reinstall drivers and applications. Then use the backup disks to reinstall all your own stuff. That too works, and it saves backup media and time as well.

Which option do you choose? How about a compromise? When you first do a backup, back up *everything* — the entire hard drive. From then on, just back up your own stuff. If you ever revamp the system or install upgrades, do another full disk backup.

Then again, the choices and options available for backing up are limitless, so it depends on your patience, experience, and willingness to do the backup in the first place.

✔ You can restore Windows only if you have a copy of the original Windows CD or a reinstall disk that came with the computer. Do not throw that stuff out!

✔ Keep copies of all the software you install on your computer. I keep the original CDs in the boxes the software came in.

How to Back Up

A *backup* is nothing more than a file copy. Here's how to back up any file:

1. **Open the My Documents folder.**

2. **Click to select any document.**

   It doesn't matter which one.

3. **Press Ctrl+C to copy the file.**

4. **Press Ctrl+V to paste the file.**

   The file is copied into the same folder, but given a new name with the prefix "Copy of."

What you've done is to duplicate a file. It isn't a shortcut because the duplicate is identical to the original: same size, type, dates, and contents, but different names because two files in the same folder cannot share the same name.

The problem with this type of backup is that there is no safety issue. Sure, you can use the backup if something happens to the original file. But if the folder is deleted or the entire hard drive is damaged, the backup is useless.

No, the key to backing up is to store the backup on another media: a CD-R/RW, a Zip disk, a disk drive on the network, or a second physical drive inside of or attached to the computer.

You may freely delete the duplicate file you just created.

✔ *Media* is a general term describing a place where information can be written, such as a hard drive, floppy disk, CD-R/RW, or Zip disk.

✔ Also included in backup media is the tape drive, though tape drives aren't as common (or as cheap) as they were just five short years ago.

✔ The best backups are those you can make to a separate media, such as a tape drive or any removable disk. That way, you can lock up the disk, just to be safe.

✔ Simply copying a file counts toward creating a backup. In fact, when I "back up" this book's files at the end of the day, I simply copy the files' folder to a Zip drive. I just copy and paste using Windows Explorer.

✔ If you have a second physical hard drive, you can back up your files to it rather than to a removable disk. This method isn't as safe as using a removable disk (which can be locked in a fire safe), but it's better than merely copying the files to the same disk. Refer to Chapter 15 to find out how to tell a physical disk from a logical disk.

✔ Expensive software and hardware backup solutions are available, though they're mostly used by large institutions or corporations. These solutions include DAT drives, RAID drives, and other high-end methods of data protection that you needn't worry about.

Backing up without backup software

To merely *copy* a group of files (to back up without using backup software), you just need to drag and drop the clutch of icons from one disk to another — from the hard drive to the CD-R disk or from the hard drive to a Zip disk. It's a simple file-copy operation, and it works.

This process has two limitations. The first is that it's up to you to determine that all the files will fit on the destination disk. For example, you cannot copy 1,300MB of your stuff to a 720MB CD-RW disk. It just doesn't work. Ditto for copying 400MB of files to a 250MB Zip disk. No amount of suitcase-sitting will get those extra bytes on the disk. No way!

The second limitation is simply automation: "Real" backup software automates the process. Plus, it may even let the backup span across multiple disks, which certainly saves some time.

In any event, suppose that you want to back up using the old file-copy method:

First, decide what you want to back up. Because space is limited, perhaps you should back up only the contents of the My Documents folder. Or, if you suppose that's too big, back up perhaps only a handful of folders in which you have current projects.

Second, determine the size of those folders. You can do this task by examining the folder's Properties dialog box. The following steps assume that you're trying to gauge the size of the My Documents folder:

1. **Open the My Documents icon on the desktop.**

   To calculate the folder's size, you must visit the *parent* folder, the folder that contains the folder you're working in. You do that by clicking the Up Folder button.

2. **Click the Up Folder button.**

3. **Right-click the My Documents folder.**

4. Choose Properties from the pop-up menu.

If you see the Target tab in the folder's Properties dialog box, you've stumbled across one of the many Windows shortcut icons. Heed these steps:

A. Click the Find Target button.

B. Repeat Steps 3 and 4.

You should see the General tab of the folder's Properties dialog box, as shown in Figure 22-1. Note the size! In Figure 22-1, it's 124MB, which is enough to fit on a 250MB Zip disk or a CD-R/RW disk.

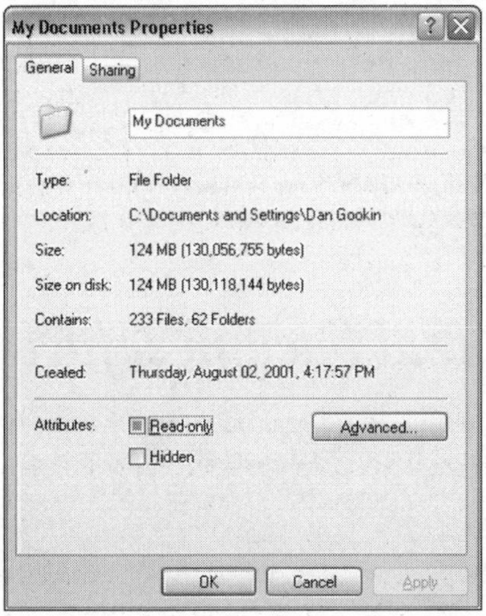

Figure 22-1:
A folder's
Properties
dialog box.

5. Close the Properties dialog box.

6. Close any other open windows, except for the original window you opened.

Third, prepare the backup disk. Insert a CD-R or CD-RW disk into the drive and prepare it for receiving information (*format* the disk). Or, insert a Zip drive or scout out a location for the files on a second hard drive.

Fourth, copy the files. Use any one of the numerous Windows file-copying commands to duplicate the files on the backup disk.

Fifth, put the disk in a safe place. Remove the disk from the drive. (*Burn* the CD-R/RW disk.) Properly label it. Date it. And then store it in a safe place.

Sixth, repeat these steps every so often. The more often you back up, the better the chances of recovery if anything nasty happens.

If these steps are all you follow to back up your stuff, that's great. The drawbacks are obvious, however. First, you can effectively back up only stuff that fits on a single disk. Second, you really can't tell the difference between what's backed up and what's new, so performing an incremental backup between major backups is fairly impossible. Third, if you're that religious about things, you may as well get real backup software anyway.

- Honestly, for backing up a single folder, project folder, or today's work, the file-copy is perhaps the best way to go.

- Not every My Documents folder handily fits on a removable disk. In fact, the computer I'm writing this book on has 1,200MB of files in the My Documents folder and its subfolders — far too many to stick on an individual disk. In those cases, you must use real backup software, which can archive files across multiple disks — and keep track of everything.

- I keep all my backup disks and tapes in a fire safe. It's not expensive or anything fancy. Most office supply stores carry them.

Backing up with real backup software

The difference between copying and using real backup software is immense. Real backup software tries as best it can to automate the process, and it can access a variety of backup devices, from special tape drives to CD-R/RW, Zip disks, and other removable disks. Plus, you have filters and other ways to select which files get backed up and how often. It's pretty amazing stuff, and most of them are easy to use.

The following steps outline how you would perform a backup of your stuff:

1. **Start the backup program.**

2. **Choose the option to back up files.**

   This sounds redundant, but remember that backup software not only backs up information but also can restore that information. You want to tell the program that you're about to back up information.

3. **Create a new backup set.**

   Most software programs ask you to create a new catalog or backup set, which contains information about the files being backed up. This step may also come after you select which files to back up.

4. **Select the files to back up.**

   Depending on the power of the program, you can back up stuff by choosing disk drives, folders, or even individual files. You can also select files based on their type, size, age, and whether they were created since the last backup.

5. **Select the backup media.**

   You need to tell the program where it is you're backing up to, either a special tape, a CD-R/RW, or a removable disk, like a Zip disk.

   Don't worry if the disk runs out of room! The program tells you whether and when to insert another disk or tape and continue the backup.

6. **Click some sort of Go button to begin the backup.**

   Sit back and watch. Or, go into another room and watch TV. Most backup programs give you an estimate of how much time the operation will take.

   You should be within earshot of the computer while it's backing up. That way, if anything strange happens, you can hear the alert sound and go try to fix it, as opposed to absorbing another hour of Oprah while the computer sits and waits for your input.

7. **Change media, if needed.**

8. **When the backup is finished, remove and label the disks or tapes.**

   Date the disks or tapes. Label them. Store them somewhere safe.

Now you can sleep easier, knowing that your stuff is backed up. That safety copy means that any accident, hardware failure, virus, or runaway 13-year-old computer genius can damage your hard drive all it wants. You can restore your stuff quickly and easily.

✔ Backup's sister, Restore, is covered in Chapter 4.

✔ Sorry about being vague here, but the nifty bitchin' backup program I just paid $170 for doesn't recognize my computer's CD-R drive or the Zip drive. Yup, I'm takin' it back for a refund.

✔ Some backup programs use compression to stick more information on the backup disk or tape. That's okay. If compression bothers you, you can turn off that feature.

✔ If you're using CD-RWs, consider rotating a set of disks. I do it this way: Two disks are labeled A, two are B, and the last two are C. I back up to set A first. Then, for the next backup, I erase set B and back up to them. Then I erase set C and back up to those disks. Then I start all over with A again the next time I back up.

When to Back Up

If you can get yourself into a regular backup schedule, great! It doesn't have to be rigorously followed. After all, if you use your computer only every so often, there's no point in backing up new stuff that doesn't exist.

Here's the schedule I recommend for diehard office environments:

- ✔ On Friday, do a full hard drive backup. Use three sets of backup media: A, B, and C. Rotate the sets so that you do a full backup with a different set every week.
- ✔ Every day, do an incremental backup, backing up only those files that were changed, modified, or added during the day.

These two steps are the most thorough way to cover all bases. Any disk mishap means that you're out of only a day's worth of work.

For the casual user, try this type of backup schedule:

- ✔ Back up the whole hard drive every month — the whole thing.
- ✔ Every Friday (or at least once a week), back up only those files that were changed, modified, or added during the week.

Because you're probably not creating as much stuff as you would in an office environment, you don't need to be as rigorous about backing up. However, if you want to be really safe — and for those folks who fall between each system — also perform this operation:

- ✔ At the end of the day, do a full backup of your main project folder.

For example, at the late evening hour when I finish today's work, I shall close down Word and back up this book's folder by copying it to a Zip disk. I could also schedule a sophisticated backup program to do that for me automatically, but it's not really a bother to perform the operation myself.

- ✔ I suppose that any schedule works as long as you stick to it.
- ✔ Also check out your backup program's automation features to see whether you can schedule backups for times when you're away from the computer.

Part IV
The Part of Tens

The 5th Wave   By Rich Tennant

WANDA HAD THE DISTINCT FEELING HER HUSBAND'S NEW SOFTWARE PROGRAM WAS ABOUT TO BECOME INTERACTIVE.

In this part . . .

I don't feel that a list has any legitimacy unless it has at least ten items in it. Top three lists? A joke. Anyone can come up with three things. It's silly. Top five? Nope. Odds are that if five things are on the list, there are most likely five more and the person concocting the list has done only half the research. Ten things? Whether they're the top ten or just ten things, you *know* that they're all good things — or at least that the list will have enough good things to make up for the mediocre things. The odds are in your favor!

In this, the traditional final part of a *For Dummies* book, I present you with various chapters that contain lists of 10 things dealing with troubleshooting your PC. Actually, I started out with 20 things in each chapter and then pared it down to only the best 10. That way, I'm certain that you won't feel ripped off.

Chapter 23

The Ten Rules of Tech Support

1 believe you'll find that the task of phoning tech support is made all the easier if you keep the following rules in mind.

Don't Use Technical Support As an Excuse for Not Reading the Manual or Using the Help System

Always look up your problem first in the manual or the online help. Second, visit the company's Web site and look for a Technical Support link, FAQ list, or troubleshooter. If you can find the answer there, great! Even if you don't, the tech support people will appreciate that you've made the effort.

Have Something to Write On

This advice not only gives you a pad to doodle on while you wait on hold, but having something to write on also means that you can take down notes and instructions as you're given them. That saves a great deal of repetition later and helps serve as a record of your tech support call.

Be Nice

Each new call is a mystery to the tech support person. The person doesn't know you, doesn't know your problem, and doesn't know how long you've been waiting on hold. None of those things is that person's fault, and they don't need to hear you scream about any of it.

The tech support person is there to help you. They did not cause the problem. They're not out to get you. The friendlier and more informative you can be, the better for them.

Be Sure to Get The Person's Name and a Number Where You Can Call Back

Before diving into the problem, get some basic information about your tech support person. Generally speaking, the person says their name when they answer the phone: "This is Richard in technical support. How can I help you?" Write down "Richard" on your notepad.

If possible, ask for a direct line on which to call back in case the call breaks off. Sometimes they have it, and sometimes they don't. Accept whatever answer the person gives you.

✔ If a tech support person says that they don't have a direct line or that they cannot be contacted directly, it's most likely a lie. Don't get mad! The company typically has a policy not to give out direct lines, so they're being forced to lie on purpose. This is policy, not an excuse to ignore you.

✔ You can also try to get an employee number up front.

Prepare: Do the Research before You Call

Exhaust every possibility and potential solution on your own before you phone tech support. Ensure that you're referring to things using the proper terms. If not, carefully describe what things look like.

Have These Items Handy: Serial Number, Order Number, Customer Number

Often, tech support needs confirmation of who you are and that you have a legitimate product before you can continue. You should get items like serial numbers beforehand — especially if the serial number is on the computer's butt and the computer's butt is up against the wall under your table.

It also helps to know which version of Windows you're using. Do this:

1. **Click the Start button.**

2. **Choose the Run command.**

    Or, press the Win+R key combination, which summons the Run dialog box.

3. **Type** WINVER **into the text box.**

4. **Click OK.**

    The WinVer program displays a dialog box that details which version of Windows you're using.

You might also see which is your CD-ROM drive, whether it's D or E or whatever.

Don't Spill Your Guts

The tech support person needs to know about the problem, not about what doom and peril await you if you can't get your computer working in time. Remember that most tech support people are under the clock; they may have only 11 minutes to deal with you, so be as direct as possible.

Be Patient

Tech support always assumes that you don't know anything about your computer. Don't bother saying, "But I really know computers. My wife calls me a 'computer genius.'" That doesn't speed things up!

Often, tech support people must follow a script and check things off despite your insistence that you've already done such a thing or another. Just follow along and eventually they catch up with you.

Get a Case Number

Before the call is over, try to get a case number, especially if the result is inconclusive or doesn't meet with your liking. The case number ensures that the next time you call, the support person can read over the incident and you have less repeating and re-explaining to do.

- ✔ You don't need a case number if the problem is solved.
- ✔ Some tech support people give case numbers whether the problem is solved or not. Do write it down and keep track of it for later.

Thank the Person

Whether your tech support person solves the problem or not, thank them for their time and efforts at assisting you. I'm not sure why, but it's just one of those things that was beaten into me as a child. (Heck, I even thanked the bullies who stole my lunch money.)

Chapter 24

Ten Dumb Error Messages

. . . .

In This Chapter

▶ Illegal operation

▶ Invalid page fault

▶ General protection fault

▶ Fatal exception

▶ Windows protection error

▶ KERNEL32.DLL errors

▶ The blue screen of death

▶ Stack overflow

▶ Divide by zero

▶ Command interpreter errors

. . . .

*H*oo, boy, this could be one long chapter! If only computers had just ten dumb error messages. But they don't. They have thousands. Back when I wrote the original *DOS For Dummies* (in 1991), I asked for and received from Microsoft a list of all possible error messages in DOS Version 5 — all 20,000 of them. And that was only DOS! Over the evolution of Windows, I can imagine that several *hundred thousand* error messages are possible — so many that I doubt Microsoft has them all listed.

This chapter lists what I consider to be the most popular, annoying, or just frustrating dumb error messages. Obviously, it's not the entire list. That would take too much room to print — and too much booze for me to write them all down.

The Program Has Performed an Illegal Operation and Will Be Shut Down; If the Problem Persists, Contact the Program Vendor

In our modern "What is legal?" society, this error message often induces uncalled-for terror in the bosom of its victims. What is *legal,* anyway?

Relax! In the computer world, the word *illegal* is used to describe a programming operation that isn't allowed. The computer programmers could have used the words *prohibited* or *corrupt* instead, but they didn't.

Another popular word to use is *invalid,* as demonstrated by the next several error messages. The word is pronounced "in-VALid," as in "not valid." It's not "IN-valid, as in "incapacitated by illness."

Anyway! The program has done something beyond your control. Too bad. Shut down the computer. Restart Windows. Start over.

Don't bother contacting the "program vendor." Odds are that the vendor doesn't want to hear from you, knows about the bug, and won't fix it. You can try if you want, but my experience has shown that they really, really don't care. And that's too bad.

Invalid Page Fault

This one has to do primarily with *virtual memory,* or disk storage that's used to bolster physical RAM. When a program attempts to access a chunk of virtual memory that doesn't exist, has been damaged, or is used by another program, you see the "Invalid Page Fault" gem of a message. There is nothing you can do about it.

Page is a term closely associated with virtual memory in Windows. Though virtual memory is one big, contiguous chunk of disk space, it's accessed through smaller chunks, called *pages*.

General Protection Fault

Who knows? Apparently, something is wrong, but Windows is unsure about the specifics; hence, the word *General*. From the word *protection*, you can assume that one program tried to stomp on some other program's turf. Windows responds by immediately killing the offending program and issuing this error message.

This is one instance where the Dr. Watson tool can be effective. Watson must be running in order to catch this one, and even if it is, good luck trying to find someone who can interpret Dr. Watson's results. (I'm not a big Watson fan; see Appendix A.)

San Andreas Fault

I'm just checking to see whether you're paying attention.

Fatal Exception 0D

The first of the Fatal Exception brothers (and I suppose that Fatal Exceptions 0A, 0B, and 0C exist, but they've apparently passed on to a higher realm — possibly UNIX), Fatal Exception 0D occurs when a program does something unusual or unexpected. In this case, the problem can be local to the display, to multimedia, or to other device drivers being corrupt or evil.

Fatal Exception 0E

A variation on the Invalid Page Fault error, this one crops up (again) when the program does something unusual or unexpected or somehow touches invalid or forbidden data. This error and the Invalid Page Fault error have subtle differences between them — subtle enough not to care about.

Perhaps the biggest difference between this error and the Invalid Page Fault error is that your Fatal Exception 0E requires that the computer be restarted in order to recover. Nasty.

Optional and fatal exceptional information

The *0D* in Fatal Exception 0D is a *number*, not a code. In this case, it's a hexadecimal number, which we humans would read as 13 — unlucky 13. Likewise, the 0E in Fatal Exception 0E is another number, 14. Here are the official Fatal Exception Family Error Numbers, their official names, and their brief meanings:

00 Divide Fault	Some idiot program tried to divide a number by zero.
02 NMI Interrupt	This hardware problem is too complex to explain in the space provided.
04 Overflow Trap	The washing machine is dumping water faster than the pipes can handle it.
05 Bounds Check Fault	Something is out of whack, so far that the whack woke up the microprocessor, which generated this error.
06 Invalid Opcode Fault	The microprocessor has encountered an instruction of a type it hasn't seen before. Yet, unlike the intrepid voyagers in a *Star Trek* episode, the microprocessor decides that it's time to cash in the chips and call it a day.
07 Coprocessor Not Available Fault	Because all Pentium computers come with a coprocessor installed, either the program is being run on a very old computer or the program is just being stupid.
08 Double Fault	The service changes sides in a tennis match.
09 Coprocessor Segment Overrun	The floating-point number is so large that it floats up and lodges in the cooling fan. The system has to stop while it unheats.
0A Invalid Task State Segment Fault	This message is rare ever since they banned alcohol from the fraternities over at Task State.
0B Not Present Fault	This message is commonly found in areas unaccustomed to earthquakes.
0C Stack Fault	See "Leaning Tower of Pisa Error."
10 Coprocessor Error Fault	The microprocessor misses the plane because the coprocessor is still in the bathroom *and* she has the tickets in her purse.
11 Alignment Check Fault	The computer sends a donation to the wrong political party.

Windows Protection Error

Whereas the other faults and errors described in this chapter seem to be rather vague (or involve virtual memory), this error is straightforward: You have a problem with a VxD, or virtual device driver. The solution is to boot into Safe mode and reinstall the virtual device driver in question (see Appendix A).

Numerous other problems can also induce a Windows protection error. The error message text states the specific source, such as memory, or a specific file or the Registry, for example.

Errors Involving KERNEL32.DLL

The kernel file gets blamed for lots of problems, but it causes relatively few of them. In fact, it's because the kernel file is so robust that many mishaps are caught and error messages displayed. In other words, KERNEL32.DLL is the messenger, and we don't kill the messenger, boys and girls.

Errors tossed back at the KERNEL32.DLL file include problems with the swap file, damaged files, injured-password lists, smashed Registry entries, microprocessor troubles, bad software programs, corrupted drivers, viruses, and even low disk space. In other words, the KERNEL32.DLL file catches lots of flack.

 ✔ As usual, restarting Windows fixes this problem.

 ✔ If you *clock* your CPU (run the microprocessor at a higher speed [MHz] than it's rated), you can get frequent KERNEL32.DLL errors.

 ✔ Hardware trouble — such as a hot PC, a broken power supply, static, or radio frequency noise — can also produce KERNEL32.DLL errors.

Blue-Screen-of-Death Errors

When it's a big and important error, Windows doesn't mess around with a dialog box or cute graphics and icons. No, it goes straight back to its soul: DOS! And the error message is displayed on a text screen; white text on a blue background. It's called the *Blue Screen of Death.* Generally, these errors are either fatal or important enough that they require immediate attention.

 ✔ If the error message says something along the lines of "Wait for window or press any key (or Ctrl+Alt+Delete) to reboot," then reboot. You can try waiting — especially if you feel that you can fix the problem or the problem will fix itself — but it's normally Ctrl+Alt+Delete+Pray.

 ✔ Sometimes the error message is simply urgent and not life-threatening. For example, you may be asked to reinsert a disk the computer was using. If so, obey the instructions and the computer continues working as before.

Stack Overflow

Technically a programmer's error, a stack overflow happens when a program runs low on a specific type of memory. The memory is called the *stack,* and it's used to store information for the program — like a scratch pad.

The problem is that the stack has only so much room and a sloppy or damaged program can use up that room quickly. When that happens, the microprocessor must take over and rescue the program, lest it bring down the entire computer system. The microprocessor steps in by halting the program and issuing a "stack overflow" error message.

No, there is nothing you can do about this other than complain to the program developer.

Divide by Zero

Another error caught by the microprocessor is the *divide by zero* error. When you try to divide something by zero on your pocket calculator, you get an *E* to indicate an error. The computer equivalent of the E is that the microprocessor steps in, stops the program, and issues a divide-by-zero error message.

No, there is nothing you can do about this error message either. You can try complaining to the software developer, but they usually blame you for it.

Bad or Missing Command Interpreter

This error is more of a DOS issue, but because the command prompt is still a part of Windows, you may see it from time to time.

The command prompt itself is a program named COMMAND.COM or CMD.COM (same thing). It's the program that displays the command prompt and runs other DOS programs and commands. Nerds would call it "the shell" program, for some obscure beach reference. Anyway.

When a DOS program closes, it's supposed to return control to COMMAND.COM. If memory space is tight or the program that was just run is corrupted, COMMAND.COM often can't be found. In that case, the DOS session hangs up and issues a "Bad or missing command interpreter" message.

Fortunately, this message doesn't mean disaster or instill the terror that it once did with DOS users. When you see the message, simply close off the DOS window and get on with your life.

Chapter 25

Ten Things You Should Never or Always Do

*Y*ou should always brush your teeth before you go to bed. No! You should always brush your teeth when you get up in the morning. No, better still, just walk around all day with a toothbrush in your mouth. Constantly brush your teeth! And floss!

Oh, boy! I hate lectures. But I thought that I would end this book with one just because I've been really good this time and haven't done much finger wagging. You see, it really isn't your fault! If you still have shame, consider reading through these ten things you should or shouldn't do. That should sate your guilt gland.

Never Run Your Computer in Safe Mode All the Time

Safe mode is for troubleshooting and fixing things. It's not the computer's standard operating mode. And though you can get work done in that mode, that's not what that mode is there for.

- ✔ I know that this advice makes sense, yet I get e-mail from people who do run their computers in Safe mode.
- ✔ Perhaps it's the name. Maybe it should be called Fixing mode or Troubleshooting mode.
- ✔ See Appendix A for more Safe mode stuff.

Never Reinstall Windows

Reinstalling Windows is a bad idea, especially considering that most problems can be fixed without having to reinstall. Only if your computer is ravaged by a virus or some other catastrophe is reinstalling the operating system ever necessary.

- ✔ Lazy tech support people suggest reinstalling Windows just to get you off the line. Don't give up that easily!
- ✔ Also refer to Chapter 19.

Never Reformat the Hard Drive

You have no reason to do this. It is not a routine chore. It is not required. It is not a part of owning a PC.

As with reinstalling Windows, reformatting a hard drive is necessary only if the system is utterly destroyed by some catastrophe. Otherwise, this is a rare and unnecessary thing to do.

Never Randomly Delete Files You Didn't Create

I think that the emphasis in this heading is more on "randomly" than on "files you didn't create." In many instances in this book, you have permission to delete certain files that you didn't create or cause to come into being. My point is merely to be careful with what you delete. Don't be hasty. Don't assume just because you don't know what something does that it's okay to delete it. That gets people into trouble.

Never Let Other People Use Your Computer

This advice is more of a Windows 98 and Windows Me rule; Windows XP is designed for multiple people to use the system — as long as each person has their own account.

No, this admonition is more of a warning: Suppose that you're having a party and one of your teenage son's friends says that he wants to use the PC in the den to do a quick check on his e-mail. The answer here is "No!" Letting strangers toy with your computer invites disaster. It's a bad idea no matter who they are.

A computer is a private thing. It's yours. If someone needs to use a computer, that person should be wise enough to carry their own portable computer or wander off to a public library, where they can use the government's computers freely. But treat your own computer like your wallet: Don't give it to just anyone.

Never Use Pirated Software

Pirated or stolen software — or any software you didn't pay for — is often the source of computer viruses. Sure, it may be "free." But who knows what idiot put what virus on that CD-R?

Pirated games are perhaps the single greatest source of viruses in the PC world. You just run a terrible risk — not to mention that it's legally and morally wrong to steal.

Always Shut Down Windows Properly

Use the Shut Down Windows dialog box to make the operating system die a peaceable death. The idea is to try to avoid the situation where you just turn off the computer. That leads to major problems down the road.

Of course, if the system doesn't let you shut down properly, you have to just flip the power switch. Refer to Chapter 20 for some help.

Always Back Up

Whether it's just copying today's files to a removable disk or using real backup software, you would be wise to have a spare copy of your data handy (refer to Chapter 22).

Always Set Restore Points after Installing New Software or Hardware

The System Restore utility in Windows Me and Windows XP is a must-use tool for whenever you upgrade your system. Remember that change introduces problems in many computers. Having the ability to "go back in time" with System Restore is a blessing. Set those restore points!

Refer to Chapter 4.

Always Scan for Viruses

I highly recommend using antivirus software. It's a must. In fact, it's shocking that such a utility isn't a part of Windows. (Oh, but I could go on. . . .) Instead, I recommend investing in a good antivirus program, such as Norton AntiVirus or any program that offers updates via the Internet.

Computing in this decade is a dangerous thing. Make it safer. Use antivirus software.

Appendix A

Useful Tools

• •

In This Appendix

▶ The System Configuration utility

▶ The Device Manager

▶ The System Information tool

▶ Dr. Watson

▶ Norton AntiVirus

• •

*W*indows has a heck of a lot of tools, or *utilities,* in it. This appendix contains my short list of what I feel are the most useful or handy tools to use.

The System Configuration Utility (MSCONFIG)

The System Configuration utility, as shown in Figure A-1, is your main weapon in fighting the PC's start-up battle. This handy dialog box covers just about anything that goes on when Windows first starts up.

To start the utility, type **MSCONFIG** in the Run dialog box.

You can summon the Run dialog box by pressing Win+R or choosing Run from the main Start menu.

The General tab contains the main start-up options:

✔ **Normal Startup:** Run the normal Windows start-up.

✔ **Diagnostic Startup:** Run the computer in Safe mode.

✔ **Selective Startup:** Choose various options to enable or disable during start-up (used mostly by tech support).

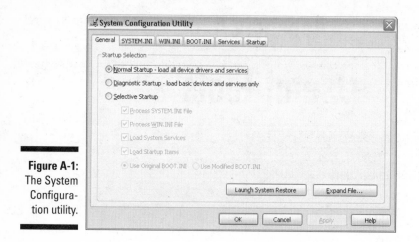

You can also use the Advanced button on the General tab (only in Windows 98 and Windows Me) to disable certain commands and options for a selective start-up.

The SYSTEM.INI, WIN.INI, CONFIG.SYS, and AUTOEXEC.BAT tabs list various options used by those programs from earlier versions of Windows. (CONFIG.SYS and AUTOEXEC.BAT do not appear in Windows XP.)

The BOOT.INI tab (in Windows XP only) is used to configure boot options that take place before Windows starts up.

Finally, the Startup tab contains programs that Windows automatically starts — programs you don't find by choosing Programs⇨Startup Menu.

Windows Me has three unique tabs in its System Configuration Utility window:

 ✔ Static VxDs provides a list of virtual device drivers for compatibility with older Windows (and DOS) programs.
 ✔ The Environment tab lists environment variables.
 ✔ The International tab shows various country-specific information.

Windows XP also sports a Services tab, which you can use to disable certain Windows elements, or services.

The Device Manager

The Device Manager is where Windows lists most of the computer's hardware and tells whether that hardware is functioning.

To open the Device Manager in Windows 98 or Windows Me, open the Control Panel's System icon. Then click on the Device Manager tab.

In Windows XP, open the Control Panel's System icon, click the Hardware tab, and then click the Device Manager button. The Device Manager is shown in Figure A-2.

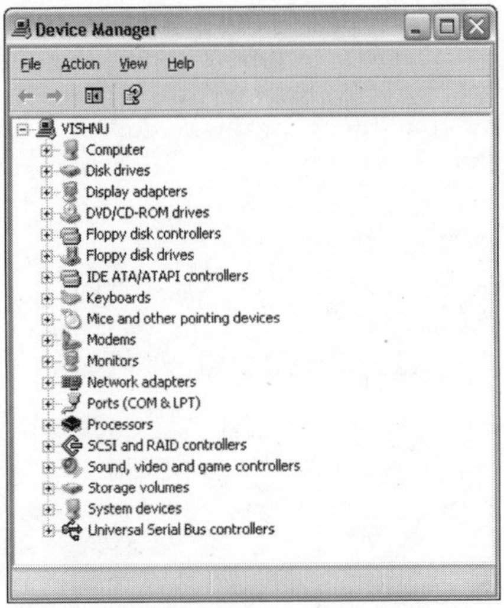

Figure A-2: The Device Manager.

Note that the Device Manager *does not* list any printers. For those, you must open the Printers window.

The Device Manager lists hardware by category. To see your PC's hardware, you must open a category, such as the Disk drives item, by clicking the plus sign [+] to the left of Disk drives. This action displays the individual hardware items.

To get more information about individual hardware items, you must double-click to open that item. That action displays the item's Properties dialog box, where you can see whether the particular device is working properly. If it isn't, a notice appears on the General tab in the Properties dialog box.

You can use the Driver tab in the Properties dialog box to install or update a new driver (software) for the device. You do that by clicking the Update Driver button (though it's assumed that you already have the driver down-loaded or available on a CD or floppy disk).

You can also disable a device, which prevents Windows from loading software or recognizing the device the next time Windows starts up. That way, you can troubleshoot the device or its driver software; if the computer works better without the device enabled, you have a problem with the device.

System Information

The System Information tool is a handy thing to have, plus it's a great launching spot for running many other tools or utilities in Windows.

Start the System Information program by clicking the Start button and choosing Programs⇨Accessories⇨System Tools⇨System Information.

The System Information tool's main job is to report about your computer, as shown in Figure A-3. This dialog box provides a central location for listing all sorts of information about your computer's hardware, software, environment, and the various applications you run.

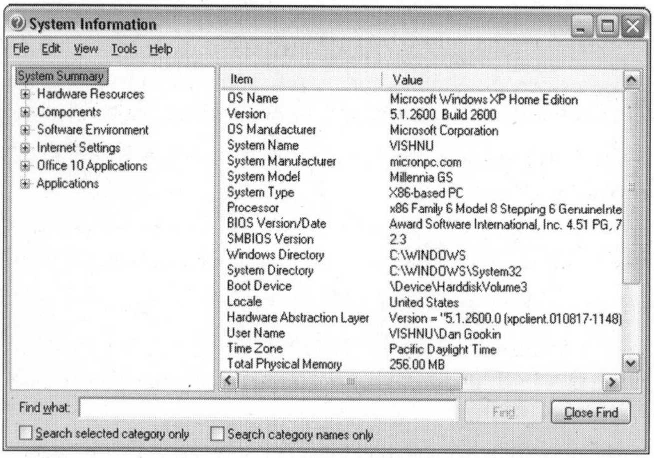

Figure A-3:
The System
Information
tool.

Note that in Windows Me, the System Information window appears as part of the help system.

For example, to see whether your computer has any hardware conflicts, open the Hardware Resources item (click on the [+] to its left) and then select Conflicts/Sharing. The System Information tool then lists any shared or conflicting devices in your computer.

Another bonus to this tool is its incredible Tools menu. On that menu are listed plenty of other handy Windows tools, including some or all of the following:

✔ **Automatic Skip Drier Agent:** A Windows 98 and Windows Me tool that helps troubleshoot problems with drivers that may be crashing the system or conflicting with other drivers. It works only when Windows notices Automatic Skip Driver failures.

✔ **DirectX Diagnostic Tool:** A massive (and relatively unknown) utility for analyzing various gaming components of your PC, as controlled by the DirectX standard.

✔ **Disk Cleanup:** Found on the menu in the Windows XP System Information tool. Refer to Chapter 21 for the details.

✔ **Dr. Watson:** Covered later in this appendix.

✔ **File Signature Verification Utility:** Confirms that signed files are valid. A *signed* file contains a digital signature, designed to ensure that the file is sent by a responsible source and performs the advertised duty (that the file isn't a virus or worm or Trojan horse, for example).

✔ **Fault log:** In Windows Me, displays a text file listing problems with the system — those "fault protection" errors. The information in the log is really technical.

✔ **Hardware Wizard:** Runs the Add New Hardware Wizard in Windows XP.

✔ **Net Diagnostics:** Runs a troubleshooter/diagnostic tool (as part of the help system) in Windows XP. It's called Network Diagnostics in Windows Me.

✔ **Network Connections:** Opens the Network Connections window in Windows XP.

✔ **Registry Checker:** Similar to ScanDisk, but used for the Registry. Also used to back up the Registry in Windows 98 and Windows Me.

✔ **ScanDisk:** Checks your disk drives for errors (refer to Chapter 21).

✔ **Signature Verification tool:** The Windows 98 and Windows Me name for the File Signature Verification utility. (Refer to Signature Verification Utility on the list.)

✔ **System Configuration Utility:** Covered earlier in this appendix.

✔ **System File Checker:** A handy Windows 98 tool that verifies the condition of Windows files and optionally restores some key files. You can also use this tool to extract a file from the Windows CD or the Windows files stored on your computer (in the C:\Windows\Options\CABS\ folder.)

✔ **System Restore:** Returns the system's condition to match an earlier time; also a great recovery tool. Used only in Windows Me and Windows XP; refer to Chapter 4.

✔ **Update Wizard Uninstall:** A tool for uninstalling various updates in Windows 98 and Windows Me.

✔ **Version Conflict Manager:** A Windows 98 tool that allows you to log newer drivers that may conflict with older drivers and to switch or rearrange the drivers to help resolve compatibility issues.

✔ **WMI Control:** The Windows Management Instrumentation tool, used for remote system management of Windows Me.

✔ **Windows Report Tool:** In Windows 98 only, an information-gathering tool to report problems to Microsoft. I do not recommend using this tool, mostly because Microsoft is dropping its Windows 98 support effective in June 2003.

Dr. Watson

I am not a Dr. Watson fan — ever since he first showed up in Windows Version 3 for DOS back in 1993. At first, he sounded like some miraculous Peter Norton–like tool for finding out what's wrong with Windows. (Yes, it had trouble even back then.) But, no, Dr. Watson is merely a disaster-reporting tool — a CNN for your computer that neither makes the news nor resolves any issues.

Running Dr. Watson in Windows 98 simply places him in the system tray. If you click his head (the icon), he snaps a picture of your PC's condition and saves it in the C:\Windows\DRWATSON folder. You can also-right click the icon and choose Dr Watson from the menu, and he gives you a brief, potentially useful, report about your PC.

Running Dr. Watson in Windows XP is a little more fruitful, mostly because you can have more control over him, what he monitors, and how he presents his reports.

Overall, I assume that the Dr. Watson tool has some value, though I personally don't find it good for much.

Norton AntiVirus

I recommend Norton AntiVirus to any Windows user who is concerned about viruses — and we all should be. However, this program isn't a part of Windows and must be purchased separately. Fortunately, the program is easy to use and update, and it does the job most adequately, which is why I recommend it.

If installed properly, Norton AntiVirus works constantly to scan your system for viruses, including incoming e-mail and attachments. It connects with the Internet to download new virus definitions, keeping the program up-to-date for free for a year after you install it. And it displays weekly reports or pops up with any important information while you're working.

A key thing to know about antivirus software is how to disable it if you ever need to install a new program or perform some activity that would otherwise be thwarted by the antivirus software. To temporarily disable Norton AntiVirus, right-click the AntiVirus icon in the system tray/notification area. Choose the Disable Auto-Protect command from the pop-up menu. Then go about your business.

To reenable AntiVirus, right-click the icon in the system tray/notification area and choose Enable Auto-Protect from the pop-up menu.

Appendix B

Working in Safe Mode

- -

In This Appendix

▶ Getting into Safe mode

▶ Using Safe mode to fix things

▶ Getting out of Safe mode

- -

*T*he only question I have is "Why does Windows need a 'safe' mode?" Shouldn't it be safe to use Windows all the time? And if it's called Safe mode, does that make the normal mode of operation Dangerous mode?"

Once again showing a knack for improperly naming things, Microsoft gives Windows users *Safe mode*. (It's an industry-wide problem with naming things, not just Microsoft's.) Safe mode really should be called Diagnostic mode or even Slim mode because in Safe mode you can run Windows with no extra drivers or options, which are often the cause of any trouble you may be experiencing.

Starting in Safe Mode

You have many ways to get into Safe mode in Windows.

The first way happens under Windows own decree: The computer just starts up in Safe mode. You can tell by the low resolution plus the words *Safe mode* in all four corners of the screen, as shown in Figure B-1. When this happens, Windows is telling you that something is wrong. Indeed, it may even announce why it's going into Safe mode before you even see Safe mode.

The second way you can enter Safe mode is manually, when the computer starts. Immediately after the "Starting Windows" text message appears, you can press the F5 or F8 key to see a start-up menu. (I cover this subject in Chapter 8.) You can select one of the Safe mode options from that menu to start your computer in Safe mode.

Figure B-1:
Safe mode.

Finally, you can direct the computer to start in Safe mode from the System Configuration utility. On the General tab, if you select the Diagnostic start-up, Windows starts in Safe mode the next time around. (Conversely, if you would rather have Windows not start in Safe mode, select Normal from the list in the System Configuration utility.)

✔ Overall, you should realize that you use Safe mode to fix things. That's it. You don't work on projects there. You don't gather and reply to e-mail. You fix something and then start the computer in Normal mode.

✔ In Windows Me, Safe mode starts with a Help system troubleshooter.

Fixing Things in Safe Mode

The idea behind Safe mode is that, with various options and features disabled, it's easier for you to work at fixing them. You can change certain settings that the computer doesn't allow you to change when you're in Normal mode.

For example, I recommend using Safe mode if someone has changed the settings on the Appearance tab in the Display Properties dialog box. Suppose that someone has changed the text to be very small or changed the graphics to be very big or use black-on-black text. You can fix all this in Safe mode and restore your settings.

If the computer just spontaneously goes into Safe mode, check the Device Manager. If your computer has a problem, the device appears flagged with a yellow circle and an exclamation point. Open that device by double-clicking it and then read what the problem is. Follow those instructions to fix the problem.

Generally speaking, disabling a device in the Device Manager or reinstalling an older device driver is the solution that puts the computer back to normal.

In Windows XP, you're given the option to run System Restore rather than enter Safe mode — a good choice! System Restore most likely gets back whatever options were changed and restores the system so that Safe mode is no longer required.

Note that you change just about any Windows settings in Safe mode. Those changes may not appear immediately, as they would when Windows is normally run. But the changes are made nonetheless; you see their effects when you restart the computer and return to Normal mode.

- Yes, many things don't work in Safe mode. Those things, such as networking, are disabled to provide a better environment for troubleshooting.

- Refer to Chapter 4 for more information on running System Restore to fix problems in Windows XP.

- The changes you make may not have any visual effect in Safe mode, but they have an effect when you return to Normal mode.

You're Done with Safe Mode

When you've finished making your Safe mode corrections, simply restart the PC. Do this part properly! Even Safe mode must be restarted the way Windows normally is.

When the computer comes back to life, the problem should be fixed. Then you can get on with your duties.

If the computer continues to boot into Safe mode, check the Device Manager. Read any start-up messages that appear. Open the System Configuration utility (MSCONF, covered in Appendix A), and switch back to the Normal Startup option to see whether that helps.

As a next-to-last resort, connect to the Internet and visit the Microsoft Knowledge Base (refer to Chapter 5) to see whether you can find a solution to your predicament there.

Appendix C

Creating and Using an Emergency Boot Disk

*W*indows 98 and Windows Me come with a nifty utility that builds a *startup disk*, though everyone I know calls it the *emergency boot disk*. It's a floppy disk you can use to start your computer. On that disk are copied a bunch of useful tools that you can use to help recover data or, if things are really bad, begin reinstallation chores.

Windows XP doesn't come with such a disk. The reason is probably that the XP operating system doesn't fit on a floppy disk, but more likely that most computers now come with recovery CD-ROMs and the era of the emergency boot disk is rapidly passing.

In addition to the Windows emergency boot disk, many utilities also come with emergency boot disks. I also discuss them in this chapter.

Creating the Emergency Boot Disk

Here's how to create the emergency boot disk in Windows 98 and Windows Me:

1. **Obtain a blank floppy disk and stick it into Drive A.**

   This disk becomes the emergency boot disk for your computer.

2. **Click the Start button.**

3. **Choose Settings⊅Control Panel.**

   The Control Panel appears in all its glory.

4. **Open the Add/Remove Programs icon.**

   The Add/Remove Programs Properties dialog box appears.

5. **Click the Startup Disk tab.**

   I could show you a figure of what you see here, but it's boring, so I won't.

6. **Click the Create Disk button.**

   A dialog box tells you to stick a disk into the floppy drive, which you've already done, so go to Step 7.

7. **Click the OK button.**

   Files are copied to the disk. This step takes some time. Floppy disks are slow.

   If the disk bombs out, replace it with another one. *Throw the bum disk out!*

   If all turns out fine, you return to the Add/Remove Programs Properties dialog box.

8. **Click OK to close the dialog box.**

9. **Close the Control Panel window as well, while you're at it.**

10. **Remove the floppy disk from Drive A.**

11. **Stick a label on the disk.**

12. **Write your computer's name, the date, and "Emergency Boot Disk" on the label.**

The disk really isn't anything special. It's merely a bootable floppy disk with certain disk recovery utilities copied to it. The only special thing is that Windows offers a command that creates the disk for you. And I do recommend creating the disk and keeping it in a safe, memorable place.

✔ I have you label the disk after it's created because not every floppy disk formats. So, labeling *after* a successful format saves you time.

✔ The files copied to the emergency boot disk comes from a special folder on the hard drive: C:\Windows\Command\EBD. The Command folder contains older DOS commands. The EBD folder, as you may guess, contains the emergency boot disk files.

Using the Emergency Boot Disk

To use the emergency boot disk, simply stick it in your computer's Drive A and restart Windows. Or, if you have a true emergency, start your computer with the disk in Drive A.

The computer should boot from the disk in Drive A, which displays a start-up menu where you can choose whether you want to have CD-ROM support. My advice: Definitely activate CD-ROM support. That way, you can use the computer's CD-ROM drive, which gives you access to any CD-ROM you have, including the Windows CD.

Sometimes, this procedure doesn't work — if you have your computer set to boot from the CD-ROM drive and ignore the floppy drive, for example. In those cases, you can enter your PC's Setup program (refer to Chapter 8) and reconfigure it so that the floppy disk boots before the hard drive or CD-ROM drive.

Or, you may have a bootable CD-ROM utility, such as Norton Utilities or a backup program. In that case, you can boot from the CD-ROM drive, and then — after the computer starts — access Drive A and run any programs from there.

After the emergency boot disk loads, you see the DOS prompt for Drive A:

```
A:\>
```

This line is where you type various commands to get things done. For example, type **DIR C:** (DIR, a space, the letter *C,* and then a colon) to see whether you can access the hard drive C. What you see should look like this:

```
A:\> DIR C:
```

Press the Enter key and you see displayed either a list of files on hard drive C or the nasty "Invalid Drive Specification" or "No such disk" message or an equally ominous and bad error message.

In a real emergency, you'll probably have a tech support person telling you what to type. For this example, merely remove the disk from Drive A and press Ctrl+Alt+Delete to restart your computer. (DOS has no official "shutdown" command.)

Emergency Boot Disk Contents

The files included on the emergency boot disk are all DOS utilities, most of which are involved with basic computer setup and initialization. The disk has few true recovery tools.

Do not run any command unless you're directed to do so by a tech support person.

Unlike the safe, warm, fuzzy world of Windows, the world of DOS can be unforgiving and cruel. If you accidentally type a command, it may march forth and alter your system without giving you a chance to change your mind. Be very careful!

Even so, here are the commands you can type at the DOS prompt and how each one works. Do not type anything here!

- ✓ **CHECKSR:** In Windows Me, this program prompts you to do a System Restore recovery. If you elect to, the last good system configuration is chosen and you're directed to restart your computer.

- ✓ **EXTRACT:** This utility is used to pull files from the special compressed CAB folders. Windows stores all its files and programs in the CAB folders. A tech support person would direct you in using this utility to restore any missing pieces of Windows.

- ✓ **FDISK:** This utility is used to partition the hard drive. Do not use it unless directed to by tech support personnel.

In Windows Me, the following utilities are installed on a RAM drive in your computer. (A *RAM drive* is a special disk drive that's created by using the computer's memory; it's an old trick from the days of DOS and one that's not used any more, other than when you're starting your computer with a floppy disk.) The RAM drive is usually given drive letter D, though it could be another letter of the alphabet.

- ✓ **ATTRIB:** You use this utility to change the attributes of a file. Specifically, in the case of a crash, you would use it to make the secret, hidden boot files secret and hidden — protecting them from tampering.

- ✓ **CHKDSK:** The old DOS version of the ScanDisk command, CHKDSK is used to "check a disk." Use the SCANDISK program instead, though.

- ✓ **DEBUG:** You use this technical utility to peer into files and memory. Use this command only when directed to by tech support.

- ✓ **EDIT:** The old DOS text editor comes in handy for editing system files.

✔ **EXT:** This special tool runs the EXTRACT utility.

✔ **FORMAT:** The disk formatting tool can be used after FDISK to format a hard drive. Again, it isn't something I recommend that you do unless you're advised to by someone else.

✔ **HELP**. This command lets you view the contents of the emergency boot disk's README.TXT file. (The command runs the EDIT program — refer to the fourth bullet in this list — to help show you the important contents of the README.TXT file.)

✔ **SCANDISK:** SCANDISK runs a DOS version of the ScanDisk program, which can help find and fix some errors on your hard drive.

✔ **SYS:** This command is used after formatting a hard drive to make the hard drive bootable. Do not use this program unless directed to do so by tech support personnel!

Other Emergency Boot Disks

Any good utility worth what you paid for it comes with some type of emergency boot disk, or at least the methods to create one.

Norton Utilities, for example, comes with an emergency boot disk that you can use to start the computer in case your system doesn't have such a disk. Also, the CD-ROM itself is bootable, should your computer be able to pull off that stunt. (Ditto for Norton AntiVirus.)

Many backup programs come with special restore floppies or CDs that can be used to start the computer and begin recovery operations. That way, you can fully restore your computer in case the hard drive becomes utterly wiped out. (I know — I've done it a few times.)

Finally, most good PCs come with a system recovery CD, which is also fully bootable. Most of these disks are merely used to reinstall Windows and rebuild the hard drive to the state it was in when you first bought the computer. This disk may also contain recovery information and utilities, though this disk gets used mostly for the old "reinstall Windows" copout.

Appendix D

Some Q&A

T he feedback I receive from readers is valuable to me because it helps me hone my books and keeps me in touch with what exactly people are having trouble with. A lot of the basic troubleshooting information and advice found in this book is based on the bulk of reader e-mail I get.

The following pages contain just a few of the many reader questions that flow into my e-mail inbox every week. I've included them here for your reference enjoyment as well as to assist you should any of your problems match those of previous readers. These examples can also show you how to put this book to work and help you solve specific problems that you may not feel are already covered.

By the way, my e-mail address is dgookin@wambooli.com. It's listed in the Introduction, which also includes information on my free weekly newsletter and my wonderful Web site, Wambooli.com. Feel free to drop me a line sometime.

General Windows Q&A

Q: Is there any way to set a default font for the entire computer? I know how to set fonts in Notepad and Word and Outlook Express. But I'd rather just set the official font in one place. Do you know where that place is?

A: Beyond the moon? Beyond the rain? Somewhere, over the rainbow. . . !

Seriously, there is no such place. There should be! But there isn't. You must set the default font for each of your applications by using commands specific to that application. Of course, after you've done that for each of your applications, you're set! But one would think that with a computer it could be done in one central, powerful place. Alas, that's just not the case.

Q: Can I still change my desktop wallpaper if I have a "theme" going?

A: Certainly. A *theme* is merely a collection of Windows visual and audio attributes that can be applied with a single command in a central place (the Themes icon in the Control Panel). Even so, once applied, you can go into any part of Windows and make adjustments, for example, to the screen fonts or sounds or the desktop background.

Specifically in the case of the desktop background, open the Control Panel's Display Properties icon. Click the Background or Desktop tab and then choose a new wallpaper from the scrolling list. Or if you'd rather not have any wallpaper, choose (None) from the scrolling list.

Q: Why does my window open up so tiny on the screen? Sometimes it's half size? What gives?

A: Windows remembers the size of its windows. Wherever you position a window, and in whatever size, that's the same location and size Windows uses when you reopen that window.

The problem people have with this is that they use the window's Maximize button to resize the window instead of using the mouse to move and resize. If you use the mouse, Windows remembers the window's new size and location.

Another problem happens when browsing the Web; annoying pop-up windows appear in a galaxy of odd sizes. Because that was the most recent window opened by Internet Explorer, any new window you open also appears in that small, annoying size. Again, you have to manually resize the window to get it back to something more pleasing.

Do not maximize! Resize!

Q: The Disk Cleanup program doesn't delete all of those temporary Windows files. I still have quite a few of them. Is it okay to go in and manually delete them?

A: No! The files are probably being used by Windows presently, so deleting them would be a bad thing. (Or you may just get a nasty warning message telling you not to delete a busy file.)

The best way to delete all of them is to start in DOS mode, where you can go and delete the files easily because Windows hasn't been started and it's definitely *not* using the files.

Even if you do manage to delete all the files, note that Windows creates more when it starts again. It's like trying to rake leaves during a windstorm.

Q: If I install both Norton AntiVirus and McAfee VirusScan, will that make me double-safe protected against viruses?

A: I suppose so, though there is overlap in the protections offered. The problem instead will be that the two programs, because they're redundant, will most likely slow down your system. I would stick with one or the other.

Q: I can't get the music CD I burned to play in my car's CD player.

A: That happens. Some CD players cannot read the CD-R disks. In fact, you have to look on the CD player to see if it's CD-R compatible. And remember that CD-RWs, though you can record music on them, are generally played only in CD-RW drives. I have seen a few portable boom boxes that claim to be CD-RW compatible, however.

Q: Is there any way to undo a Windows Update?

A: I've never tried, though you could attempt either a System Restore or restore from a recent full backup disk.

Q: I just copied a newer file over an existing file. Is there any way I can get the older file back? Would it be in the Recycle Bin?

A: Alas, when you copy over an existing file, or even save a new file to disk with the name of an existing file, the older file is completely overwritten by the newer one. There is no way to recover the older file at all. Alas.

General Internet Q&A

Q: I really don't understand the concept of a "firewall." Can you explain?

A: A *firewall* is simply hardware or software designed to ensure that the information getting into your computer is welcome and wanted. Everything else that wanders through is squished. In fact, if the firewall is good enough, nasty programs or probes attempting to enter your computer don't even know that a firewall has stopped them in the first place; the program merely assumes that there is no computer there and moves on. Spiffy.

Firewalls provide varying degrees of protection. For example, my firewall allows one of my computers to host a Web page. Only valid Web page traffic is allowed through the firewall and into that one computer. Everything else that attempts to make contact is snuffed out.

Q: The little computers that once appeared when I connected to the Internet are gone! They used to show up down in the System Tray, but now the tray is empty. How can I get that icon back? It was really handy for when I had to disconnect.

A: Sorry that you miss the little guys. If you have Windows Me or Windows XP, consider doing a System Restore. Otherwise, you can manually summon them back by following these steps:

1. **Open the Control Panel's Internet Options icon.**

2. **Click the Connections tab.**

3. **Highlight your ISP in the list.**

4. **Click the Settings button.**

   The ISP's Properties dialog box appears.

5. **Click the Properties button.**

6. **Finally, put a check mark by the Show Icon in Notification Area When Connected check box.**

   (Look at the bottom of the dialog box.)

7. **Close the various dialog boxes and windows you opened.**

That will fix it.

Web Browsing Q&A

Q: Some Web sites seem to have extremely small fonts. I can't read them! Is there anything I can do about this?

A: Sure, get glasses. No, seriously, your Web browser, like many other programs in Windows, has a Zoom command, which you can use to enlarge the text on the screen. In Internet Explorer, the commands you're looking for are in the View⇨Text Size submenu. Choose the Larger command from the menu, for example, to see all the text in a Web page in a larger size.

This command will not fix smaller images or text that is in reality a graphical image.

Also note that each new Web page that loads resets the text size. (If the problem is on one of your favorite Web sites, consider e-mailing the Webmaster at that site and have him or her change the size. The e-mail address is typically *webmaster@* followed by the name of the Web page's domain, such as `webmaster@wambooli.com`.)

See Chapter 17 for more Web browsing information.

Q: I'm having a heck of a time trying to print this Web page. Any help?

A: Web pages are tough to print. Webmasters realize that and often create printer-friendly versions of a page, which you can find by looking for a printer-friendly link.

If there is no printer-friendly link, and your attempts at printing the page are less than spectacular, then do what I do and save the entire Web page archive to disk: Choose File⇨Save As from the menu bar. Use the drop-down list in the Save As dialog box to tell Internet Explorer that you want to save the Web Page Archive. (That means everything: graphics, text, all of it.) Click the Save button.

After the page is on disk, then you can open it by using a program such as Microsoft Word or Microsoft Excel, both of which can read Web pages. Excel is a better choice, in fact, for printing wide Web pages because, like spreadsheets, Web pages can be wide, and Excel knows how to print such things. Word, on the other hand, is better for longer documents.

When you have the document open in Word or Excel, use the Print Preview command to check out how it's going to look. If things need adjusting, use Word or Excel to adjust whatever needs it (by using the various commands and controls in those programs). Then print as you would any Word or Excel document.

Q: What is the square icon that often appears on a Web page? It has a little box with a red square, green circle, and blue triangle in it?

A: That's the *missing picture* icon. It means that either the Web page didn't have time to load that graphic image or the image couldn't be found. (Typically when an image can't be found, a red icon with a white X in it appears.)

You can try to reload the Web page; the reload command is the F5 key in Internet Explorer. Or you can right-click on the icon and choose the Load Image command from the pop-up menu.

Q: If a Web page can save a cookie on my computer, what's to stop it from putting a virus into that cookie?

A: Nothing. Cookies generally do not contain executable code. Even if they do, the cookie file itself ends up as a plain old text file on disk. To be technical, the file is ASCII, not binary. Even if it did contain nasty code, the file would have to be renamed and then run, which is beyond the scope of any Web browser to do.

Q: The Web page didn't load! It can't be gone! I was just there yesterday.

A: Some pages do go away, but more likely the browser just got tired of waiting. Remember that the entire Internet does slow down from time to time, and your Web browser *times out* after a spell. Just click the Reload button and try again. Oftentimes, the page will come right up.

Q: For some reason, I've lost all the pictures on the Web.

A: Pictures are, if you can believe it, optional. You can turn them off or turn them on. In this case, something probably turned them off. To turn them back on again, follow these steps:

1. **Open the Control Panel's Internet Options icon.**
2. **Click the Advanced tab.**
3. **Scroll through the list of options until you get to the Multimedia section.**
4. **Find the Show Pictures item.**
5. **Put a check mark by that item.**
6. **Click OK.**

That will get your pictures back.

E-mail Q&A

Q: I've created dozens of e-mail "rules" in Outlook Express, most of which help me eliminate common spam. Unfortunately, my mail rules also delete messages from people I legitimately correspond with. How can I make the rules less severe?

A: When it comes to Mail Rules, there is a pecking order. Refer to Figure 18-4 to see an example of a list of many Mail Rules. See how they appear in the list? That's the order in which they're processed. So, from Figure 18-4, you see that the Dr. Fred rule is processed first, then the "spam — you cannot beat this deal" rule, then the "credit card" rule, and so on.

To save messages from your friends first, you need to create a Mail Rule for your friend's name, similar to the Dr. Fred rule in Figure 18-4. Create a rule that states when the From line contains *"your friend's name"* the rule should move that message into a specific folder. For example, you could have a folder just for that friend or a folder that contains all your friendly e-mail — whatever! Just create a rule that saves the legitimate e-mail. Then put that rule *at the top* of the list: Highlight the rule and use the Move Up button to put it first. That way the rule sifts out legitimate e-mail before the anti-spam rules have a chance to squash things.

Q: I tried to send e-mail to my friend, and the message came back. It's never done that before!

A: The message bounced, eh? That happens, and it could be for a number of reasons. If it's an address you send to often, then just resend the message: In Outlook Express, go into the Sent Items folder and right-click the bounced message. Choose Forward from the pop-up menu and then resend the message as a forward. You can add something like, "This originally bounced from your account. I don't know why."

Q: I have a friend who swears she knows someone who got a $4,000 check from Bill Gates for forwarding her e-mail. I doubt it myself, but how can I convince my friend that it's bogus?

A: You're correct that it's bogus. It's an official e-mail myth, in fact. Such things are easily verified by checking a few sources on the Internet. My favorite places are

    www.truthorfiction.com/

and

    www.vmyths.com/

When you get to either page, search for the myth in question, and that will verify that it's untrue. Then send that Web page address (copy it from the Web browser and paste it into your e-mail program) to your friend as proof. If you do this enough, then these rumors will stop.

Q: I have a message stuck in my e-mail inbox. The message has an attachment, which I think may be a virus, but I can't tell; whenever I try to open the message — even to click it — my computer crashes, and I have to restart Windows. I've turned the preview pane off, and the computer still crashes. What can I do?

A: Obviously the message contains something vile enough to turn the computer into stone when you try to open it, most likely because your e-mail program (and I'm guessing it's Outlook Express here) is trying to display the attachment — even with preview off, which is odd. But the problem can still be cured in a rather brutal and final way:

1. **Clean out your inbox, but leave the offending message untouched.**

   Read all the mail in your inbox. Delete the messages you don't want to keep. File the rest away into other folders. But do not click or highlight the offending message. Leave it alone!

2. **Quit Outlook Express.**

3. **Search the computer for your inbox file.**

   Outlook Express stores the mail messages in your inbox in a special folder on disk. The exact location varies with each release of Windows, but the filename is the same: `INBOX.DBX`. Use the Windows search or Find Files command to locate the file `INBOX.DBX`.

   If you're using Windows XP, then it may find several such `INBOX.DBX` files. Choose only the one that belongs to your account on the computer.

4. **Click to select the found `INBOX.DBX` file.**

5. **Press the F2 key.**

   F2 is the Rename command keyboard shortcut.

6. **Change the name to `INBOX.DBX.BAK`.**

   Just add `.BAK` to the name.

7. **Close the Search Results window.**

8. **Restart Outlook Express.**

   Because Outlook Express is rather smart, it will restart and recreate the missing `INBOX.DBX` file, giving you a brand-new, empty e-mail inbox. Problem solved.

If you really want to be final about things, then go back and find the `INBOX.DBX.BAK` file and delete it from your computer. Then the problem message will be gone forever.

Q: Is there any way to compress a video clip to send it through e-mail?

A: No. Video is pretty compressed already, so it cannot be compressed further. Zipping the file, or putting it into a Compressed folder, doesn't actually save any space. And many ISPs limit the size of individual e-mail messages, so you cannot send such bulky files.

There are, however, two solutions. The first is to burn the video onto a CD-R and then use the regular mail to send a CD of your video to your pals. That's pretty common.

The second solution is to use video-editing software and clip down or edit the image to a shorter segment that can be e-mailed. It's not much, but it does get the idea across.

Index

• C •

• *E* •

• *F* •

Notes

Notes

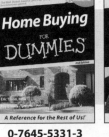

FOR DUMMIES®

A world of resources to help you grow

TRAVEL

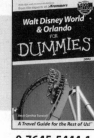

0-7645-5453-0

0-7645-5438-7

0-7645-5444-1

EDUCATION & TEST PREPARATION

0-7645-5194-9

0-7645-5325-9

0-7645-5249-X

HEALTH, SELF-HELP & SPIRITUALITY

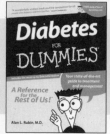

0-7645-5154-X

0-7645-5302-X

0-7645-5418-2

FOR DUMMIES®

Helping you expand your horizons and realize your potential

GRAPHICS & WEB SITE DEVELOPMENT

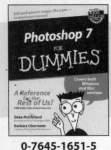

Photoshop 7 For Dummies
0-7645-1651-5

Creating Web Pages For Dummies
0-7645-1643-4

Macromedia Flash MX For Dummies
0-7645-0895-4

Also available:

Adobe Acrobat 5 PDF For Dummies
(0-7645-1652-3)

ASP.NET For Dummies
(0-7645-0866-0)

ColdFusion MX for Dummies
(0-7645-1672-8)

Dreamweaver MX For Dummies
(0-7645-1630-2)

FrontPage 2002 For Dummies
(0-7645-0821-0)

HTML 4 For Dummies
(0-7645-0723-0)

Illustrator 10 For Dummies
(0-7645-3636-2)

PowerPoint 2002 For Dummies
(0-7645-0817-2)

Web Design For Dummies
(0-7645-0823-7)

PROGRAMMING & DATABASES

C++ For Dummies
0-7645-0746-X

Visual Studio .NET All-in-One Desk Reference For Dummies
0-7645-1626-4

XML For Dummies
0-7645-1657-4

Also available:

Access 2002 For Dummies
(0-7645-0818-0)

Beginning Programming For Dummies
(0-7645-0835-0)

Crystal Reports 9 For Dummies
(0-7645-1641-8)

Java & XML For Dummies
(0-7645-1658-2)

Java 2 For Dummies
(0-7645-0765-6)

JavaScript For Dummies
(0-7645-0633-1)

Oracle9i For Dummies
(0-7645-0880-6)

Perl For Dummies
(0-7645-0776-1)

PHP and MySQL For Dummies
(0-7645-1650-7)

SQL For Dummies
(0-7645-0737-0)

Visual Basic .NET For Dummies
(0-7645-0867-9)

LINUX, NETWORKING & CERTIFICATION

Red Hat Linux 7.3 For Dummies
0-7645-1545-4

TCP/IP For Dummies
0-7645-1760-0

Networking For Dummies
0-7645-0772-9

Also available:

A+ Certification For Dummies
(0-7645-0812-1)

CCNP All-in-One Certification For Dummies
(0-7645-1648-5)

Cisco Networking For Dummies
(0-7645-1668-X)

CISSP For Dummies
(0-7645-1670-1)

CIW Foundations For Dummies
(0-7645-1635-3)

Firewalls For Dummies
(0-7645-0884-9)

Home Networking For Dummies
(0-7645-0857-1)

Red Hat Linux All-in-One Desk Reference For Dummies
(0-7645-2442-9)

UNIX For Dummies
(0-7645-0419-3)

Available wherever books are sold.
Go to www.dummies.com or call 1-877-762-2974 to order direct